BRITISH COLUMBIA
ADVENTURES IN NATURE

Holly Quan

JOHN MUIR PUBLICATIONS
A DIVISION OF AVALON TRAVEL PUBLISHING

John Muir Publications
A Division of Avalon Travel Publishing
5855 Beaudry Street
Emeryville, CA 94608

First edition. First printing March 2000.

Library of Congress Cataloging-in-Publication Data

Quan, Holly.
    British Columbia : adventures in nature / Holly Quan.—1st ed.
    p.   cm.
    Includes bibliographical references.
    ISBN 1-56261-443-6
    1. Ecotourism—British Columbia—Guidebooks. 2. British
    Columbia—Guidebooks. I. Title.

    G155.C2 Q36 2000
    917.1104'4—dc21   99-044804

Editor: Peg Goldstein, Chris Hayhurst
Graphics Editor: Ann Silvia
Production: Janine Lehmann
Design: Janine Lehmann
Typesetting: Marcie Pottern
Maps: Kathleen Sparks—White Hart Design
Printer: Publishers Press
Front cover photo: Bob and Ira Spring—Mt. Sir Donald, Glacier
  National Park
Back cover photo: Kirkendall/Spring—Exploring Indian fish traps in
  Broken Island Group
Title page photo: D. Leighton

Distributed to the book trade by
Publishers Group West
Berkeley, California

CONTENTS

This book is dedicated with love to KDW, my travel buddy.

A WORD OF THANKS

For generous support, ideas, stories, transportation, information, photos, and encouragement, my hugs and thanks to the following: Ken Wong, Chandra, Adrienne, and Karin Wong, Sue Staker, Doug Leighton, Donna Giberson and Pat Crawford, Andrew Hickinbotham, Gail Maslak, Paul Clark, Steve Neill, George Otcenasek, Fred and Jan Williamson, Patrice Haan, Cherry Holand, Mich and Dorothy Palmer, Kelly and Gwen Palmer, Scott and Nancy Palmer, Gord Lussier, Laura Miller, Margot McMaster, Artesano the Wonder Horse; the many tour operators and outfitters who answered my requests for information, and the staff at John Muir Publications.

ABOUT THIS BOOK

British Columbia: Adventures in Nature is a guide to British Columbia's most exciting destinations for active travelers who are interested in exploring the province's natural wonders. Along with the best places for hiking and whale watching and the prime spots for skiing and canoeing, author Holly Quan recommends outfitters and local guides who can provide gear and lead you to the more remote parts of the province. She also points out places to eat and stay that will help you enjoy local cultures and cuisine. (All prices in this book are given in Canadian dollars.)

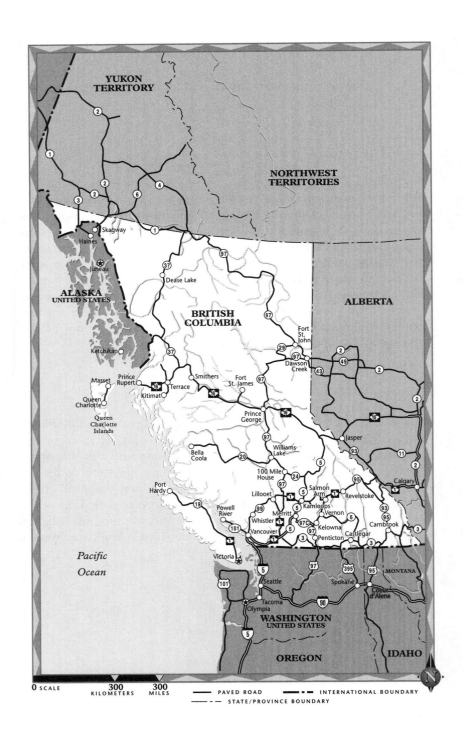

YUKON
TERRITORY

NORTHWEST
TERRITORIES

Skagway

Haines

Juneau

ALASKA
UNITED STATES

Dease Lake

BRITISH
COLUMBIA

ALBERTA

Ketchikan

Fort
St.
John

Masset

Prince
Rupert

Smithers

Fort
St. James

Dawson
Creek

Terrace

Kitimat

Queen
Charlotte

Queen
Charlotte
Islands

Prince
George

Jasper

Bella
Coola

Williams
Lake

100 Mile
House

Port
Hardy

Lillooet

Salmon
Arm

Revelstoke

Calgary

Powell
River

Merritt

Kamloops

Vernon

Whistler

Kelowna

Carnbrook

Vancouver

Penticton

Castlegar

Pacific
Ocean

Victoria

MONTANA

Seattle

Spokane

Coeur
d'Alene

Tacoma

Olympia

WASHINGTON
UNITED STATES

OREGON

IDAHO

N

0 SCALE   300   300
         KILOMETERS   MILES   ———— PAVED ROAD   ■—■-■ INTERNATIONAL BOUNDARY
                                            — - — STATE/PROVINCE BOUNDARY

CHAPTER 1

Welcome to
British Columbia

"Diversity." It's the first word that comes to mind when describing British Columbia. Urban and suburban parks to the most remote and untouched of wild places; peaks well over 4,000 meters to sea level and below; Canada's wettest place (Henderson Lake on Vancouver Island) to the driest (Osoyoos Pocket Desert); rivers to ranches, streams to streets . . . It's this amazing jumble of geography, climate, development, and wilderness that is BC's stock in trade.

British Columbia is also a place that lends itself to superlatives. The province's own tourism slogan is "Super, Natural British Columbia"—a clever juxtaposition of the notions that this land often defies description, that much of it remains unspoiled, and that it holds a particular spiritual fascination.

British Columbia embodies such a sweeping range of landscapes and challenges that to comprehend the place as a whole is problematic. How can a human mind grasp the fact that blue-ice glaciers, karsts, enormous trees, waterfalls 10 times the height of Niagara, surf-pounded beaches, desert, sagebrush ranch country, and rich farmland all occur within the boundaries of this single province? The key to understanding BC is to focus on one area, then another, until a picture emerges, just as a jigsaw puzzle is gradually assembled piece by piece. To me, the most astonishing fact about British Columbia is that its natural wonders are *accessible.* With relative ease and comfort, it is possible to experience truly wild places.

The essence of place is what remains in memory once we get home. We can describe the weather, tell of the people we met and our conversations, meals, activities, and discoveries. But travel is greater than the sum of these parts. Travel is learning, growing; it is spirit and heart. Travel is epiphany. Travel is unique to the traveler. So, ultimately, the best way to describe a trip is not to describe it at all, but to say, "Go there."

LAY OF THE LAND—MOUNTAINS AND MORE

British Columbia's geology is a mess. According to the theory of plate tectonics, BC's many parallel mountain chains were created by succeeding collisions of the North American continental plate with numerous eastward-moving plates, smashing and sandwiching one another for millions of years. The tremendous pressures that lifted ocean bottoms high into the air also transformed rock through metamorphic and volcanic processes. With repeated glaciation further sculpting the surface, it's a wonder geologists can make any sense of this complex and puzzling landscape.

At a glance you might dismiss British Columbia as a mass of mountains and nothing else. While mountains define the province's geography, there are distinctive regions. Besides mountain ranges, there are broad valleys and rolling plateau areas. The great plains of North America's interior reach out to snatch a corner of BC. And, of course, there's the ocean.

Starting from the Pacific Ocean and moving east across BC, you cross six physiographic zones that run roughly parallel, northwest to southeast. The most westerly of these is the Insular Mountains, a range that rises steeply from the ocean floor to create Haida Gwaii (the Queen Charlotte Islands) and most of Vancouver Island.

The eastern side of Vancouver Island and the western coast of the mainland where the city of Vancouver is situated are a separate physiographic region known as the Georgia Lowland. The Strait of Georgia itself is a glacier-carved passage bulldozed and gouged out of the lowland during the most recent Ice Age. To the east lie the

BC AT A GLANCE

Location: *Canada's most westerly province, bounded on the west by Alaska and the Pacific Ocean, on the north by the Yukon, on the east by the province of Alberta, and on the south by the Canada/U.S. border.*

Population: *3.76 million people (Canada's third-most-populous province)*

Official languages: *English and French are official languages throughout Canada, although French is not widely spoken in BC.*

Currency: *The Canadian dollar is the basic unit of currency.*

Taxes: *Federal Goods and Services Tax (GST)—7 percent— plus 6 percent provincial sales tax*

Area: *947,800 square kilometers (369,642 square miles) or approximately 10 percent of Canada's land-surface area*

Coastline length: *27,200 kilometers/16,320 miles*

Time zones: *Pacific and Mountain time*

Official bird: *Steller's jay*

Official tree: *Red cedar*

Official stone: *BC jade*

Climate: *Extremely variable, from semi-arid Mediterranean to desert, from temperate rain forest to alpine tundra, from relatively frost-free to near-Arctic. BC's record high temperature was recorded at Osoyoos on July 27, 1998, when the mercury hit 42.8 degrees Celsius (113.3 degrees Fahrenheit).*

Coast and Cascade Mountains (including all offshore islands except Haida Gwaii and Vancouver Island). Collectively known as the Western System, these mountain ranges are steep-sided and composed largely of hard, weather-resistant granite.

The next zone to the east is the Interior System, a mixed bag of rolling hills and plateau areas in the south, gradually giving way to mountains in the north—the Skeena, Hazelton, Cassiar, and Omineca ranges. East of the southern plateau are the Columbia Mountains, including the Monashee, Selkirk, and Purcell ranges. Separating the Columbia Mountains from the Rocky Mountains is the Rocky Mountain Trench, a remarkable physical feature that is visible from orbiting spacecraft. The trench is North America's longest valley and may represent a zone where two crustal plates collided.

The Rocky Mountains are known as the Eastern System. Geologically young, composed primarily of relatively soft sedimentary rock that has not been subjected to volcanic activity, the Rockies are extensively folded, faulted, splintered, and cracked. The Rockies form the Continental Divide of North America, with water on the west side flowing to the Pacific, water on the east flowing to the Atlantic (via the Hudson Bay in Canada).

The northeast corner of BC lies east of the Rockies. This corner is part of the Interior Plains that stretch across the middle of North America. The region is generally flat or gently rolling and has BC's only significant deposits of petroleum and natural gas.

Much of British Columbia has experienced volcanic activity, both underground and at the earth's surface. Flows of molten magma deep under the surface resulted in the granite that is now exposed as the rugged Coast and Cascade Mountains. Although there are no active volcanoes in BC, the Coast Mountains contain many cones and vents that may only be dormant. The most recent lava flow in BC occurred in approximately 1750, in the Nass River region north of Terrace. Earthquakes in BC's coastal regions, while generally not severe, are common, and there are many hot springs throughout the province—testament to underlying heat and turmoil.

Almost the entire province has been heavily glaciated. As the earth's climate grew cooler, huge ice sheets formed at the higher elevations and in the far north. The ice sheets began to flow, coalescing like great rivers inching their way over the landscape, gouging and grinding, changing the face of the land forever. Only the mountains of Haida Gwaii and some of the Rockies' highest peaks escaped the ice. Then the earth's climate began to warm and the great ice sheets melted, first along the coast, then gradually retreating from the interior valleys. Huge glaciers and ice fields remain in some areas, a link to the not-so-distant past that shaped the land and its inhabitants.

As you might expect in a rough and difficult landscape, rivers have provided people, wildlife, and vegetation with the easiest, sometimes only, means of moving from place to place. The province is drained by several major river systems: The Fraser is BC's longest river and has the largest drainage basin, extending from the Rocky Mountains to the Pacific; the Columbia River drains most of the southeast portion of the province on its way to the Pacific; and water from the northeast part of the province drains east by the Peace River and north into the Mackenzie River.

The landscape we see today is the result of these mountain-building and erosional forces. The saga continues, with sudden ferocity in the case of landslides or earthquakes, or with subtlety and finesse in the case of constant erosion by wind, water, and winter.

ABORIGINAL CULTURES

Human habitation in BC dates back approximately 12,000 years. Evidence from archaeological sites indicates that humans began to populate coastal areas following the retreat of the Ice Age glaciers. It is possible that Haida Gwaii (the Queen Charlotte Islands) was not glaciated and that human habitation on these remote islands is among the oldest and longest in the province. Where these first coastal dwellers came from is debatable. They may have migrated from what is now Siberia—during the Ice Age, the sea level was much lower than it is today, and the Bering Strait between Alaska and Russia was dry land and possibly relatively free of ice.

Aboriginal peoples of the province's interior may have had different origins. Peoples of the northeast may be descended from Inuit (northern peoples) or from the peoples of the northern plains and eastern boreal forests. Native peoples of the mountains and southeastern BC may be descendants of people migrating north after the retreat of the glaciers approximately 10,000 years ago.

Because the food supply along the coast was so rich and abundant, coastal peoples gradually established permanent villages and developed a very sophisticated, highly ritualized society. Art, dance, music, and storytelling all flourished in these societies. Interior peoples had to be more mobile, moving from place to place in search of food, often returning to favorite camps year after year but moving on again following the migration patterns of game animals.

Separate tribal groups evolved, with territories of varying size. Boundaries between tribal territories fluctuated and sometimes overlapped, but were generally based upon landscape features such as rivers and mountain ranges. Languages evolved too; of the 11 aboriginal language groups found in Canada, 8 occur in BC. Some of these are "isolates" spoken by only one tribe—Haida is one of these, as is Ktunaxa (Kootenay).

Despite wars and raids between neighboring tribes, trade was strong. A large proportion of the aboriginal diet depended upon salmon, but the quality of the fish was better at the coast. Interior peoples sought salmon and oolichan grease (oolichan, also spelled eulichan, is a small oil-bearing fish similar to smelt), and trade routes developed. Among these was the Nuxalk Grease Trail, which remains today as a long-distance horseback and hiking trail from the interior to the Native town of Bella Coola on the Pacific coast.

Because aboriginal languages were numerous and mutually unintelligible, a "trade lingo" gradually came into use. Europeans called this language "Chinook jargon." The language consisted of about 700 words, some of which are in common English use today in BC and elsewhere in the West: *chinook* (a warm westerly wind, also a species of salmon), *camas* (a flowering plant with edible roots), *salal* (a coastal shrub), *tyee* (a species of salmon), *skookum* (money or power), *muckamuck* (the upper crust, upper management).

The names by which BC's aboriginal peoples call themselves are revealing: names such as Haida, Dene, and many others translate simply as "people," "us," or "we"—there were no other "people" except for other First Nations. When Europeans arrived on the west coast in the 1700s, the aboriginals living there had no means of understanding where these newcomers came from. One coastal tribe called the white men "suddenly they're there;" another called them "men who live in a boat." When white fur traders first entered aboriginal territories in the interior, they were variously called "real whites" (for those Europeans who abided by Native laws and traditions) or "King George men" (for the British, as opposed to "Boston men" for Americans).

Regardless of names, the arrival of Europeans spelled doom for the traditional ways of all aboriginal peoples in British Columbia.

Even before whites arrived on the Pacific coast, BC Natives had a taste of European culture in the form of smallpox. Brought to the New World by the Spanish in the 1500s, the disease gradually moved north, devastating aboriginal populations across North America and arriving in the lower Fraser River area in approximately 1780.

At first, Europeans were interested only in exploiting the area's riches and saw Native peoples as a means to obtain furs, food, and other supplies. Europeans "claimed" lands and established trading posts and settlements, forming alliances with aboriginals. Gradually, however, the European view of the aboriginal peoples shifted; the presence of Natives was seen as an impediment to settlement and further exploitation. In 1849, to thwart potential American expansion, the British declared ownership of Vancouver Island and made James Douglas the first governor of the new Crown Colony. Douglas set about negotiating treaties with local First Nations in the area now occupied by Victoria and Nanaimo. Until 1998 these were the only treaties west of the Rocky Mountains. (In the 1880s the government of Canada negotiated a treaty that encompassed a wide area of the northern plains, including the Peace River district of northeastern BC.)

In 1858 Victoria became the main port of entry for gold seekers. Aboriginals had also come to Victoria from nations and villages far northward along the coast, to trade and to obtain European goods. Sadly, they also contracted smallpox, which spread rapidly. Sick with fever, many fled home to their northern villages, taking the disease with them. The resulting smallpox epidemic virtually wiped out entire villages, decimating the aboriginal population. Some estimates claim that up to 90 percent of the aboriginal population of coastal BC vanished.

Sick and starving, their societies in tatters, aboriginals were needy and vulnerable. To the "rescue" came both church and state. Missionaries from various denominations came to work among the Natives, converting them to Christianity and abolishing their traditional beliefs. The government established reservations and residential schools to further isolate and dismantle the traditional ways. From the age of six, Native children were required by law to leave their homes and live at the schools, often located very far from their homes and families. The tiny reserves disconnected aboriginal peoples from their resource base—hunting, fishing, and trading were replaced by poverty and dependence on the state. In 1876 the government of

Canada passed the infamous Indian Act, which dictated all aspects of Native life, even marriage. Native people could not vote in municipal elections until 1947 or in national elections until 1960. Residential schools continued their nefarious work until the 1980s.

Since the 1960s and 1970s, Native peoples have attempted to revive their culture, language, and traditional ways. In 1973 the Canadian government recognized that First Nations peoples had "long-time occupation, possession and use" of their lands, opening the door for Native land claims. The BC government refused to negotiate land claims, saying it was a federal issue, until 1990 when the provincial government decided to join negotiations between the Canadian government and various First Nations. The first among these claims to successfully be signed by all sides was the 1998 agreement between the federal and provincial governments and the Nisga'a First Nation of northwestern BC. Other land claims continue, oh so slowly.

Today, there are 197 First Nations bands in BC, with a total population of about 175,000. There are 1,650 reservations totaling 3,440 square kilometers (1,352 square miles)—0.37 percent of the province's land base. Many bands are members of tribal councils, political allegiances struck to facilitate land-claims negotiations. Aboriginal peoples call themselves bands, tribes, First Nations, First Peoples—but the term *Indian* is not commonly used. Band names are changing, too, either reverting from English to traditional names or to new names chosen by the people to better reflect their modern identities. Throughout this book, both modern and Anglicized band or tribal names are used.

The once-thriving coastal cultures are undergoing a renaissance, due in no small part to the popularity of Northwest coastal art forms. Carvings, jewelry, weaving, basketry, prints, and other art forms are widely available in art galleries throughout BC. These contemporary art forms are based on traditional artistic expression, which was in turn based on spirituality and mythology. Two traditions most commonly associated with coastal aboriginal culture are totem poles and potlatch ceremonies.

Totem poles were never objects of worship, but of commemoration. Carved poles were raised in celebration for such passages as marriage or the formal conferring of leadership, to commemorate events, and to explain kinship and family histories. Carved mortuary (memorial) poles were also created for the burial and remembrance of important people. House posts were carved too, usually with the crests of the family or clan that inhabited the house. Totem carving began around A.D. 1000 and truly flourished once the coastal peoples obtained iron and could fashion durable woodworking tools, beginning in about 1740. The "golden age" of totem poles occurred all along the coast from approximately 1830 until 1890.

Totem pole traditions are slowly reviving.

With the devastation of Native populations resulting from smallpox and other diseases in the 1860s and 1870s, the traditional ways, including the carving and erection of totem poles, began to disappear. Missionaries and government officials also discouraged totem carving; by 1910 pole carving had virtually ceased. Also, beginning in about 1870, many standing totems were confiscated and removed, some into private hands, many to museums around the world.

A handful of carvers remembered the old ways and taught their children and grandchildren how to carve. Among these was Charley James of Alert Bay; his granddaughter Ellen Neel became the focus of a revival movement funded in part by the University of British Columbia, which was planning to construct a major museum devoted to coastal aboriginal traditions and arts. Neel persuaded her step-uncle, Mungo Martin, to participate in the project. His excellence and abilities revived interest in carving among his nation, the Kwakwaka'wakw (Kwakiutl) of northern Vancouver Island. Martin is recognized today as the modern father of totem carving in BC. Today, carving and raising of totems has regained its importance in the spiritual and family life of coastal aboriginal peoples.

Among coastal cultures, the potlatch ceremony was a vital part of political, spiritual, and family life. Family groups and clans would gather to determine leadership succession, to engage in songs, dances, storytelling, and feasting that served to educate and instruct, and to carry on a family's oral history and traditions. Gatherings could last for a few days or a few weeks. Potlatches were marked by what Europeans considered a bizarre and immoral custom—that of giving away valuable goods and sacred items. Usually a high-ranking family member or elder would impoverish himself and his family by giving away all their possessions, an act that served to strengthen family ties through a ritual redistribution of goods. The recipients were then honor-bound to reciprocate and even outdo the gift giving by hosting the next potlatch. Hosting a potlatch was among the most important events of a Native person's life.

All this free exchange of goods was too much for European sensibilities, and potlatching was officially banned in 1884. Ceremonies continued to be conducted in secret but the feasting, dancing, and storytelling suffered and nearly died out. William Halliday was an especially zealous government administrator who waged war on potlatching between 1914 and 1920.

In 1921 Doug Cranmer held a large gathering of his kin from Alert Bay and Cape Mudge (settlements on the small islands between Vancouver Island and the mainland). Among other things, Cranmer gave away food, blankets, canoes, and sewing machines. The potlatch resulted in 34 arrests. The accused were given the option of signing a document agreeing to give up potlatching and have their ceremonial items such as masks, headdresses, and blankets placed in museums in return for their freedom. It almost goes without saying that some artifacts went missing and never made it to any museum. Halliday also sold several items to a New York museum for the princely sum of $200.

The potlatch law was repealed in 1951. In 1970 many items were repatriated and placed in the U'Mista Cultural Centre in Alert Bay and the Kwagiulth Museum in Cape Mudge. Items confiscated from the Nisga'a people (of the Nass River area north of Terrace on the mainland) and kept in the Royal British Columbia Museum in Victoria were returned to their rightful owners following the signing of the Nisga'a agreement in the summer of 1998.

Contemporary potlatch ceremonies are considered private family affairs to which outsiders are seldom invited. Potlatches usually last for a weekend (instead of several weeks) and still consist of songs, dances, storytelling, feasts, and gift giving.

EUROPEAN SETTLEMENT

European contact first occurred from the west. Juan Perez Hernandez came ashore long enough to claim Vancouver Island for Spain in 1774, but he did not establish a colony or Spanish presence. In 1778, Captain James Cook, exploring and claiming territory on behalf of England, sailed into Nootka Sound on Vancouver Island's west coast and proclaimed the area was henceforth under British rule, in spite of the prior Spanish claim. The obvious happened: Spain and Britain haggled, and several skirmishes occurred in BC coastal waters. The matter was settled in 1794, in England's favor.

Meanwhile, England dispatched Captain George Vancouver to explore and map the entire west coast of North America from Oregon north. It took Vancouver three years to complete his survey. Word was out by that time concerning the amazing bounty of whales, seals, and sea otters on the west coast, and soon the region was overrun. With single-minded ruthlessness, whales, sea otters, and other sea life were all but exterminated.

Europeans also began to infiltrate British Columbia from the east. The Hudson's Bay Company (HBC) had long been exploiting the woodlands north of the Great Lakes for furs. Gradually the HBC spread its influence westward. The HBC sent out traders and explorers overland from the east to establish trading posts and forts through the west, setting up trading links and partnerships with Native peoples. The company's archrival, the North West Company (NWC), was similarly engaged. Together these two companies were largely responsible for the early exploration and first European contact throughout the Canadian west, including British Columbia.

Alexander Mackenzie, a NWC man, was the first white person to travel across North America, arriving at Bella Coola on the west coast of mainland BC in July 1793. Simon Fraser and David Thompson were perhaps the most active explorers and fur traders through the interior in the early 1800s. In the mid 1850s, John Palliser and a group of scientists were sent out from England to determine whether western North America held any potential for settlement and agriculture. Palliser and his men explored much of the southern Rocky Mountain region of BC.

With the discovery of gold on a gravel bar of the Fraser River in

1858, attention turned from the dwindling fur and whale resources of the coast to the potential for quick riches from the interior. Discoveries of gold in the Cariboo region brought even more prospectors and began to open the difficult territory north of Lillooet in the upper Fraser Canyon. The promise of gold lured Europeans and Americans ever farther into the wilderness of north-central BC. By the 1860s, the largest community in western Canada was Barkerville, with a population of some 25,000.

Victoria was declared the capital of the combined island and mainland Crown Colonies, named British Columbia by Queen Victoria, in 1868. The new colony was being courted by the distant and equally new country of Canada, which had been formed just the year before by an act of the British parliament. Canada wanted to establish a clear presence in the west to protect the vast interior plains and riches of BC's mountains from the Americans. In 1871 BC agreed to become a Canadian province on the condition that the government of Canada build a railroad to link British Columbia with the rest of the country.

It took 15 years, cost many lives and the personal fortunes of several prominent Canadian businessmen, and brought down at least one federal government, but the Canadian Pacific Railway (CPR) was eventually built. In keeping with the federal government's desire to maintain a Canadian presence as close to the U.S. border as possible, the railway's path was changed from an easier but more northerly route over the Yellowhead Pass through the Rockies to a more difficult southerly route that used the steep Kicking Horse Pass and the snow-choked Rogers Pass through the Selkirk Mountains. The last spike was driven at Craigellachie, west of Revelstoke, in November 1885.

The railway spawned numerous settlements, not the least of which was Vancouver. Even though Victoria was the province's political capital, Vancouver became a thriving port, surpassing Victoria's population by 1901. As the enormous natural wealth of the region was exploited, roads and settlements were built and established. The fishing industry gave rise to literally hundreds of canneries and villages all along the coast. Mineral exploration and mining opened the interior. But it was logging that really brought white settlers into the interior of BC.

A second trans-Canadian railway, the Grand Trunk Railway, was completed in 1914, using a northern route to the Pacific. The towns of Prince George and Prince Rupert were established along this second

A NOTE ABOUT NAMES

With the recent reawakening of aboriginal pride and rights, the true names of many First Nations have come into common general use. However, because aboriginal languages use sounds not found in English, the written form of tribal names can be really confusing, a disturbing splatter of consonants punctuated by double, even triple vowels, underlined letters, apostrophes, and colons. In most cases, rather than provide a guide to pronunciation, this book provides the Anglicized tribal name.

rail route. With the building of new railways came greater potential for moving goods and resources from isolated interior locations to ports on the Pacific and markets in eastern Canada and the United States. It wasn't until the 1950s that BC's transportation networks were extended again, this time with the building of roads. The Alaska Highway was completed in the early days of the Second World War; the Trans-Canada Highway was completed through Rogers Pass as late as 1962.

Major population concentrations today are in the Vancouver-Victoria-Nanaimo triangle of the lower mainland and the southeastern portion of Vancouver Island. Of a total provincial population approaching 4 million, about half live in the greater Vancouver area. In the interior, the Okanagan and Thompson Valleys are heavily populated. In the north, Prince George (close to the geographical center of BC) and coastal Prince Rupert have become relatively large settlements, while Fort St. John has the largest population in the northeast. Northwestern BC remains sparsely settled.

Until the gold-rush era began in 1858, the non-Native population of BC was virtually all British. But the influx of gold rushers brought many European and Asian nationalities to BC, as well as many American citizens. Native populations dwindled due to smallpox and other diseases. The Canadian Pacific Railway brought many Chinese and Japanese workers to North America as cheap labor. Today the province demonstrates a cultural mosaic dominated by whites of British origin, followed by a strong Asian presence, especially in Vancouver and Victoria. Elsewhere in the province the cultural mix is mostly white and aboriginal.

British Columbia, as a province of Canada, is governed at the federal level by the Canadian parliament in Ottawa. Federal jurisdictions include health care, fisheries management, and taxation. The provincial legislature in Victoria is responsible for managing more regional concerns, including regulation of the logging and mining industries, agriculture, road-building, education, and taxation. Municipal governments concern themselves with local issues such as sanitation, schools, and taxation. If you're beginning to think that British Columbians suffer from too much government and too many taxes, you might be right.

An interesting experiment is currently unfolding in the realm of First Nations' self-government. The Nisga'a people have negotiated a land-claim and self-government settlement with the federal and BC governments which will allow the Nisga'a to govern themselves in accordance with their own cultures and customs. The Nisga'a treaty will establish a form of local government similar to municipal government, although some powers formerly belonging to the federal and provincial levels have been transferred to the Nisga'a.

Exploitation of natural resources remains the foundation of the province's economy now as it has been for over two hundred years. In order of importance, BC's economic drivers are forestry, mining, tourism, agriculture, and fishing. Other sectors are services, financial, and manufacturing. In the late 1990s, BC's financial links with Asia, and the province's dependence on exploitation of natural resources, especially trees, have led to widespread declines in the traditional economic forces in the province. In particular, forestry has declined significantly; related declines in other economic sectors could follow.

FAUNA

When it comes to wildlife, BC is much like Africa—the critters are out there, all around you, roaming free and just waiting for you to take their picture. The whole point of adventuring in remote (and even not-so-remote) areas of the province is to witness wild animals in their natural surroundings. You will not be disappointed.

As BC's wilderness becomes more accessible and as logging and other extractive industries make inroads to even the most remote areas of the province, the result is a growing list of threatened or endangered animal species due to reduced, destroyed, or altered wildlife habitats. Overfishing is taking a serious toll on many salmon stocks. Poaching of rare or endangered species further tightens the noose of impending extinction.

Plant-eating land mammals range from the tiny mountain-dwelling pika to the moose, the largest member of the deer family anywhere in the world. Among BC's most commonly seen herbivores are deer (two species, white-tailed and mule), elk (also called wapiti), moose, and caribou. Bighorn sheep come in several varieties, including Rocky Mountain bighorns with their massive curling horns and white Dall and dark-brown stone sheep, both found in the north. Shaggy white mountain goats can be seen throughout BC, especially in the Rocky and Coast Mountains.

A few notes and cautions about BC wildlife: Although deer may appear timid and gentle, approaching and feeding them is risky at any time, especially during the fall rut. Deer will strike with their front hooves, and can inflict broken bones. Keep your distance and take pictures instead. Elk and moose can be extremely dangerous during the mating season and will charge without warning; females will also defend their calves. Due to their weight and size, these animals can also be lethal if struck by a vehicle. Always exercise caution when driving, especially at dawn, dusk, and at night. Sheep seldom charge humans, but are hazards on the roads where they come to lick salt. They don't seem to get the car-as-predator concept and will stand stubbornly in the path of oncoming vehicles. Refrain from nudging them with your bumper—go around. Sheep habituated to humans can be aggressive.

Where herbivores dwell, predators are sure to follow. Two major species of bears are found in BC. The larger of the two species is the grizzly, so named because the dark-brown fur is tipped with white, giving the bear a grizzled appearance, as though it sports a layer of frost. Grizzlies are easy to identify by their prominent shoulder hump and

Woodland caribou can be seen frequently in northern BC.

D. Leighton

dished face, very long claws, and by their size—males can be two and one-half meters (eight and one-half feet) long and weigh 385 kilograms (850 pounds). Grizzly bears are found throughout BC but are most common in remote areas, especially the northern and coastal regions. Open avalanche slopes are prime grizzly habitat. During salmon runs, bears frequent salmon streams.

Black bears are smaller than grizzlies, ranging up to 270 kilograms (600 pounds). They have a flat back (no shoulder hump), a straight nose, and big, round ears. Despite their name, these animals can be black, chocolate, cinnamon brown, even white or bluish. Black bears are common throughout BC. Kermode bears deserve a special mention. The white coats of these black bears are caused by a recessive gene. While they can be found just about anywhere, the Kermode bear population is concentrated on Princess Royal Island and the nearby islands north of Bella Bella and on the mainland near Terrace.

Both black and grizzly bears enter a period of dormancy in winter (not true hibernation). For black bears, the nap can last up to six months, and the bear's metabolism, although slower than when the bear is active, can consume up to 40 percent of its body weight. Bears are dangerous and will vigorously defend their young. For tips on safety from bears, see Appendix A.

Foxes, coyotes, and wolves roam BC's forests and grasslands. Of these, the one you are most likely to see is the coyote. About the size of a German shepherd, these dusty-brown, sharp-nosed and curious critters have learned to adapt and thrive in human company. Coyotes are not dangerous to humans unless they are cornered or threatened. However, a coyote will take a small dog, so keep an eye on your pets. The gray wolf ranges throughout BC, including the coast, but these shy animals are much less fond of humans than their smaller cousins. Similarly, red foxes are widespread but not common, and are not found at all on the coast except in the Fraser Valley.

British Columbia's wild cats are reclusive and seldom seen. Bobcats are restricted to the lower mainland and southern portions of the province. The larger lynx, recognizable by their short, black-tipped tails, tufted ears, and muttonchop whiskers, range throughout BC but are wary. Cougars are found in remote areas throughout the province except for in the extreme northwestern section. Cougar attacks on humans are extremely rare.

British Columbia is also home to numerous members of the weasel family, including wolverine, mink, marten, fisher, and various smaller weasels. You may also encounter badgers, skunks, raccoons, river otters, beavers, and porcupine. Contrary to popular belief, porcupines do not "shoot" quills—but a quick slap from a bristling tail can leave you (or your child or dog) looking like a pincushion. Porcupines are attracted to salt, so don't urinate close to a trail, a cabin, or your tent, lest you wish to find a "porky" nibbling your tent lines. Porcupines are small and move about at dusk when they are really hard to spot—be careful not to stumble over them on the trail if you're walking around near sunset.

If you're roving through a west coast rain forest, it won't be long before you encounter your first banana slug. Among the world's largest (25 centimeters/10 inches long), these beauties are harmless but will crawl up anything, including your tent. Slugs eat bracken fern; toxins from the ferns enter the slug's system and render the slug inedible, or at least unappealing, to most predators.

Sad but true, BC is home to a number of pesky bugs. Female mosquitoes need blood in order for eggs to develop. Mosquitoes search for carbon dioxide, a sure sign that an animal is in the vicinity. Body heat also attracts these insects. The mosquito inserts her long, tubelike mouth into her victim, along with a dose of nerve-deadening enzyme, so that her pinprick puncture goes undetected and she can feed in peace. With 45 species of mosquito present in BC, your chance of evading them is slim to none. Repellents containing DEET are effective but harsh to skin, plastic, and some fabrics. Citronella is gentler but not as effective and needs to be refreshed frequently

Black flies (which can be can be black, gray, even reddish-orange) go for the thin skin of wrists, throats, faces, and scalp. The fly's saliva contains an anticoagulant that encourages the victim's blood to flow easily from the bite. Black flies swarm in massive hordes in summer, especially in the northern areas of the province and near swamps and wetlands. Your best defense is a good bug repellent and clothing with tight cuffs and a neck closure. A high tolerance for crawling insects helps, too.

From April through June, Rocky Mountain wood ticks are a danger throughout the Rocky Mountains and Kootenays. These eight-legged relatives of the spider perch on leaves or blades of grass and grab anything that brushes by. The tick—flat and about the size of a match head—then searches for a spot to puncture the victim's skin and begin sucking blood. If undisturbed, the tick will bury its head under the skin and continue sucking for several hours. When fully gorged with blood the tick will relax its jaws and fall off to search for a suitable spot to lay its eggs.

Ticks can carry a variety of diseases, from Lyme disease to Rocky Mountain spotted fever and even the potentially fatal tick paralysis. The best defense is to wear a hat, a long-sleeved shirt, and long pants, with firmly buttoned cuffs, socks pulled well up over your pant hems, or high gaiters. A bandana around your neck can help prevent a tick from crawling inside your shirt. Always check yourself thoroughly after every spring outing, no matter how brief (and don't be shy about getting a companion to check your back). If you find a tick that has already attached itself, gently remove it with tweezers. (Some schools of thought recommend plastering the tick with petroleum jelly or kerosene, but extraction with tweezers is the best course of action.)

WHERE ARE THE ANTLERS?

Male deer, elk, and moose and both male and female caribou grow a new set of antlers every year. Once the fall mating season is past, the antlers fall off. So shouldn't the woods be full of discarded antlers? Well, no. Antlers break down naturally. The process is aided by rodents, which gnaw away at the antlers to obtain their phosphorus and other minerals.

There are at least 450 bird species in British Columbia, ranging from tiny hummingbirds to majestic eagles, from ducks, geese, and other water birds to cranes, herons, swans, songbirds, sea birds, owls, hawks . . . the list goes on. The most spectacular bird in the region is the bald eagle, which can be found anywhere there are salmon. Juvenile birds are mottled brown; the characteristic white head and tail feathers denote a mature bird. The wingspan can reach 3.5 meters (12 feet). Among the best places to see bald eagles is the Brackendale Bald Eagle Reserve near Squamish. Each autumn eagles come here to hunt salmon in the Squamish River; their population grows to a maximum in January and February, when more than 2,000 birds may congregate here.

It is difficult to escape gulls anywhere along the coast, and in many inland locations, too. There are several species of gulls and terns that migrate through BC or make the province a year-round home. Other common bird species in BC include great blue heron, great horned owl, Canada goose, gray jay, loon, osprey or "fish eagle," and numerous seabirds such as guillemots, cormorants, and puffins.

British Columbia's coastal waters are cool to cold as they are continually refreshed with cold northern water from the Gulf of Alaska. The marine environment is so rich with plankton that the area is known as the Emerald Sea—the water is literally green with life.

Plankton (microscopic plants and animals) is at the bottom of the marine food chain; where plankton is plentiful, the resulting abundance and diversity of higher marine life is astonishing.

British Columbia's coastal waters are home to numerous species of whales, dolphins, and porpoises. Many of these are either rare or seldom venture into nearshore waters, and are not commonly seen; these include the sperm, blue, fin, and sei whales. Other species tend to stay closer to the coastline. In BC coastal waters, the most commonly seen members of the cetacean tribe are the Pacific gray whale, Pacific white-sided dolphin, and orca (killer whale). Possibly the west coast's most sought-after creature, almost synonymous with British Columbia, orcas are distinctively marked black-and-white members of the dolphin family. Researchers now know that there are two separate orca populations in BC: migrants, which move up and down the coast; and residents, which tend to stay within a known range year-round. Orcas are common in Haida Gwaii and the Inside Passage between Vancouver Island and the BC mainland, especially in Johnstone Strait and Robson Bight. Orcas are toothed carnivores. Favorite foods include squid, salmon, seals, and other whales.

The west coast is also home to elephant, northern fur, and harbor seals, along with California and Steller's sea lions. Sea otters spend their entire lives in the water, almost never coming to land. Their luxurious pelts—up to 800 million hairs per animal—made them the object of intense hunting in the 1800s, when the species was extirpated from Canada. The sea otters that live along Canada's west coast today were reintroduced from the remaining populations in Alaska. The species is now protected and is making a slow comeback. The best place to view sea otters in BC is at Nootka Sound.

The Pacific coast is rich in marine life, due to the wide variety of environments, from open ocean to rocky outcrops to sand beaches, mud flats to salt marshes. The common sea and tide-pool creatures include purple sea urchins, starfish (also called sea stars), jellyfish, mussels and other bivalves, nudibranchs, anemones, and sponges. The beaches are home to snails, worms, clams, and crabs.

In BC, salmon is king. All salmon hatch in freshwater streams where the young fish live and grow for a year or two. Young salmon gradually make their way downstream toward the ocean, their bodies undergoing significant chemical changes to allow them to live in salt

A Pacific gray whale breaches off the coast of Vancouver Island.

water. Salmon spend from two to five years in the ocean. When they have reached maturity, the salmon begin their final migration back to fresh water, swimming upstream to find the very pool or stream where they were born. These migrations, called "runs," occur in spring, summer, and autumn, depending on the species. Most rivers experience several salmon runs each year, as different species return to the rivers to spawn. Once they have left salt water, the fish do not eat again; instead, they rely upon stores of fat to see them through the perilous journey to the spawning grounds. Physical changes also occur, including coloration—sockeye salmon, for instance, turn a brilliant red with green heads. When spawning is completed, the exhausted fish die.

British Columbia is home to five species of salmon, all of which are fished commercially. The most sought-after species are sockeye and coho. Other important fish include rainbow, cutthroat, lake, brook, and Dolly Varden trout. Rainbow trout that spend some of their lives in salt water are known as steelhead trout; Dolly Varden can also be found in marine waters.

FLORA

Topography, elevation, latitude, and climate combine to create an incredible diversity (there's that word again) of vegetation communities in BC. Forested regions of the province can be divided and differentiated based on the dominant tree species. The coastal-hemlock and mountain-hemlock zones are found on the coasts and slopes of the Coast Mountains, where trees grow tall and ancient. Also known as the temperate rain forest, this zone includes tree species such as western red cedar, yellow cedar, Sitka spruce, and Douglas fir, plus mosses, ferns, salal, berries, and devil's club. The southeastern portion of Vancouver Island and parts of the Fraser Valley are occupied by mixed-wood forests including Douglas fir, reflecting the somewhat drier climate. Pockets within this zone are occupied by the Garry oak/arbutus zone, now among Canada's most endangered ecosystems.

East of the Coast Mountains is an extensive rain shadow where moisture levels are the lowest in the province. Here the trees are widely scattered, the forest floor is open, and sage is the most common shrub. This is the dominant vegetation zone in the central Fraser Valley, the lower Thompson, and the Nicola, Similkameen, and Okanagan regions. In the extreme south end of the Okanagan Valley this zone gives way to near-desert vegetation communities with cactus and sage. In the upper reaches of the Fraser Canyon and on into the Cariboo and Chilcotin regions the zone is dominated by grass, with trees growing only in coulees or depressions where water collects.

At upper elevations in the Rocky and Kootenay Mountains and throughout the inland mountain ranges is the spruce/subalpine fir zone. A portion of this zone is occupied by the montane zone, where lodgepole pine mingles with spruce. A band in the interior is characterized by a dense, lush growth of large trees and heavy underbrush, in response to a wet climate caused by the high Columbia Mountains. This is the most diverse of BC's vegetation zones—there are at least 57 tree species, plus shrubs, grasses, flowers, moss, and fungi.

The sub-boreal spruce zone dominates the northern interior plateau. The dominant trees are Engelmann and white spruce and a hybrid of these two species. In the far northeast where winters are long and harsh, the scrubby, tough-as-nails white spruce grows on the drier sites while black spruce thrives in the bogs and low-lying areas.

The drier sites have extensive lichen growth, and as a result attract large numbers of caribou. The northwest part of the province is covered by a mix of spruce, willow, and birch; white spruce, lodgepole pine, and subalpine fir predominate. Above the tree line throughout the province there is a narrow alpine-tundra zone dominated by hardy, low-growing plants and brilliant wildflowers.

The big news in BC is trees—really big trees. Over 63 percent of the province is forested. Some of the forests are lush and productive; some are struggling for survival at the brink of the northern and alpine tree lines. Seeing a really big tree is humbling. They do not announce themselves like roaring waterfalls; they do not necessarily dominate the skyline like mountains. Big trees simply stand in their remote, silent realms and wait. They're often very old—most are more than 1,000 years old, and some particularly long-lived individuals have been around for 1,500, even 2,000, years. Being in the presence of such antiquity engenders contemplation, reverence, respect.

The primal forests that nurture really big trees are known as old-growth forests. In a province full of complex ecosystems, the old-growth forests are remarkable for their complexity. The chains of interdependence that exist between the trees, creatures, and their environment is astonishing. Old-growth forests exhibit four key parameters that set them apart from other forests: the presence of very large, very old trees; very large and standing dead trees; very large fallen trees, also called nurse logs; and a multitude of layers in the branches supporting birds, insects, and other plants at various heights above the forest floor. For a complete list of record-holding trees in BC, write the BC Register of Big Trees, c/o Lynn Canyon Ecology Centre, 3663 Park Rd., North Vancouver, BC V7J 3G3.

If big trees are the main attraction on land, kelp beds are the coast's claim to fame. Kelp beds can be very dense and extensive. These immense kelp forests reduce the strength of the ocean's swells and currents, providing shelter and protection to many species of animals and fish.

There are a few poisonous plants in BC. "Three leaves, stay away!" is the child's rhyme that accurately identifies poison ivy. The leaves have wavy edges and are attached to the branches in groups of three. Poison ivy is common on sunny, dry sites in the Columbia, Kootenay, and Okanagan Valleys. All parts of the plant contain an oil that causes

MARBLED MURRELET

British Columbia has two murrelet species—the ancient and the marbled. Both are coastal birds. The marbled murrelet was a mystery for many years, for while the bird itself had been sighted, nobody had ever seen a nest.

While the ancient murrelet is known to lay its eggs on seaside cliffs, this is not the case with marbled murrelets. It turns out that they lay their eggs on the soft moss that grows on high tree limbs in the depths of the coastal rain forests. Thus, clear-cutting in old-growth forests has had a devastating effect on marbled murrelet populations. Though the birds are protected under various Canadian laws, their habitat remains at risk.

severe skin irritation. Treat by soaping and rinsing the affected area, using fresh water for each rinse. Chamomile lotion is also a well-known remedy.

Death camas is common in damp meadows and forested areas, primarily in the middle to high elevations. The spike of white flowers, supported on a tall stalk, smells awful and deters most people and animals from consuming the plant. Cattle and horses, however, sometimes can't resist, and can die as a result. Prickly pear cactus is found in the southern interior and in the arid section of the Fraser Valley north of Lytton. A species is also found on the north bank of the Peace River.

As for mushrooms, unless you're an expert, don't pick and eat wild varieties. Several poisonous mushrooms grow in BC, including the false morel. The true morel has a short and thick white stalk topped by a cone-shaped cap with distinctive pits separated by raised ridges. The false morel is also called "brain mushroom," an apt description of the folded and wrinkled surface that ranges from dark brown to purplish.

OUTDOOR ACTIVITIES IN BC

When it comes to recreation in British Columbia, even the sky is no limit if you're into skydiving or hang gliding. An excellent source of information on common terrestrial and water-based activities is the Outdoor Recreation Council (ORC) of BC, which was established in 1976 and has more than 50 member organizations throughout the province, including several educational institutions. The ORC supports several province-wide programs such as the Rails-to-Trails Strategy (turning abandoned rail beds into hiking, cycling, and horseback trails), the River Recreations Strategy for BC (working with the provincial government for long-term management of BC rivers), and land-use planning initiatives.

The good folks at the ORC can supply you with activity maps showing where to hike, ride, boat, climb, and more throughout the province. The ORC puts out a quarterly newsletter, *The Outdoor Report*, and maintains a list of publications of interest to outdoor activists and ecotravelers. It also publishes an excellent map series depicting topography, trails, and other recreation opportunities for several regions in the province. Brochures outlining codes of ethics for wilderness, water recreation, trail use, and backcountry sanitation are also available, and are great sources of practical information. In addition, every year the ORC publishes a list of BC's 10 most endangered rivers.

The ORC can also put you in touch with specific sports associations for more detailed information. Each of the member organizations is listed on the ORC's Web site, www.orcbc.bc.ca/; or you can contact the Outdoor Recreation Council of BC, Suite 334, 1367 W. Broadway, Vancouver, BC V6H 1A9, 604/737-3058, fax 604/737-3666.

Many of British Columbia's colleges and universities offer extension programs and noncredit courses on the province's natural history and aboriginal culture, and courses specifically geared to outdoor activities such as climbing and kayaking. Generally speaking though, unless you're a BC resident it can be difficult to find and register for these courses, which can be very popular and fill up quickly. If you are interested in educational opportunities of this kind, contact the local university or college in the region you're planning to visit, or contact the Outdoor Recreation Council (see above).

More accessible alternatives for visitors who wish to learn about the land, wildlife, history, or culture of the province are the many interpretive programs offered at the national and provincial parks. Park interpretive programs are well worth attending, especially for families—often the naturalist will have items and objects that kids can handle and examine closely, or will lead a nature walk where you can see geological features, vegetation, and wildlife firsthand.

Interpretive programs are available in summer (May through September) in BC's national parks. These programs range from beach walks to fireside talks and slide shows and are usually held in the early evening in national park campgrounds. The larger provincial parks employ naturalists who give fireside lectures, storytelling sessions, and hands-on demonstrations. BC Parks also publishes pamphlets on the larger provincial parks, including some interpretive information.

A unique learning opportunity is offered by BC Ferries on their longer coastal voyages (such as the Discovery Coast and Inside Passage voyages) through their artist residence summer program. Writers, painters, photographers, sculptors, and carvers set up shop in a quiet corner, usually the ferry's cafeteria or a sheltered outside deck, to read from their work, lecture on history or culture, or carve a mask. Passengers are encouraged to ask questions and interact with the artists. Interpreters and naturalists from the BC Forest Service are also frequently aboard the longer ferry trips and give periodic lectures on regional wildlife, plants, and forestry practices.

Self-guided trails and interpretive centers are scattered everywhere in BC. You can take a hike through a logging company's domain and learn about reforestation, courtesy of signs along the trail. You can stop at the roadside and watch the beehive of activity at a dryland log-sorting yard and learn about the process and equipment from a roadside sign. There are a number of museums and interpretive centers, both staffed and unstaffed, where you can learn about the forest-products industry, railroading, fish canning, fish spawning, local history, and more. You will find museums and interpretive centers listed throughout this book. Check them out—they're worth the time to explore and learn. And here's a tip: if anyone in a local museum offers you a tour of their facilities, consider taking them up on the offer. When it comes to learning and really getting a glimpse of life in BC, nothing beats talking to a local.

Of course, the advantage of employing the services of a private guide, tour operator, or outfitter is the potential for learning about the region through which you're traveling. Most tour guides take great pride in their knowledge of their particular area and share it willingly with their clients. A selective list of local and regional tour guides and outfitters appears in each chapter in this book.

To learn a specific skill or activity, consider taking a course while you're visiting BC. Courses provide a perfect opportunity to experience a sport for the first time or to build your aptitude during an intensive multi-day experience. At the same time, you'll see some great places and benefit from the instructor's knowledge of the local area. Courses are often inclusive, meaning that instruction, accommodation, meals, and transportation are all part of the package. Several schools (climbing, horseback riding, kayaking, outdoor leadership) are listed throughout this book.

Elderhostel Canada offers numerous travel/study opportunities on a variety of topics. There is no minimum age—the only requirement for membership is retirement. Programs combine meals and accommodation at hostels, conference or study centers, or university/college residences with lectures, workshops, visits to Native sites, outdoor activities, and more. Among the programs offered in BC are Okanagan University College/Spring Wine Festival, Sea Lion Safari in the Gulf Islands, and People of the Potlatch on Vancouver Island. Some programs are specifically tailored for physically challenged or visually impaired participants. A catalog of programs is available from Elderhostel Canada, 4 Cataraqui St., Kingston, Ontario K7K 1Z7, 613/530-2222, fax 613/530-2096, e-mail ecclaire@elderhostel.org.

Hiking on a beach or an alpine meadow, in an urban park or in utter wilderness, with a group or on your own, is perhaps BC's most common and most accessible recreation. You don't really need special equipment for a simple walk—just open the door and get going. For more remote areas or longer trips, obviously preparation and the right boots and backpack are just the beginning.

There are hiking trails everywhere in BC, especially in the national and provincial parks. These range from short nature walks, often with self-guiding information signs or brochures, to major backcountry expeditions. Be aware that even on a short walk you can encounter such hazards as bad weather and bears. Helicopters offer a quick means of access to high alpine terrain and backcountry lodges. Check out Purcell Lodge, Selkirk Lodge, and Mount Assiniboine Lodge.

An interesting national millennium project is the Trans-Canada Trail (TCT), a hiking trail that, when completed, will link the Atlantic, Pacific, and Arctic Oceans. The total length of the trail will be 15,926 kilometers (9,329 miles). The British Columbia portion of the TCT hugs the U.S. border from Victoria to the Kootenays, then heads north to link with hiking trails in Banff National Park. For information on the TCT, check out the Web site devoted to the trail at www.tctrail.ca, or call 800/465-3636. Trails BC is the provincial body responsible for acquisition and construction of the BC portion of the TCT. For specific information about the BC portion, contact 24208-102 Ave., Maple Ridge, BC V2W 1J1, 604/486-8456.

Cycling and mountain biking is another sport that can be pursued just about anywhere—all you need is wheels, and if you don't own a cycle you can usually rent one. Within the provincial and national parks, some trails are off-limits to mountain bikers; check with park officials before setting out. Note that logging roads are not suitable for cycling. For detailed information, check with local cycle shops for trail maps and information, or contact the Bicycling Association of BC, Suite 332, 1367 W. Broadway, Vancouver, BC V6H 1A9, 604/737-3034.

It's pretty obvious that in a mountainous region such as BC, mountaineering and rock climbing are popular pastimes. There are books, clubs, climbing organizations, and outfitters galore. However, climbers being an independent lot, there is currently no central organization or information source. Your best bet is to check with guides or local sport shops in the area you're visiting. For information on climbing courses, contact the Federation of Mountain Clubs, Suite 336, 1367 W. Broadway, Vancouver, BC V6H 4A9, 604/737-3053. You can get contact information for regional offices of the Alpine Club of Canada through the Federation of Mountain Clubs or through the Outdoor Recreation Council.

If you're interested in spelunking, you've come to the right place, although most of BC's caves are uncharted, undeveloped, and can be difficult to access. Carry the right equipment, including helmet, lights, and spare batteries. Never go caving alone, and be aware that hazards abound and rescue is difficult. Several caves are accessible

RED TIDE

Single-celled microorganisms called dinoflagellates occasionally color the nearshore waters a rusty red. Dinoflagellates are always present in seawater, but under the right conditions, usually in late summer, a "bloom" occurs. Dinoflagellates carry a toxin that can accumulate in shellfish as they filter these tiny animals from the water. Butter clams can retain the toxin for up to two years; mussels usually release the toxin in a few months.

The toxin can cause a condition known as paralytic shellfish poisoning (PSP). If humans eat clams, oysters, or mussels containing the toxin, symptoms of PSP can appear within a few minutes: tingling of the lips, tongue, and mouth, advancing to tingling in the fingers and toes, numbness in the arms and legs, and paralysis in extreme cases. PSP can be fatal. Always check for red-tide warnings before gathering and consuming shellfish.

only in the company of guides. The eerie and beautiful formations found in many caves, though made of rock, are delicate and easily damaged. Stalactites, stalagmites, and other such features depend on the evaporation of water and consequent deposition of dissolved minerals and grow at an exceedingly slow rate. Don't touch these formations, as sweat and oils from your hands can prevent further calcite deposition. Information sources include the BC Speleological Federation, Box 733, Gold River, BC V0P 1G0, 250/283-CAVE; and the Cave Guiding Association of BC, Box 897, Gold River, BC V0P 1G0, 250/283-7144 or 250/283-2283.

Riding horseback for an hour, an afternoon, or a full day is an activity widely available in BC. Watch for signs along the highway indicating stables, trail rides, and horses for hire. Infocentres will also point you in the right direction. For a more in-depth taste of cowboy life, or for multiday pack trips, check out one of the many guest

K. D. Wong/Blackbird Design

Both novice and expert kayakers can explore BC's rivers and extensive coastline.

ranches in the province, many of which are located near Clinton in the Cariboo-Chilcotin region. Several of these are listed in Chapter 11. For information, contact BC Guest Rancher's Association, Box 4501, Williams Lake, BC V2G 2V8; or the Horse Council of BC, 5746 B, 176 A St., Cloverdale, BC V3S 4C7, 604/576-2722.

Have canoe, will paddle. In a land of lakes and streams, paddling should almost be a mandatory occupation. A variety of paddling experiences awaits, from remote and rugged whitewater trips for experts to easy lake excursions for novices. Remember that every river in BC is connected with a glacier somehow—the water is cold. On hot summer days, lakes in the interior can be warm enough for comfortable swimming. Generally speaking, though, you don't want to spend a long time in the water, so canoeists should be familiar with self-rescue and group-rescue techniques. You should also wear a personal floatation device (life jacket) at all times while on the water. For information, contact Canoe Sport BC, 1367 W. Broadway, Vancouver, BC V6H 4A9, 604/275-6651.

Kayakers looking for whitewater or surf, or for extended wilderness-exploration trips, will be well rewarded in BC. Experienced whitewater kayakers can negotiate virtually any river in the province, with the exception of the Grand Canyon of the Stikine, a stretch that contains several impossible rapids. If you are going to attempt to run any whitewater, be experienced and prepared, and remember to inform someone of your whereabouts. Sea kayaking is continuing to grow in popularity. It's possible to rent kayaks at many coastal locations, or you can take an all-inclusive kayak trip. Again, if you're going to kayak, a life jacket is a must, as are a spare paddle, bailing device, and the ability to get your kayak upright and yourself or your companion back into the boat if you capsize. Common sense is your best defense against accidents. Staying out of trouble is easier, and much more fun, than getting out of trouble. For information, contact the Sea Kayak Association of BC, 7955-161 St., Surrey, BC V3S 6H9, 604/597-1122.

If you're simply looking for an easy way to see lots of remote territory, you can opt for float trips by raft. A number of serious whitewater rafting accidents in the early 1990s resulted in stringent requirements for rafting safety. All raft outfitters are now licensed, and their equipment is inspected annually. Rafting is currently among the most closely regulated sports in the province—which is not to say that the thrills have been legislated out of existence. For more information, contact the Registrar of River Rafting c/o BC Parks, 800 Johnson St., Victoria, BC V8V 1X4, 250/387-5002.

There are some great spots to pursue surfing and windsurfing. Remember that the ocean is generally cold—experienced BC surfers use full wetsuits including hood, gloves, and boots. Strong tides and currents can carry the unwary far out to sea or along the coast, where rocky headlands make landing impossible. Pay attention to your surroundings and don't go out any farther than you can swim back to shore. Also beware of large rogue waves, especially in coastal areas exposed to the Pacific. Before venturing out on your board, ask locally for information on submerged hazards. Never surf alone.

With more than 27,000 kilometers (17,000 miles) of coastline and 18,000 square kilometers (7,000 square miles) of inland waters, BC offers spectacular opportunities for sailing and boating. Sailboat and motorboat cruises and charters are easy to find and to book; ask at visitor infocentres or look in the yellow pages. Amenities and services run the full range, as do prices. If you're into bringing your own boat and going it alone, the Sailing Association of BC can provide you with lots of information. Call them at 604/737-3113. Note that there are restrictions on importing boats into Canada, even for your own recreational use. For information, contact Canada Customs, First Floor, 333 Dunsmuir St., Vancouver, BC V6B 2R4, 604/666-3228.

Both *National Geographic* and Jacques Cousteau rated diving in BC as second only to diving in the Red Sea. Now *there's* an endorsement! The cold, oxygen-rich waters off British Columbia's west coast provide exceptional habitat for an astonishing array of marine life. Known as the Emerald Sea due to its concentration of plankton containing chlorophyll, the water holds a variety of marine life, from whales to starfish, nudibranchs to sea urchins, anemones, enormous octopus, squid, fish, and a myriad of invertebrates. Winter diving is fantastic, thanks to improved visibility. The waters are clear and light can penetrate to 45 meters (150 feet).

Powell River, on the Sunshine Coast north of Vancouver, is known as the Dive Capital of Canada—for good reason. Not only are there endless opportunities for diving but there is a vibrant and enthusiastic dive community in this small city. If you've arrived in town eager to fill your tanks and get down (so to speak), just call one of the dive shops in town and ask for its list of dive buddies—locals who are ready and willing to venture out with you. You can contact a buddy via e-mail at deepbreathers@hotmail.com. There are also numerous dive charters in the Powell River area.

Among BC's recreational and ecotouring opportunities, whale watching is perhaps the fastest growing and the most easily accessible to a wide variety of participants. You don't have to be fit or active; you just need a sense of adventure, a bit of patience, and good binoculars. Because marine life in BC coastal waters is so plentiful, it's a rare expedition that comes home without seeing anything. But even if you don't spot whales, there are plenty of porpoises, dolphins, seals, sea lions, and birds to watch.

So many fish, so little time. Anglers eager to test their skills in both salt and fresh water will find that BC offers varied and rewarding fishing opportunities. Five salmon species, plus cod, halibut, and numerous other fish inhabit coastal waters. BC's lakes and rivers are alive with several varieties of trout (native and introduced), perch,

C. L. Wong

Whale watching is an eco-friendly way to get close to many oceanic species.

whitefish, and char, not to mention steelhead (sea-run trout) and kokanee (landlocked salmon). Fishing in BC is big. You'll find tackle shops, boat rentals, charters, everything you might want. Catching the fish is up to you.

To catch fish legally in BC you need a license, available from most sporting goods stores and tackle shops. Licenses are required for saltwater fishing regardless of age (even kids need a license); in fresh water, anyone over 16 must have a valid license to fish. Catch limits are in effect and vary depending on species and area. Some species are designated as catch-and-release only. To keep up with current regulations, and to get the lowdown on great fishing spots, lodges, operators, and more, get the *Freshwater Fishing* and *Saltwater Fishing* guides, available from Tourism BC, 800/663-6000, or contact BC Fishing Resorts and Outfitters Association, Box 3301, Kamloops, BC V2C 6B9, 250/374-6836.

For 24-hour information on open and closed coastal areas, call the federal Department of Fisheries and Oceans (DFO), 604/666-0383 or 604/666-2268. Remember that certain size and catch limits also apply to shellfish and crustaceans, and that shellfish cannot be

P. R. Clark

Enjoy panoramic views by chartering a plane.

harvested during red tides (paralytic shellfish poisoning). Red-tide warnings are posted on popular beaches. Always ask a local before collecting shellfish to eat.

After a tough day of hiking, skiing, climbing, cycling, or whatever, sometimes there's nothing better than to soak away those aches and bruises in one of British Columbia's many natural hot springs. The province's 95 known hot springs attest to BC's violent volcanic past. Surface waters trickle down through cracks and fissures in the earth's crust to be heated deep underground and bubble upward again, emerging as hot, mineral-laden water.

Several developed hot pools are scattered throughout BC, but there are also many sites where the pools are simply natural depressions and there are no change rooms, towel rentals, or admission fees. Undeveloped sites tend to be clothing-optional. Never use soap or shampoo in a natural hot spring; even biodegradable cleaning fluids leave a residue and can damage delicate ecosystems.

Air charters are widely available. Seeing BC from the air is like looking at a huge three-dimensional map, complete with color and movement. Heli-skiing and hiking are variations on this theme—as long as you have the cash you can access remote areas quickly and with little effort. In northern BC and along the coast, air access is often the only means to get to where you want to be.

To charter a plane, simply drop in to the local airport or airstrip and talk to the pilots, or consult the local yellow pages. You can charter a plane for a few hours' sightseeing, to take you and your gear to a remote lake or river and pick you up again at the other end, or to drop food caches for a long hike or canoe trip. Pilots are usually able to give excellent commentary about the landscape over which you are flying.

Both downhill and cross-country skiing are wildly popular in BC. As for snowboarding, BC produced an Olympic champion in 1998, due in no small part to the first-rate riding available at Whistler. When it comes to skiing, variety is the theme once again. You can enjoy a quiet glide with the kids in an urban park, a major glacier traverse, tony world-class glitter and downhill-racing events, family-run ski hills, helicopter access to the world's best powder, and, of course, plenty of extreme skiing and riding.

Nordic skiing on groomed backcountry trails is among the most popular and widely accessible sports in BC. You can rent skis virtually anywhere, and the skiing is nearly unlimited. All you need is snow (and there's plenty of that). For more information, contact Cross-country BC, 106, 3003-30 St., Vernon, BC V1T 9J5, 250/545-9600.

Whether or not downhill skiing can be considered in the same category as ecotravel is debatable. Never mind. In most parts of BC, winter comes early and stays late—and dumps a whole lot of snow while it's here. Residents have learned to make the best of the situation. As a result, downhill skiing is ubiquitous; there are 35 developed downhill ski resorts in the province. Helicopter and snowcat skiing offer participants easy access to incredible powder bowls, tree skiing, and trackless high-alpine terrain in the company of experienced guides. For many, this is the ultimate ski experience. Classics in this realm are Canadian Mountain Holidays (Blue River) and Bugaboo Lodge. Snowcat skiing is available from several operators in Golden and Revelstoke.

PRACTICAL TIPS

British Columbia has a well-developed tourism industry and associated tourist information system. For information on the province, including accommodations reservations and excellent regional guides, call Super, Natural British Columbia, 800/663-6000 (throughout North America) or 604/663-6000 (international). You can also check out their Web site at www.travel.bc.ca.

For tourism marketing and information, BC is divided into nine destination regions: Vancouver Island/Gulf Islands; Vancouver Coast and Mountains; Okanagan-Similkameen; Kootenay Country; High Country; Cariboo-Chilcotin; North by Northwest; Peace River-Alaska Highway; and British Columbia Rockies. Contact information for each of these regions is in Appendix B of this book.

A really handy service is the Travel Infocentre Network. More than 130 communities throughout BC maintain Infocentres, which are staffed by helpful people who can book tours, give you maps and brochures on local attractions, parks, and activities, help you find outfitters and tour operators, and even make hotel reservations for you. Note, however, that many Infocentres operate only during the summer.

When to travel depends on where you intend to go. Generally, the farther north you go (or the higher in elevation) the shorter the travel season. Summers are pleasant throughout BC, and even in the mountains and far north the days can be hot and sunny. Therefore, summer is the busiest time regardless of where in the province you are, although remote locations are relatively less crowded than the Gulf Islands, Okanagan, and Rocky Mountain regions.

May and June can be great times to travel in BC. The weather is usually acceptable even for camping and outdoor activities, and the highways, hotels, campgrounds, and hiking trails are less busy than in July and August. Many attractions and activities are only available during the summer. September brings gorgeous autumn colors and cooler weather. October through March or April can bring wet, cold, and stormy weather.

Ski season varies depending on where you are. The mega-ski resorts of Whistler and Blackcomb enjoy an elongated season due to their altitude—it's possible to ski in June at Blackcomb, though the regular season is generally from late November until late April. In the interior and the Rockies the season can begin as early as October and last until late April. Many resorts offer discounts for early and late-season skiing, and some offer deals during January, which tends to be the coldest month.

What it costs to travel in BC depends on where you travel and what you do. It is possible to travel inexpensively, camp, purchase your own food (as opposed to restaurant meals), and generally have a low-budget vacation. Conversely, if you opt for an all-inclusive package tour with a guide or outfitter, stay at guest ranches, lodges, or hotels, and participate in any number of attractions and activities, you can literally spend thousands of dollars. One saving grace, for American visitors at least, is the current low value of the Canadian dollar. Nonetheless, travelers tend to find BC expensive, especially when federal and provincial sales taxes are added to nearly everything. Bring money.

You will find a full range of accommodations styles and prices throughout BC. Generally speaking, the more remote the location, the fewer amenities you can expect and the fewer accommodation choices you may have—though some remote mountain lodges are luxurious. Also, be aware that many remote facilities operate seasonally (summer only).

For specific information on accommodations, write to Tourism BC (see Appendix B) and request the *BC Accommodation Guide* or write to the tourism region that you intend to visit (also in Appendix B). Infocentres throughout the province can also help you find accommodations.

The BC tourism ministry operates a toll-free accommodations and reservations line: 800/663-6000. Use this number to make reservations and to obtain advice on travel, events, and points of interest. Accommodations available include everything from bed-and-breakfasts to luxury hotels. This is a terrific and highly recommended service, and it's free. You can get specific information on bed-and-breakfasts by calling the BC Bed and Breakfast Association, 604/276-8613.

Low-cost accommodations are widely available, although there are more choices in large urban centers than in the smaller communities of the interior and the north. Further information is available from Hostelling International, BC Region, 402, 134 Abbott St., Vancouver, BC V6B 2K4, 800/661-0020 or 604/684-7111; or from the YMCA, 955 Burrard St., Vancouver, BC V6Z 1Y2, 604/681-0221. Many outfitters and tour companies also provide accommodations as part of their packages.

Tent, trailer and RV camping is widely available in BC. As with fixed-roof accommodations, campgrounds run the gamut from luxurious to basic. BC Parks and Parks Canada operate campgrounds within the provincial and national parks. There are more than 11,000 campsites in BC's provincial and national parks. Basic facilities at most of these campgrounds include flush or pit toilets, firewood (for sale), fire pits or barbecues, picnic tables, and potable water.

Commercial campgrounds are located in some provincial and national parks and at or near many major natural and recreational destinations throughout the province. These campgrounds tend to have more facilities and amenities than provincial or national park campgrounds, but generally they cost more, too. The BC Forest Service has established numerous primitive campgrounds—with minimal facilities—throughout the province, usually with logging roads for access. Although the Forest Service started charging fees for the sites in 1999, they are still a bargain. For more information on camping fees, see Appendix A. Some Native reserves and villages also operate campgrounds, with varying facilities and fees.

The *Accommodation Guide*, available from Tourism BC (see Appendix B), lists campgrounds. Infocentres are also good sources for camping information. You can make reservations in over 50 selected provincial and national park campgrounds. Information on parks and the reservation system can be found on the Web at www.discovercamping.ca. To reserve a spot in BC's great outdoors, call 800/689-9025. Do take full advantage of this reservation service, especially for popular campgrounds during the summer—otherwise you may find that all spots are taken. Note that some parks contain more than one campground, but not all campgrounds in a given park may accept reservations. Campgrounds accepting reservations place limits on party sizes (number of vehicles and number of people per campsite). If you arrive at the campsite with more vehicles or people than your reservation allows, the reservation may not be honored, or you may be assessed additional fees. For campgrounds not on the reservation system, it's a good idea to find a campsite early in the day.

Anyone using a national park, even for a day-hike or overnight RV camping, must purchase a park-user pass, available at the entry gates or from the warden's office/visitors information center in the national park you are visiting. You can also purchase a pass by phoning 800/748-7275—have your credit card ready. Failure to purchase a pass can result in a fine.

Wilderness-camping passes must also be purchased by anyone venturing into the backcountry in a national park. See the wardens, do the paperwork, and stay out of trouble. The registration/pass system was created to regulate and minimize impact on the backcountry, and the fees collected are used to improve facilities and interpretive programs within individual parks. For more information about national park passes and wilderness-camping passes, contact Canadian Heritage, Parks Canada Information Services, Western Regional Office, Room 522, 220-Fourth Ave. SW, Calgary, Alberta T2P 3H8, 403/292-4401, www.parkscanada.pch.gc.ca.

Obey fire bans, which are placed on designated areas in times of high risk of wild fire. Always inquire about fire bans prior to venturing into the backcountry. Burn carefully, never leave a fire unattended, don't set a fire when the wind is high (especially if the wind is blowing toward heavy, dry brush), and keep water handy in case you need it quickly. Put out the fire thoroughly (douse with water, stir the ashes, douse again).

Protection of water bodies is another very important part of camping and backcountry use. Try to avoid wading in streams, where your actions will stir up sediment that could affect fish and insect eggs and other water-dwellers. Use a biodegradable soap for washing clothes, dishes, and yourself. Never wash anything directly in a stream or lake, because even biodegradable soaps can damage organisms and vegetation. Sand and gravel work well as abrasives for cleaning pots.

As for drinking water, although the quality of water in most places is excellent, you should always boil it prior to drinking it or cooking with it. Doing so helps prevent "beaver fever"—abdominal discomfort and diarrhea caused by giardia, a microorganism that lives in cold, moving water. In some dry areas, many Forest Service camping areas, and on some of the Gulf Islands, fresh water is very limited and you should bring your own supply. It's always a good idea to have a large bottle of water with you.

Hornby Island

CHAPTER 2

Conservation and Responsible Tourism

The province's travel authority uses "Super, Natural British Columbia" as its slogan, and the tagline seems to work. British Columbia records an average of 24 million overnight stays each year, with travelers spending more than $5.5 billion annually. Tourism is big biz in BC. In fact, according to some statistics, tourism is second only to forestry for generating income and employment in the province.

British Columbia's provincial parks record more than 20 million visits annually. As such near-urban parks as Manning Provincial Park and Pacific Rim National Park Reserve become ever more crowded and less like wilderness, travelers venture farther afield in search of the soul and essence of BC. A recent survey indicated that the fastest-growing tourism regions are the Chilcotin and Cariboo, formerly the haunts of only a handful of rugged wilderness-seekers. The Tatshenshini River, which rises in the Yukon and flows through the very remote northwest corner of BC before crossing into Alaska, sees more than 1,000 rafters in the brief summer season—an incredible number considering the river's isolation. Take a look through any good bookstore in BC and you'll find entire sections devoted to travel within the province. No doubt about it: Even the far corners of British Columbia are receiving a steadily increasing stream of people.

WHAT IS ECOTOURISM?

Ecotourism is synonymous with self-discovery. Who can regard a mountain sunrise without a shiver? Who can hear a loon and not ache? Who can climb laboriously to the top of a ridge and not spare a thought for the glaciers that carved the edge? Ecotravel gives ordinary people the chance to see, feel, smell, and touch nature. It allows them to develop a bond with nature, to understand that the natural realm is worth preserving. From the most humble wander through an urban park to a challenging journey through a remote and beautiful place, ecotravel serves to promote an appreciation for the natural environment that sustains us.

Are you an ecotraveler? If you are a curious traveler, someone who wants to know the story behind the scenery, then you're certainly a cut above the average tourist. If your curiosity is tempered by respect for vegetation and wildlife (you don't pick flowers, feed potato chips to deer, or pluck creatures from streams or tide pools), you could definitely count yourself among the ecologically aware and responsible. If you have respect for and even seek out local cultures, customs, and sacred sites, you can take your place among a growing legion of enlightened travelers. And if your heart quickens at the sight of a huge cedar in a dim, damp forest, if your eyes sting when thunder rolls above a canyon, you are perhaps an ecotraveler. Maybe I'm overly romantic. Then again, if dreamers like me had the upper hand here at the beginning of the twenty-first century, maybe ecotravel wouldn't be a craze—it would be a way of life.

By any definition, ecotravel encompasses the notion of responsibility. Sensitivity to the natural and cultural environments through which you are traveling, combined with an interest in landscape, vegetation and wildlife, human history, and environmental issues, creates a traveler with both curiosity and respect.

Of course, all this awareness and respect doesn't mean that you're not up for a little adventure. Being an ecotourist also implies that you're willing to get out of your car and walk, cycle, ski, or paddle your way into the heart of the place you're visiting. You're smart enough to know your limits (you don't endanger yourself or others), but you're not afraid to push yourself; you know that challenge brings rewards such as breathtaking scenery, new knowledge, and a deeper understanding of your surroundings and yourself.

"Adventure" travel, on the other hand, does not necessarily attract people with this combination of curiosity and respect for nature. An adventure traveler is someone seeking an experience outside the ordinary, a challenge, a thrill. Certainly, most adventurers are acutely aware of their environment, because often it's the environment itself that provides the challenge. Too often, though, adventurers are simply looking for another peak to conquer, another trophy to mount on the wall, another tale of adversity and triumph to share with their buddies back home.

Ferries are popular modes of transportation in BC.

There is an essential conundrum to ecotravel: You are sensitive to your natural surroundings, but your very presence can be a disturbance. For instance, the only access to some remote locations in BC is by plane, helicopter, or powerboat, all of which disturb wildlife and cause pollution. Horses can cause trail deterioration and import foreign plant species. Even hiking and camping can create erosion.

Once in the backcountry, humans have the potential to seriously harm the very ecosystems they've come to experience. However, if you have the knowledge and tools to minimize your impact and maximize your enjoyment, you stand to gain a life-changing experience without having a similar effect on the wildlife. Such experiences can motivate people to go back home and put time, effort, and dollars into preserving threatened areas or species on a local, regional, or national level. In this way, promoting responsible adventure and ecotourism promotes conservation and environmental awareness on a broad scale.

ENVIRONMENTAL ISSUES

With British Columbia's astonishing natural endowments, broad spectrum of environmental and recreation/education opportunities, vibrant Native culture, and vast wealth of natural resources, it's no wonder that opinions on how the province should be managed are divergent and often in direct opposition. To exploit or preserve? To save jobs or save trees? Not only is British Columbia a major tourist destination, but it's also a major international supplier of minerals, agricultural, and forest products. Thus are the seeds of controversy sewn!

A heavenly veneer coats the surface of British Columbia. If you don't look too closely, you might think that natural wonders are appreciated and protected, that the woods are full of wildlife, the streams jump with fish, the air is clear and the water fit to drink. You'd mostly be right, but . . .

Look closer. Under the surface, ecological destruction is widespread, sometimes cruelly blunt and obvious, other times extremely subtle and long-term. In some places, BC is an ecological hell. Among the major issues are: logging in old-growth forests; logging practices in general (clear-cutting, slope erosion and damage to streams, road construction, reforestation); recent provincial government initiatives to attract more mining to BC; dam development (new plans and the ongoing effects of existing dams); and dwindling wildlife and fish stocks.

The environmental movement has strong roots in BC. The internationally recognized group Greenpeace was founded in Vancouver in the 1960s, initially in opposition to whaling, then branching into anti-logging, anti-mining, and anti-nuclear activism. Other groups, some very radical, have coalesced around specific or local issues. It's a safe bet that any proposal for mining, logging, mineral exploration, or other development in BC will run smack into opposition, often well organized and well funded. Tactics can include international boycotts, civil disobedience, court injunctions, and more.

The forest-products industry is a significant economic factor in BC. The industry directly and indirectly employs 17 percent of BC's workforce, brings in $15 billion annually in revenues, and generates $4.3 billion in taxes (1998). On the other hand, in the late 1990s the industry suffered economic setbacks: mills closed, exports were reduced, jobs lost. As the economic underpinning of the entire province, the forestry sector is in trouble.

In British Columbia, forest preservation battles with economics all the way from the highest government offices to the lowest common denominator: personal lifestyle. The story of the BC forest industry includes governments and big business, but essentially it's a story of one-industry towns, of passionate individuals, of spiritual quests, of people simply trying to provide a livelihood for their families. There are many views, some moderate, some extreme.

Since the 1940s there has been a considerable increase in logging activity in the province, with little regard for habitat and watershed destruction or for preservation of aboriginal cultural and spiritual places. The province's timber resources once seemed endless, and most logging was carried out in rugged and remote areas where the clear-cuts and ecological damage were seldom seen. Environmental damage from logging is caused by the removal of trees and from poorly constructed logging roads, both of which can create massive

K. D. Wong/Blackbird Design

The logging industry has had a major impact on environmental issues in the province.

45

erosion on steep mountain slopes, degrading soil and polluting streams. The practice of clear-cut logging—removing every tree within a cut block and leaving a denuded, open scar littered with stumps, broken timber, and waste—has become widespread.

Since the 1970s the forest-products industry has come under closer scrutiny, thanks in no small part to improved access to remote areas coupled with environmental awareness, the conservation movement, aboriginal actions to protect sacred lands, and ecotourism. The conservation movement has gained momentum and has put logging in BC in the worldwide spotlight. According to the Sierra Club of Western Canada, over 75 percent of the old-growth forest that existed on southern Vancouver Island in 1954 had been logged by 1990. If that pace of logging continues, all unprotected old-growth timber between Port Alberni and Victoria will be gone by 2002.

Among the threatened regions is the north coast of the mainland, an area known as the Great Bear Rain Forest. Utterly remote and highly inaccessible until recently, the region now includes logging roads that allow the plunder of previously uneconomical old-growth forest. The forest is now deemed feasible to log as more-accessible timber supplies become depleted. The Western Canada Wilderness Committee has been mounting a major campaign against further logging in the Great Bear region, including lobbying for an international boycott of forest products created from old-growth timber. Check out the Great Bear Web site at www.wildernesscommittee.org/gbear.html#a1.

Lobbyists are also trying to preserve an area north of Vancouver in the Squamish/Whistler area known unofficially as the Randy Stoltmann Wilderness, an area that encompasses the drainage of the Elaho River and includes several very large trees.

In the summer of 1998 Macmillan-Bloedel (MacBlo), among the largest of BC's forest-industry corporations, announced that it would cease clear-cutting in old-growth forests. This declaration came in response partly to European boycotts of the company's lumber and wood products. The forest-products industry in general is critical of MacBlo's move, while environmental activists hail it as a bold step in the right direction. The declaration does not mean that MacBlo will cease logging in old-growth forests, but it does mean that alternatives to clear-cutting will be used in the future.

FACTS ABOUT FORESTRY

- *Canada is the world's largest exporter of forestry products.*
- *Approximately half of Canada's timber production is based in British Columbia.*
- *Vancouver Island has 89 watersheds covering more than 5,000 hectares (12,350 acres). Of these large watersheds, only five remained untouched by logging in 1997.*
- *Approximately 1 out of every 10 BC residents is directly employed by the forest industry.*

Who can say what forest giants and unique ecological resources were lost before people started to notice that British Columbia's forests are finite? Perhaps it's best not to look back with regret, but to look forward with insight.

British Columbia is rich in ore deposits, from aluminum to zinc. Mining requires ecological disturbance, if not destruction, regardless of the mine's size. Gold panners may trample fish eggs in streams; huge open pits and tailings ponds are the legacy of large-scale extraction of such ores as molybdenum, copper, lead, and coal. To give the mining industry its due, environmental practices are currently much improved from earlier days. Mining companies also continue to fund and conduct significant research in the areas of reclamation, erosion control, wildlife-population dynamics, and water management.

The fact remains, though, that ore deposits are where you find them, and often you find them in places that have other uses and other values. Thus, mining is on a constant collision course with nature conservancy. Take the Windy Craggy development, for example. Geddes Resources of Toronto wanted to extract the rich copper deposits situated above the Tatshenshini River in northwestern BC, among the most remote, rugged, and pristine regions anywhere on the planet. Activists maintained that opening the area to mining would mean the irreversible destruction of wildlife habitat and damage to the wild river. Eventually the provincial government came to the river's rescue, declaring the area a provincial park.

Contemporary global economics in the late 1990s slowed and even stopped the exploitation of mineral resources, at least for the time being. With commodity prices at all-time lows, many BC mines are closing. Even the giant Highland Valley copper mine near Logan Lake south of Kamloops—said to be Canada's largest open pit mine, covering a total area of 16,000 hectares (40,640 acres)—announced that operations would cease in 1999.

British Columbia's electric power is generated from several very large hydroelectric developments located throughout the province. While it might be argued that the power generated from these developments is nonpolluting, the truth is that no industrial facility can be built and operated without an environmental cost. In the case of dams, the cost is the permanent flooding of land, destruction of habitat and aboriginal sacred sites, and the alteration of stream-flow characteristics that affect vegetation, wildlife, and fish populations downstream from the dam—sometimes far downstream.

Williston Lake is an enormous reservoir created by the W. A. C. Bennett Dam on the Peace River. The lake is BC's largest reservoir and the ninth-largest reservoir in the world. It took five years to fill. Creation of the reservoir drowned the traditional homeland, settlements, and burial grounds of the Tsay Keh Dene people.

Perhaps the biggest impact of the Bennett Dam, however, occurred hundreds of miles to the east in Alberta. The Peace River formerly carried tons of silt suspended in the swift water. When the river encountered Lake Athabasca and the current slowed, sediment was deposited in the rich Peace-Athabasca Delta, home to enormous populations of waterfowl. When the Bennet Dam was built, downstream fish and wildlife populations decreased, and bogs and wetlands dried up. Only after weirs were constructed on the free-flowing Athabasca River, to imitate the effect of the Peace River's spring floods in the delta, did wildlife and waterfowl populations begin to recover.

Elsewhere in BC, Kinbasket Lake is a sinuous reservoir that floods much of the northern portion of the Rocky Mountain Trench at the former "Big Bend" of the Columbia River (the Columbia flows north from its headwaters at Columbia Lake, then makes a sharp turn around the Selkirk Mountains to begin its southward journey toward

GOING, GOING . . .

Among the world's rarest animals is the Vancouver Island marmot. The total wild population is just 70 individuals. These chocolate-brown cousins of the woodchuck are confined to a few slopes in the mountainous interior of Vancouver Island.

In 1999, the BC government and MacMillan Bloedel (a large forest-products corporation) announced the creation of a $2 million program designed to capture, breed, and release marmots. The Calgary and Toronto Zoos are currently conducting the captive-breeding program.

Washington and Oregon). The reservoir was created by the Mica Dam. At 242 meters (799 feet) high, this is the highest earth-fill dam in North America. Farther downstream on the Columbia, the Revelstoke Dam holds back Revelstoke Lake, which covers 120 kilometers (75 miles) of river valley from Revelstoke to the Mica Dam.

The Kootenay region in southeastern BC has several dams and reservoirs, including the Upper and Lower Arrow Lakes created by the Hugh Keenleyside Dam on the Columbia River at Castlegar. The lakes stretch a total of 220 kilometers (138 miles) from Castlegar northward to Revelstoke. Several settlements had to be relocated to higher ground; some towns were completely abandoned.

Whether or not Pacific salmon stocks are truly endangered, what might be causing fish populations to decline, and what should be done to remedy the situation are topics for endless debate in British Columbia. It seems certain that several salmon species, especially coho and sockeye, are in trouble. The cause for dwindling fish stocks is a combination of overfishing; the degradation of spawning streams resulting from industrial pollution, dams, and poor logging practices; and environmental factors such as El Niño. Discussion on how to resolve the problem is bogged down in arguments between commercial, sport, and aboriginal fishers; between provincial and federal governments; and between Canada and the United States. The issue is characterized by acrimony and greed, endless research studies, high-level international meetings, and newspaper headlines. Meanwhile, salmon become ever more endangered. In 1998 the federal government banned the commercial coho fishery in Canadian waters and severely restricted the commercial sockeye fishery.

Also in the summer of 1998 the British Columbia government announced a multimillion-dollar program to begin the painstaking task of bringing spawning streams back into production. The program will enhance streams through physical clean-up programs, and through the creation of artificial spawning beds and channels. Project leaders say that it could be 10 years or more before results of the program are realized, and even longer before natural salmon-production levels approach traditionally high numbers. The jury's still out on this one.

Meanwhile, as revenues from commercial fishing decline (estimated to be $100 million in 1998, down from $500 million in the 1980s), sportfishing has gained. In 1998 sportfishing brought $500 million into the province. The provincial government has given sport-fishing outfitters and lodges access to salmon stocks that are off-limits to commercial fishermen—but often on a catch-and-release basis.

The international spotlight also shines on BC wildlife, specifically bears. With a steady demand in some areas of the world for bear parts, especially paws and gall bladders (thought by some cultures to have medicinal or aphrodisiacal powers), poaching is an ongoing problem. Even without illegal hunting, bears are threatened by habitat destruction, increasing human encroachment in previously remote and unreachable places, and legal hunting.

In 1998 the international conservation group Environmental Investigation Agency, based in London, England, published a report that condemned legal grizzly bear hunting in BC. The report said the provincial government had vastly overestimated the number of grizzlies in the province and that hunting, combined with other stresses, would push the grizzly toward extinction. The BC government countered the allegations by saying that between 200 and 400 bears are legally shot every year, out of an estimated population of 10,000 to 13,000 bears. (This population figure is disputed, even by biologists working for the provincial government; estimates from other sources range from a high of 8,000 bears to a low of 4,000.) Despite the lack of a solid estimate of the number of grizzly bears in the province, the government has no plans to restrict or ban the legal shooting of grizzlies.

According to the British Columbia Endangered Species Coalition, BC has the highest biodiversity in all of Canada but also the highest number of species that are vulnerable, threatened, or endangered— 743 species are in some danger, including mammals, birds, fish, amphibians, reptiles, and plants. For the most part, habitat loss is the main reason for dwindling populations. Pollution, disease, hunting, and overfishing are other reasons. For more information on Canada's endangered species, visit the Web site of the Committee on the Status of Endangered Wildlife in Canada: www.cwsscf.ec.gc.ca.

PARKS AND PROTECTED AREAS

Now for the good news: In 1986, in an effort to protect wildlife and promote biodiversity, the United Nations passed a resolution calling on member countries to preserve and protect 12 percent of their land

Grizzly bears, an endangered species, need to roam large territories.

D. Leighton

51

base by 2000. Canada adopted the resolution, and British Columbia is leading the way in meeting the UN's objective.

Canada established national parks in the Rocky Mountains of BC in the 1880s and 1890s. In the spirit of the times, lands of particular scenic beauty and recreation/tourist potential were set aside, but logging and resource extraction were allowed to operate within park boundaries for many years afterward. By 1900 less than 0.5 percent of BC's apparently endless wilderness was protected.

Logging and resource extraction escalated after World War II, but preservation did not keep pace; by the 1950s about 4 percent of the province was protected, but this amount decreased as some parks were actually reduced in size to allow resource development. Between 1970 and 1990, protected areas in BC increased to 7 percent of the land base, thanks in large part to the actions of various environmental groups that resulted in pro-park policies by the government.

Then came the 1986 UN resolution. The BC provincial government of the day responded with the Protected Areas Strategy, an ambitious policy to set aside at least 12 percent of the province by 2000. Since 1992 the BC government has been legislating an average of about 810,000 hectares (2 million acres) of new protected areas per year. By comparison, approximately 224,000 hectares (553,000 acres) are actively logged throughout the province in any given year. By early 1999 approximately 11 percent of the province's land base was protected in parks or reserves of various types, with the BC government committed to set aside another 250,000 hectares (618,000 acres) by the end of the year. Within the Lower Mainland (the province's most heavily populated region, encompassing the metropolitan area of Vancouver) about 14 percent of the land base is now protected. Protected areas in the Muskwa-Kechika region of the northern Rockies alone accounts for about 1.2 percent of the province's total land area.

Of the 59 million hectares (145.7 million acres) of forested land in the province, about 33 million hectares (81.5 million acres) are either protected, preserved, or otherwise unavailable to logging. That's an area larger than England and Scotland combined. Yet conservationists continue to hammer the government and to protest logging companies' activities, saying that while the amount of land preserved is important, the *type* of land preserved is equally vital. In the

Lower Mainland, for example, while 14 percent of the land base is preserved, the majority of the forested land under protection is upper-alpine and not the productive old-growth forests found at low- and mid-elevation slope positions. Furthermore, creating a system of disconnected "island parks" in no way serves to protect endangered wildlife species such as wolves and grizzly bears that require large territories. Conservationists charge that park creation is still based on scenic features and not on ecological principles.

Despite environmentalists' claims to the contrary, British Columbia's newest parks seem to represent a shift in thinking, toward protection of habitats and biodiversity instead of the former focus on recreation and tourism. Parks are now being established based on protecting representative ecosystems, even aboriginal cultural sites, regardless of location, accessibility, or recreation potential.

The present-day parks system in BC works like this: National parks, including national historic sites, are of national significance and are owned and operated by the Canadian federal government. National parks in BC include Kootenay, Yoho, Mount Revelstoke, Glacier, Pacific Rim National Park Reserve, and Gwaii Hannaas National Park Reserve. (Unresolved aboriginal land claims mean that the latter two parks have not been fully declared and legislated; however, both are operated as national parks, complete with user fees.) The Rocky Mountain national parks (Kootenay and Yoho), the Tatshenshini-Alsek region, and the abandoned Haida village of Sgun Gwaii (Ninstints) are BC's three UNESCO world heritage sites.

Throughout BC, provincial parks exist for many reasons: to preserve a particular natural or cultural feature, for example, or to provide recreation opportunities. As discussed above, provincial parks are increasingly being established to preserve representative ecosystems. Some are cooperatively managed by BC Parks and local First Nations—the Nisga'a Memorial Lava Bed Park is a good example. In other areas, the province comanages parklands with regional, municipal, and federal concerns. The Lower Mainland Nature Legacy near Vancouver and the Commonwealth Nature Legacy in and around Victoria are assemblages of regional and municipal parks, while the Pacific Marine Heritage Legacy includes a commitment for a new national park combined with ecological reserves and marine parks in the Strait of Georgia. Recreation areas are set aside for fishing, boating, and wilderness

Holly Quan

*Totem poles, Gwaii Haanas
National Park Reserve*

hiking, but are not fully protected and are subject to development from mining and logging. Most recreation areas are on Crown land (see below).

More than 100 ecological reserves throughout the province protect a variety of vegetation and wildlife communities. These areas serve as research sites and as benchmarks against which environmental change (degradation) can be measured. Ecological reserves also protect rare, unique, or endangered species. Camping is not allowed in ecological reserves—in fact, access to many reserves is restricted in order to preserve the fragile ecology they encompass.

Coastal marine parks may be developed (offering services, toilets, designated campsites) or undeveloped. Camping is allowed in most marine parks, and generally there is no fee for use or camping. The same rules apply to camping in marine parks as in any other campsite—control your fires, use the outhouses or privies (or use the woods, away from the beach), and pack out your garbage. Be aware that foreshores above the high-tide line are often private property; "no trespassing" signs should be honored. However, in Canada all beaches below high-tide line are public; people can walk and paddlers can pull ashore anywhere, except where leases have been granted to private wharves, marinas, port facilities, or log booms. Marine parks and recreation reserves offer the best choices for hiking, beaching your craft, or setting up camp.

The provincial government owns much of BC. Government-owned areas are known as Crown land (also called public land) and are usually leased to logging companies for tree farming (logging) or to ranchers for grazing cattle. In theory, Crown lands are available for public access; however, you may find "no trespassing" signs posted.

Don't just ignore them. Instead, get permission to hike, ski, camp, or whatever it is you wish to do.

For more information on parks in British Columbia, contact BC Parks, 800 Johnson St., Victoria, BC V8V 1X4, 250/387-5002; or Canadian Heritage Parks Canada, Information Section, Western Regional Office, Room 522, 220-Fourth Ave. SE, P.O. Box 2989, Station M, Calgary, Alberta T2P 3H8, 403/294-4401.

CONSERVATION GROUPS

The world's largest environmental organization, Greenpeace, was founded in a church basement in Vancouver in the 1960s. By 1986 Greenpeace was established in 26 countries and had an annual income of over $100 million (CDN). Initially committed to activism based on public education and awareness building, and effective political lobbying and media use, the organization has increasingly taken a "no compromise" stance. In 1990 Greenpeace called for a "grassroots revolution against pragmatism and compromise."

Protests and civil disobedience are among the conservation movement's main sources of action and publicity. The first such action in BC occurred in 1984 on Meares Island near Tofino on Vancouver Island's western shore. Since then similar protests have occurred in Haida Gwaii (the Queen Charlotte Islands), the Stein Valley, and the forests of Clayoquot Sound. Recently, environmental activists and loggers squared off in the Stoltmann Wilderness, an unofficial wilderness area at the head of Jervis Inlet and encompassing Princess Louisa Inlet, just three hours north of Vancouver. (See Appendix B for a list of BC's major environmental and conservation groups.)

TIPS FOR RESPONSIBLE TRAVEL

No matter how fit and well equipped you are, or how well you know the territory or how long you've been visiting a particular spot, as an ecotourist some things will always be beyond your control. Accidents happen, the weather changes, people suddenly become seriously ill. Be aware that even for apparently mundane or routine activities, an

NEW PARKS IN BRITISH COLUMBIA

Among BC's recently declared parks are:

Tatshenshini-Alsek Wilderness Park—958,000 hectares (2.36 million acres) in the heart of North America's largest protected wilderness; also a UNESCO world heritage site

Spatsizi Plateau Wilderness Park—656,785 hectares (1.6 million acres) in northwestern BC; includes the Grand Canyon of the Stikine River

Khutzeymateen Grizzly Bear Sanctuary—Located in the Coast Mountains north of Prince Rupert, this was the first area in Canada to be specifically preserved for grizzly bears and their habitat.

Scott Islands Marine Park—No development (campgrounds, trails, etc.) is planned for this rugged northern tip of Vancouver Island, one of the world's windiest places.

Akamina-Kishinena Provincial Park—This mountain wilderness in the southeast corner of the province protects habitat for a dense population of mountain goats.

Muskwa-Kechika region—Declared wilderness in October 1997, this northern Rocky Mountain region encompasses an area the size of Switzerland and is the largest intact wilderness south of the 60th parallel. More than 1 million hectares (2.64 million acres) are protected; in addition, the wilderness is surrounded by 3.24 million hectares (8 million acres) of special management lands.

Stein Valley Nlaka'pamux Provincial Heritage Park—This pristine wilderness watershed, sacred to the Nlaka'pamux First Nation and just hours from Vancouver, was the site of a protracted and bitter dispute between activists and loggers. It was declared a park in November 1995.

element of risk is always present. Travel can give you the thrill of a lifetime, but it can also lead to danger.

It is your personal responsibility to ensure that you are adequately prepared and equipped for the adventure you are about to undertake. For your own safety and the safety of others, it is essential that you assess your abilities, equipment, and plans honestly and accurately. There is no room in the backcountry for bluffing and bravado.

Many of the destinations in this book are described as "wilderness"—and it is meant as a warning. *Do not* venture into remote backcountry areas unless you are experienced and self-reliant. Increasingly, as the cost for backcountry rescue operations goes up, the person requiring the evacuation or rescue receives a bill for services rendered. And in some very remote areas of the province, rescue is all but impossible.

If you have limited time, resources, or experience, hiring a guide or outfitter is an excellent idea. Guides can enrich your experience by providing information while you travel; they can provide specialized equipment that you may not own or wish to purchase; and they can often obtain access to areas that may be off-limits to unescorted adventurers. Not all guides are created equal, though. If you are considering using the services of a guide or outfitter, research the company carefully before committing yourself to its care. How long has the operator been in business? Can you contact previous clients for an assessment of the operator's service? Does the operator's literature or Web site emphasize safety and environmental responsibility?

Courtesy and respect are essential for sharing British Columbia's unique natural splendors with other adventurers. The notion of "leave-no-trace" camping should dictate where and how you establish your camp, how you live in the woods, and how diligently you pack out waste (even other campers' garbage). As the demands on BC's wilderness increase, with more and more people able and willing to access ever more remote places, clean camping has become an essential practice for ensuring that the wilderness remains wild.

Several destinations described in this book are on aboriginal lands. While First Nations generally welcome and encourage visitors, remember that you are a guest and that courteous and respectful behavior is appropriate. When traveling through Native lands, obey all signs and restrictions.

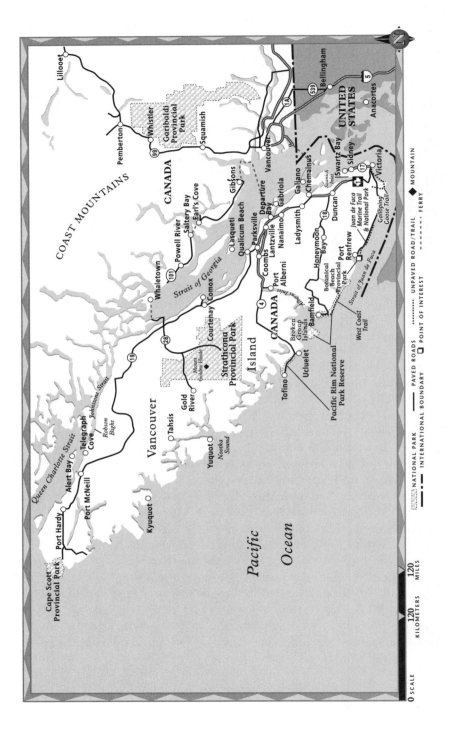

CHAPTER 3

Vancouver Island

Vancouver Island is a study in extremes, from the wet and windy west to the Mediterranean climate of the sheltered eastern shore. The island is home to one national park and several stunning provincial parks, as well as some of the world's oldest and tallest trees. Other natural wonders include Canada's highest waterfall, Della Falls; the Upana Caves, an extensive underground cavern system; and Robson Bight, an ecological reserve where orca whales come to perform a strange belly-rubbing ritual on the gravel bars not far from Telegraph Cove.

Despite extensive urban development on the south and east coasts of the island and continuing controversies associated with logging, mining, and fishing, Vancouver Island embodies British Columbia's outstanding environmental, recreational, and cultural heritage perhaps more than any other part of the province. You'll find a lifetime of things to do and see on the island—the information in this chapter only scratches the surface.

LAY OF THE LAND

Vancouver Island, the largest island off North America's west coast, is a long, thin chunk of rock. It's 460 kilometers (287.5 miles) long,

K. D. Wong/Blackbird Design

The west coast is exposed to the Pacific Ocean's full force.

and varies in width from 50 to 80 kilometers (31 to 50 miles). The island's west coast is deeply incised with fjords, inlets, and bays; countless islands, islets, and rocks dot the shattered coastline. The east side of the island exhibits a different character, with many sandy beaches and only one major inlet. Vancouver Island is separated from the mainland by (from north to south) Queen Charlotte Strait, Johnstone Strait, and the Strait of Georgia, collectively known as the Inside Passage. Juan de Fuca Strait lies between Vancouver Island and the Olympic Peninsula of Washington State.

In the southeastern portion of Vancouver Island, the climate is mild and relatively dry, even in winter. Golfers hit the links in February, just as daffodils and crocuses begin to bloom. Summers can be deliciously warm, cooled by ocean breezes and almost never humid. This Mediterranean climate is caused by the rain-shadow effect, created by the Olympic Peninsula and mountains in Washington. Average annual rainfall at Victoria is 619 millimeters (24.75 inches), a mere trickle in comparison with the 3,943 millimeters

(157.72 inches—more than 13 feet) that douse Port Renfrew on the island's west coast. Farther north, Vancouver Island's east coast becomes increasingly maritime, but it is still not as wet and wild as the Pacific side of the island.

The west coast of Vancouver Island is exposed to the full, unhindered force of the Pacific Ocean. Freezing temperatures are rare, but wet weather is not—rain is the defining characteristic of the west coast all year. Winter storms can be fierce, with enormous surf driving into the headlands, tossing logs onto the beach as though they were toothpicks. Fog is also common, even in summer.

The Insular Mountains run the length of Vancouver Island, and the island's interior climate varies with altitude—cooler and wetter at higher elevations. The highest peak on the island is Mount Golden Hinde at 2,200 meters (7,260 feet). Snow arrives at the higher elevations in November and lingers until April.

Victoria, the largest city on the island and BC's provincial capital, is situated on the dry southeastern tip of Vancouver Island. Nanaimo, the island's only other major city, is located on the east coast, 113 kilometers (70 miles) north of Victoria.

HISTORY AND CULTURE

Aboriginal people have lived on Vancouver Island since shortly after the last Ice Age, when glaciers melted and retreated from the lowlands. Petroglyphs (rock art) found south of Nanaimo are believed to be 10,000 years old. Major First Nations on the island are the Nuu-chah-nulth on the west coast, Kwakwaka'wakw (Kwakiutl) in the northern and eastern portions of the island, and Lekwammen (Coast Salish) in the southeast. These Native peoples developed art forms such as wood carving and basketry, along with complex social structures, spiritual beliefs, and rituals. At the time of European contact, perhaps 15,000 Native people lived on Vancouver Island.

The west coast of Vancouver Island was first visited by Europeans in the 1770s, when Spanish explorers dropped anchor to trade with the Natives. Russian, British, and American traders, lured by the abundance of sea otters off the west coast, soon followed, as did whalers and sealers from several nations. England gained control of

61

the island in 1794. The Hudson's Bay Company (HBC) built a trading post in the area of present-day Victoria in 1843. In 1849 the island became a British Crown Colony.

Mineral exploitation on the island began in 1850 with the discovery of coal at Nanaimo. When gold was discovered on the Fraser River (on the mainland) in 1858, the tiny settlement of Victoria—the main access and supply center for gold seekers—suddenly became a boomtown. (Vancouver didn't exist at the time.) Logging and sawmill operations served to open up the island's west coast. The HBC built the island's first sawmill in 1849. Logging fueled the exploration and settlement of the island's northern half.

Victoria's prosperity grew steadily, fueled by lumber and coal. Over on the mainland, the Canadian Pacific Railway chose Burrard Inlet as the western terminus of the transcontinental railway and established a new town, Vancouver. It quickly became a busy port and surpassed Victoria as the region's economic powerhouse. Victoria had to be content with retaining political power in the province.

On Vancouver Island the lifestyle tends to be casual, especially on the west coast. The northern half of the island is the territory of loggers and fishermen; you'd be smart to keep your environmental opinions to yourself when visiting the northern towns.

FLORA AND FAUNA

The big news on Vancouver Island is big trees. Canada's largest known red cedar, Douglas fir, and Sitka spruce trees are all on the island. Unfortunately, where there are big trees, logging companies are soon to follow. The extensive old-growth rain forest that once blanketed the southwest portion of the island is all but gone, and bitter conservation battles rage over the fate of the few remaining untouched watersheds on the west coast. The northern portion of the island is similarly in the grip of forest-products companies, with significant areas of clear-cutting and reforestation—and more disputes.

As you might expect, the dry and mild southern climate has given rise to plant communities not found elsewhere on the island—or elsewhere in Canada, for that matter. The rare Garry oak ecosystem once thrived in this region. This community—grassland with thickets of

Garry oak and arbutus (also called madrone) and laced with flowering plants such as camas—has now nearly disappeared due to urban and agricultural development.

Only 33 species of mammals inhabit the island; notable for their absence are coyotes, moose, and chipmunks. Among the island's mammals are black bears, cougars, the extremely rare Vancouver Island marmot, black-tailed deer, and marine mammals such as sea lions, seals, and several species of whales.

The Pacific Flyway passes over Vancouver Island. As a result, the island becomes a temporary home to huge populations of migratory birds, in addition to summer-only and year-round resident bird populations. Approximately 150 species stop over on their way to northern breeding grounds or wintering areas to the south.

Bald eagle

K. D. Wong/Blackbird Design

VISITOR INFORMATION

Access to Vancouver Island is by ferry, bus, or air. BC Ferries links Vancouver Island with the mainland. Major ferry terminals are located at Victoria, Nanaimo, Courtenay/Comox, and Port Hardy. Swartz Bay, at the northern tip of Saanich Peninsula, is the BC Ferries terminal closest to Victoria—32 kilometers (20 miles) north of the city. Crossing time from Vancouver takes about an hour and a half.

Another great way to access Victoria is via the *Victoria Clipper* from Seattle, a passenger-only hydrofoil (see Appendix A). The *Victoria Clipper* docks in Victoria's Inner Harbour, just steps from the visitor infocentre, shopping, restaurants, the Royal BC Museum, and accommodations. Washington State Ferries, operating from Anacortes,

Washington, land at the Sidney ferry terminal, five kilometers (three miles) south of the Swartz Bay terminal. Ferries operating from Port Angeles, Washington, dock in Victoria's Inner Harbour.

There are two ferry terminals at Nanaimo: Departure Bay and Duke Point. Ferries from Departure Bay link with Horseshoe Bay northwest of Vancouver. Crossing time is approximately an hour and a half. Ferries operating from the terminal at Duke Point link Nanaimo with Tsawwassen, south of Vancouver. Crossing time for that trip is about two hours.

Ferries link Port Hardy on the island's northern end with Prince Rupert on the mainland, just south of the Alaska Panhandle. This ride is a magnificent trip through the Inside Passage—you get the same scenery as the big cruise ships at a fraction of the cost. Crossing time is approximately 14 hours.

You can take a bus from downtown Vancouver to either Victoria or Nanaimo, with connections to other island destinations from either of these cities. The fare includes your ferry passage. See Appendix A for a list of bus companies.

Victoria and Nanaimo both have airports. Several flights per day link both cities with Vancouver and other destinations in Canada, the United States, and overseas. The island has numerous small airstrips—you can fly from Vancouver to Tofino on the island's west coast in just 45 minutes. For a list of commercial and charter airlines, see Appendix A.

Once on the island, the best way to get from point to point is by driving. The Sooke Road (Highway 14) leaves Victoria and winds 95 kilometers (60 miles) around the southern end of Vancouver Island to the village of Port Renfrew. En route are several exceptional beaches for surfing, windsurfing, and beachcombing, and the Juan de Fuca Marine Trail. Port Renfrew is the southern end of the West Coast Trail, which extends 76 kilometers (47.5 miles) up the coast to Bamfield.

For alternative access to Vancouver Island's west coast, travel north from Victoria on Highway 1 to Duncan, then west on Highway 18. This route also gives access to Cowichan Lake, the Ditidaht First Nations and Nitinat Lakes, and the northern terminus of the West Coast Trail at Bamfield. Highway 18 is paved as far as Honeymoon Bay. After that it's a logging road—rough but well traveled. Bamfield is 141 kilometers (88 miles) from Duncan.

ESQUIMALT AND NANAIMO RAILWAY

A wonderful way to see southern Vancouver Island, the E&N avoids much of the over-urbanized sprawl and zips up the "back way" between Victoria and Courtenay (up the coast from Nanaimo), crossing canyons and rivers, passing ghost towns, and diving in and out of dense forest. Passengers can take a round-trip excursion or travel one way. To cut costs, take your own food and beverages (no alcohol), sit back, and enjoy the scenery. The train departs from the VIA Rail station in downtown Victoria, next to the Johnson Street bridge. For schedules and reservations, call 250/383-4324 in Victoria or 800/561-8630 elsewhere in Canada.

Highway 4, also called the Island Highway, crosses the width of Vancouver Island from Parksville on the east side to Tofino and Ucluelet on the west coast. This highway, complete with its rock-and-roll climbs and drops, hairpin turns (when the signs say "Slow Down" they're not kidding), and views of ice-cold green rivers, clear-cut logging, old-growth forest, glaciers, and mountain lakes, is truly a spectacle—for passengers. Drivers must pay strict attention to the road. Despite the narrow, winding character of Highway 4, literally hundreds of thousands of people travel it every summer on their way to the beaches of Pacific Rim National Park Reserve.

A scenic day-excursion rail line links Victoria with Courtenay. The Malahat Railiner (also called the E&N for Esquimalt and Nanaimo, the railway's former name) completes one round trip daily. For information, see VIA Rail's Web site at www.viarail.ca. Other contact information is listed in Appendix A.

For detailed information on Vancouver Island, contact Tourism Vancouver Island, 302, 45 Bastion Square, Victoria, 250/382-3551, fax 250/382-3523, e-mail tavi@islands.bc.ca, www.travel.bc.ca/region/island.

NATURE AND ADVENTURE SIGHTS: VICTORIA

Victoria is situated at the southeastern tip of Vancouver Island, at one end of the Saanich Peninsula. The setting is stunning, with rolling and occasionally steep hills overlooking the sparkling waters of Juan de Fuca Strait and, beyond it, the snowy Olympic Mountains.

The city wraps around a sheltered embayment called Inner Harbour. The small downtown is pedestrian-friendly, with lots of cafés, galleries, shops, and attractions. Major streets are Government and Douglas (the main shopping streets, east of the harbor), Wharf (along the harbor, with more shops and cafés), Belleville (along the south side of the harbor, offering access to provincial government buildings and the Royal BC Museum), and Pandora and Johnson (east-west one-way streets crossing the harbor via the Johnson Street bridge at the north end of downtown).

The Visitor Infocentre, open daily, is located downtown on the harbor. The staff can provide you with local information and help with booking accommodations, charters, and activities in Victoria and the surrounding area. Contact the Victoria Visitor Infocentre, 812 Wharf St., 250/953-2033, or go to its Web site at www.travel.bc.ca.

Beacon Hill Park

This 74-hectare (183-acre) park overlooks Juan de Fuca Strait and the mountains of the Olympic Peninsula. In spring the hill is covered with yellow daffodils and blue camas. First Nations peoples called the hill Meequan and harvested the edible camas bulbs. Much of the park remains relatively wild, and it is a great place to stroll and escape the noise of the city. The world's tallest totem pole, the 56.4-meter (185-foot) *Spirit of Lekwammen*, stands at Songhees Point in the park.

Details: Dallas and Douglas Streets. Open daily until dusk. Admission is free.

Galloping Goose Trail Regional Park

This network of cycle and hiking trails extends 60 kilometers (37.5 miles), from Saanich in the north, through downtown Victoria, and onward to the old gold-mining settlement of Leechtown west of the city.

The trail wanders through a variety of landscapes—urban, suburban, agricultural, and coastal. Trails are constructed on the former Canadian National Railway right-of-way; thus the grades are easy and the trails are wide. Some sections are paved and wheelchair-accessible. Shops, restaurants, snack bars, and even rest rooms are located along the trails. Contrary to what you might be thinking, the trail is named Galloping Goose after a gas-powered rail bus that once transported passengers between Victoria and Leechtown.

Details: The trailhead is located at the west end of the Johnson Street bridge near downtown, but there are numerous access points. Get a map from the Victoria Infocentre.

Royal British Columbia Museum

In Canada, the designation "Royal" indicates that a place has been opened, dedicated, visited, or otherwise blessed by British royalty. The Royal British Columbia Museum has three floors of excellent displays on First Nations culture and traditional lifestyles, a great collection of artifacts and masks, and totem poles on the grounds. If you intend to travel extensively along BC's coast, this museum will greatly enhance your experience and your appreciation of the cultural diversity, intricacy, and impact of the coastal First Nations. Adjacent to the museum is **Thunderbird Park**, famous for totem poles from many coastal nations including Haida, Tsimshian, and Nuu-chah-nulth.

Details: 675 Belleville Street, 250/387-3014. Open daily. Adults $5–$7, with discounts for seniors, children, and families. Admission to Thunderbird Park is free.

NATURE AND ADVENTURE SIGHTS: SOUTH VANCOUVER ISLAND

Duncan

With a population of more than 5,000, this town is the main service center for the Cowichan Valley. This area is the traditional home of the Cowichan First Nation, famous these days for their heavy wool sweaters, caps, mitts, and other items. The clothing comes in soft shades of cream, gray, and brown and is ideal for a damp west coast winter. Duncan is also known as the "City of Totems." Thirty-seven poles have been erected along the highway and in downtown since 1985, and another 80 poles (some privately owned) are scattered throughout the Cowichan Valley. A guidebook available from the city's chamber of commerce shows where the poles are located and explains their symbology. The **Native Heritage Centre** (200 Cowichan Way, 250/746-8119) has exhibits on the Cowichan people, including a multimedia presentation, storytelling, dance demonstrations, and artists working on-site. A large selection of crafts (including those fabulous cozy sweaters) and carved items is for sale in the gift shop.

Details: 62 kilometers (39 miles) north of Victoria on the Trans-Canada Highway (Highway 1). Contact the Visitor Infocentre at 381 Trans-Canada Hwy., Duncan, 250/746-4636.

Juan de Fuca Marine Trail Provincial Park

This park was created in 1994 when Western Forest Products Limited donated 264 hectares (650 acres) of their land to the provincial government. China Beach and Botanical Beach, at the south and north ends of Juan de Fuca Marine Trail, were already parks.

The **Juan de Fuca Marine Trail** is the little sister of the famous West Coast Trail, but it's in no way inferior, except that portions pass through logged forests and clear-cuts. To hike the whole route takes four days. The trail parallels the shore for 47 kilometers (30 miles), from China Beach in the south to Botanical Beach just south of Port Renfrew. There are four access points to the trail, so if you aren't prepared to hike the entire length you can still enjoy a day or overnight outing. Each section of the trail is different, allowing you to choose a beach walk, forest hike, or combination.

The trail passes through lands that have been occupied by humans for perhaps 6,500 years. The southern portion of Vancouver Island is home to the Pacheenaht First Nation, who traditionally lived on the coast during summer (you can see evidence of an ancient village at Jordan River on the Sooke Road), moving inland during winter to avoid horrific Pacific storms. The Pacheenaht claim the entire area, from Point No Point to Port Renfrew. Claim discussions with the provincial government are still in the early stages.

Hiking the Juan de Fuca Marine Trail brings you face-to-face with

BC's number-one land-use and conservation issue: logging. Although the trail passes through old-growth forests of red cedar, logging and clear-cutting and the associated habitat destruction is evident in some areas. One spot was logged in the 1860s and again in the 1950s; trees in another portion were cut as recently as 1986. If nothing else, this trail is a condensed lesson in BC politics—ecological issues, pressures from increasing numbers of tourists and hikers, and Native land claims. Another point of contention along the trail's route is Sombrio Beach, a squatters' community that's a throwback to the freedom-loving spirit of the 1960s. The last remaining family, which lived in the area for more than 20 years, was evicted in 1998 from a tiny sliver of privately owned land adjacent to the Sombrio River.

The trail offers much more than an exposure to controversy, though. Besides the dense rain forest south of Botanical Beach, you'll find beaches to comb, whales to watch, and sunsets to contemplate. You'll see unique rock formations, seabirds, black bears, sunny days, and mist-shrouded mornings. This hike is no breeze—you need to be properly prepared, even if you're venturing out for just a day—but you'll be rewarded by the astonishing beauty of Vancouver Island's southwest coast.

Portions of the trail are cut off at high tide, so it's *essential* that you have tide tables for Sombrio and Tofino (see Appendix A). Waiting on the trail for the tide to fall can delay your hike and prolong your journey. And getting trapped by rising tidewater with unclimbable cliffs above you is no joke. Plan your hike around the rising and falling tides to avoid delays and danger. When using the tide tables during summer, remember to add one hour to the published times to adjust for daylight saving time.

The southern access point to the trail is at **China Beach** (a favorite landing spot for illegal Chinese immigrants during the time of the Oriental Exclusion Act). Even if you're not hiking the trail, China Beach is an excellent choice for a day trip from Victoria—great for picnics and beachcombing.

The trail from China Beach to **Sombrio Beach** is the most difficult section, with some steep and slippery climbs. Reasonably fit hikers can complete this portion in two days (with one or two overnights, depending on tides). The section from Sombrio to Parkinson Creek is mostly an easy walk of eight kilometers (five miles), with a few steep, difficult, and potentially slippery slopes. This section passes through the most recently logged area, now prime habitat for black bears. The final section, Parkinson Creek to Botanical Beach, is a 10-kilometer (six-mile) wonderland of temperate rain forest that can be hiked in a day (get an early start and watch those tides).

Botanical Beach Provincial Park is a terrific destination in its own right, known for excellent beachcombing and tide-pool exploration. If you intend to spend the day here—especially with kids—be aware that high tides cover most of the tide pools; incoming tides can block your retreat to shore if you're exploring marine life and not watching the rising water level. In addition, rogue waves have been known to occur here, as elsewhere on the Pacific coast. Tide pools are as fragile as any other ecology—minimize your disturbance.

Details: China Beach is accessible from Sooke Road (Highway 14), just west of Jordan River. Parkinson Creek can be reached via the Minute Creek Forest service road, which leads west from Highway 14. For Sombrio Beach, follow a dirt road west off the highway. Look for the BC Parks kiosk. For Botanical Beach Provincial Park, take Highway 14 to Port Renfrew and turn left onto Cerantes Road; it's another four kilometers (two and one-half miles) to the park. A Pacheenaht First Nation bus runs between access points. Call for a schedule and reservations: 250/647-5521 or 250/647-5556.

Port Alberni

Alberni Inlet is a long, thin arm of the Pacific that nearly cuts Vancouver Island in two. The inlet is spectacular: It's cloaked with forests, with the high peaks of the Insular Mountains rising straight from the water's edge and freshwater streams pouring down to the sea. The fishing here is superb—Port Alberni calls itself the "Salmon Fishing Capital of Canada" (but then, so does Campbell River on Vancouver Island's east coast).

Port Alberni, 40 kilometers (25 miles) from the Pacific Ocean, is a saltwater port at the head end of the inlet. Initially established as a mining and mill town, Port Alberni today is fueled by logging (the city has both a sawmill and a pulp mill) and fishing and retains an honest, working-class character.

Harbour Quay on Argyll Street has a collection of waterfront galleries, shops, and restaurants. It's also where you'll find **Alberni**

AUTHOR'S TOP PICKS:
WHALE WATCHING

- *Johnstone Strait—Johnstone Strait and Robson Bight are orca hot spots.*

- *Tofino and Ucluelet—These two towns are the best places to see Pacific gray whales during their early-spring migration (mid-March). There's also a resident population of orcas.*

- *Victoria—Pods of orcas cruise the Juan de Fuca Strait between Vancouver Island and the Olympic Peninsula of Washington State.*

Marine Transport Company (250/723-8313 in winter, 800/663-7192 April to September), operators of the MV *Lady Rose* and the MV *Frances Barkley*. These two freighters ply the waters of Alberni Inlet to Bamfield and on into Barkley Sound, carrying mail, goods, passengers, and their cargo of kayaks and camping gear. This is *the* way for West Coast Trail hikers to access Bamfield and for kayakers to access the Broken Group Islands. You can even rent kayaks from Alberni Marine. If you're not a hiker or kayaker but are interested in seeing the Broken Group and Alberni Inlet, take a full-day cruise. This service is very popular during summer. Don't plan on just dropping in to take a cruise. Book ahead—way ahead!

On your dirve to Port Alberni you'll pass right through **MacMillan Provincial Park (Cathedral Grove)**. A donation from MacMillan Bloedel, a giant forest-products corporation based in Vancouver, created this 136-hectare (336-acre) park in 1947. A self-guided nature trail leads through a stunning grove of towering Douglas fir, a tiny remnant of the forests that once blanketed southern Vancouver Island. Highway 4 runs through the park, 31 kilometers (19 miles) west of Parksville.

Details: Port Alberni is located on Highway 4, 47 kilometers (29 miles) west of Parksville. Contact the Port Alberni Visitor Infocentre, 2533 Redford St., 250/724-6535.

Port Renfrew

This community of about 400 is situated at the mouth of the San Juan River on the south side of the inlet known as Port San Juan. For such a small and relatively isolated place, Port Renfrew is an important tourist crossroads and service center. It's the southern access point to the West Coast Trail and near the northern end of the Juan de Fuca Marine Trail. In winter the town reverts to its true character as a logging and fishing community. In summer, the place can be overrun with hikers, beach-combers, and day-trippers from Victoria. West Coast Trail wannabees should go have a beer at the Port Renfrew Hotel's pub and listen to the tales of sweat and glory from those just completing the odyssey.

Canada's tallest known Douglas fir, the Red Creek fir, is located just east of Port Renfrew. The tree stands 73 meters (241 feet) tall, with a circumference of 12.6 meters (41.2 feet). This tree, probably a thousand years old or more, stands within a small reserve set aside by Fletcher Challenge Canada, the logging company that owns rights to the tree.

To find the Red Creek fir, take Highway 14 south from Port Renfrew (toward Victoria) for 2.4 kilometers, turning left at the Red Creek mainline road. Head east for 14.5 kilometers until you come to a parking area. Ditch the car and walk along the level road beyond the parking lot. You'll come to a trail marker. Turn right and hike up the hill, then turn left onto the road you encounter and keep walking. You'll see three big red cedars, then the Red Creek fir.

Details: To reach Port Renfrew, take Highway 14 (Sooke Rd.) 95 kilometers (59 miles) from Victoria around the southern end of Vancouver Island.

NATURE AND ADVENTURE SIGHTS:
NORTH VANCOUVER ISLAND

Alert Bay

Located on an island just a short ferry ride from the town of Port McNeill, Alert Bay was once the site of the world's tallest totem pole—

53 meters (175 feet). Raised in 1972, the pole was carved by six Native craftsmen from Alert Bay and depicts the history of the Kwak-waka'wakw (formerly known as Kwakiutl) people. The current tallest pole in the world is in Victoria.

Alert Bay has many excellent (but much shorter) totems and is home to the **U'mista Cultural Centre**. *U'mista* carries a meaning similar to "prodigal" and refers to the many artifacts within the building—masks, coppers, ceremonial, and everyday items—that were confiscated after the Cranmer potlatch in 1921 (see Chapter 1) and later returned to Alert Bay. Besides offering an extensive display of artifacts, the center holds lectures and demonstrations. Kwakwaka'wakw children come here to learn traditional songs, stories, and dances.

To get to Alert Bay, take the BC Ferry from Port McNeill to Cormorant Island. The ferry docks in Alert Bay, then carries on to Sointula on an adjacent island before returning to Port McNeill. There are several departures each day.

Details: Alert Bay Infocentre, Box 28, Alert Bay, BC V0N 1A0, 250/974-5213. Port McNeill is located on Highway 19, 194 kilometers (121 miles) north of Campbell River.

Gold River

Gold River was an "instant town," built in 1967 to provide accommodations for workers at the nearby pulp mill. Closure of the mill in 1998 has brought hard times to Gold River, and some services may no longer be available.

If you're interested in First Nations culture, take a tour to Nuchalitz (Nootka) Island. The town of **Yuquot** (Friendly Cove) on the island is a national historic site and an excellent place to witness contemporary aboriginal culture. You can also take a wilderness hike on the island. For a very cool tour of **Nootka Sound**, take the MV *Uchuck III* (Nootka Sound Service Ltd., P.O. Box 57, Gold River, BC V0P 1G0, 250/283-2325 or 250/283-2515, www.island.net/-mvuchuck/), a converted navy minesweeper that now does freight, mail, and passenger duty between Gold River and several fishing and Native villages along the coast.

The nearby **Upana Caves** offer extensive exploring through a series of underground passages and chambers. You can go alone (take a good flashlight and extra batteries and wear non-slip shoes) or visit the caves in the company of a tour guide. The caves are located 17 kilometers (10.5 miles) west of Gold River (take the Head Bay forestry road off Highway 28, travel west toward Tahsis, turn at Branch H27, and park in the lot a short distance up the branch road. Take the access trail to the self-registration area). For guided cave tours contact Cave Treks, Box 897, Gold River, BC V0P 1G0, 250/283-7144. The BC Ministry of Forests publishes a useful pamphlet on the caves, including information on access, cave routes, and passages. To obtain a copy, contact the Gold River Chamber of Commerce.

If you're in search of a coastal wilderness hike, free from fees, quotas, reservations, designated campsites, and other hikers, **Nuchalitz Island** is the place for you. The upside is that you'll see the west coast of Vancouver Island as few have—undisturbed and utterly beautiful. The downside is that the creek crossings are tough, slogging through the slick and slippery rain forest is tougher, and nobody will be there to patch you up or catch you if you fall.

Start your hike from Louie Lagoon at the north end of the island. You can go with a group, in the company of experienced local guides, or alone (once you've obtained permission from the Mowachaht band office, 250/283-2532). Six days of hiking will allow you to comfortably (OK, strenuously) cover the 35 kilometers (22 miles) to Yuquot (Friendly Cove). En route you will trek through salal-choked forest, saunter along shingle and sand beaches, wade thigh-deep across Beano Creek, rock climb over headlands, and explore tide pools teeming with life. With any luck you'll arrive at Yuquot full to the brim with life and challenge. To arrange for a guided hike on Nootka Island or elsewhere in the Nootka Sound area, contact Sea to Sky Expeditions, 800/990-8735, e-mail seatosky@netcom.ca.

Details: Take Highway 28 west from Campbell River. After 48 kilometers (30 miles), the road branches at Buttle Lake. Take the right branch for Gold River. Gold River Chamber of Commerce, P.O. Box 39, Gold River, BC V0P 1G0, e-mail goldriv@island.net.

Port Hardy

Just about—but not quite—as far north as you can go on Vancouver Island, this rough town is the home of unemployed miners, loggers, and fishermen who are beginning to turn their hands to other work, notably sportfishing, diving, and kayaking charters. Daily ferry service links Port Hardy with Prince Rupert on the mainland's north coast. When the ferry arrives the few local hotels fill up quickly, so if you're planning to stay in town during summer, hotel reservations are a must.

From Port Hardy it's a trip by logging road and foot to rainy, windswept **Cape Scott Provincial Park** at the very northwestern tip of Vancouver Island. Cape Scott is rugged, isolated, uncrowded, and starkly beautiful. There is a small campground on the San Josef River. Several hiking trails radiate from the campground, including a 40-minute walk to the sandy beaches of San Josef Bay and an eight-hour trek out to Cape Scott. Views from the lighthouse at Cape Scott are astounding. Recently there have been increased reports of humpback whale sightings from the cape. You'll also have a good chance of seeing peregrine falcons and hundreds of shorebirds. Due to heavy rainfall at all times of year, the trails are usually muddy. Carry a walking stick or ice ax to help you keep your balance, and bring fresh water (although the water at Cape Scott is safe to drink once boiled, it's brownish and unappealing).

For access to the park, take the logging road west from Port Hardy for 42 kilometers (26 miles) through the town of Holberg, then turn right and continue another 16 kilometers (10 miles) to the San Josef River campground.

Details: 230 kilometers (144 miles) north of Campbell River on Highway 19; Port Hardy Infocentre, P.O. Box 249, Port Hardy, BC V0N 2P0, 250/949-7622. For more information on Cape Scott Provincial Park, contact BC Parks, 800 Johnson St., Victoria, 250/387-5002. For guided hikes, contact Sea to Sky Trails, 105C, 11831-80 Ave., Delta, BC, 800/990-8735 or 604/594-7701.

Strathcona Provincial Park

Vancouver Island's largest park and the first provincial park anywhere in BC (established in 1911), Strathcona currently encompasses over 253,000 hectares (627,000 acres) and almost spans the width of the island. Within the park are the island's highest peak, Mount Golden Hinde, at 2,200 meters (7,260 feet); only icefield, Comox Glacier; and Canada's highest waterfall, Della Falls, at 440 meters (1,452 feet). Alpine meadows with carpets of wildflowers, glaciers, and isolated lakes

K. D. Wong/Blackbird Design

Telegraph Cove

share the park with coastal rain forests and marine environments where the park meets the west coast at Herbert Inlet. Strathcona is popular year-round for hiking and wilderness camping, climbing, and nordic skiing. The very rare Vancouver Island marmot inhabits several areas within the park. Although Strathcona is, in theory, a protected area, special logging and mining licenses have recently been issued by the provincial government, sparking furious debate and protests.

Details: Take Highway 28 west from Campbell River. After 48 kilometers (30 miles), the road branches at Buttle Lake—take the left branch to Strathcona Park. Park headquarters and visitor information are found at Buttle Lake. Information is also available from BC Parks Strathcona District, P.O. Box 1479, Parksville, BC V9P 2H4, 250/248-3931.

Telegraph Cove

With a population of less than 20, this tiny, obscure village is undergoing a huge expansion courtesy of a longtime resident and his family. Once a fishing and sawmill town, just a collection of weather-beaten houses on stilts at the water's edge, Telegraph Cove was all but abandoned. The town's owner closed the mill and sold the whole town in the 1980s, just as the whale-watching craze began to develop.

Telegraph Cove is perfectly situated for whale-watching expeditions on **Johnstone Strait**, a body of water that literally swarms with orca whales from mid-June until October. Nearby **Robson Bight** is the site of a mysterious orca ritual, where whales swim close to shore to rub on the gravel bars (an ecological reserve, Robson Bight is off-limits to whale-watching boats).

Approximately 15,000 eager whale watchers annually make the trip to Telegraph Cove for half- and full-day cruises. An additional 7,000 kayakers visit the strait independently or with group tours to see the whales up close. To provide food, lodging, and other services for this horde of visitors, the town's current owners are expanding the marina and have renovated many of the old buildings into self-contained suites; one of the original residences is now a five-bedroom hotel. A pub and restaurant opened in 1998. The property also includes a campground, and there are plans to develop a golf course.

The whole enterprise, at the end of a rough logging road that leads east from the North Island Highway, is almost a surreal surprise. You'll find bright houses, barrels and baskets of flowers, a broad boardwalk leading to the whale-watching office, even interpretive signs and pictures of the town's early residents. Eagles steal fish from the docks, acrobatic ravens dive and frolic overhead, logging trucks roll by, and people launch powerboats in the sheltered bay. It's absolutely amazing.

Hanson Island, just offshore from Telegraph Cove, is shaping up to be yet another logging battleground. TimberWest Forest Ltd. has plans to remove approximately 125 hectares (318 acres) of trees using several clear-cut blocks. Though the company has promised to leave a buffer zone to reduce the visual impact of logging, opponents say the logging will be destructive to the local ecotourism industry and to the orcas of Johnstone Strait. In addition, Hanson Island is said to have thousands of culturally modified trees—cedar trees from which aboriginal peoples stripped bark before European contact.

Details: From Campbell River take the North Island Highway (Highway 19) approximately 180 kilometers (112.5 miles). A side road leads to Beaver Cove and Telegraph Cove. The road is 19 kilometers (12 miles) long and rough in places, with several one-lane bridges; watch for logging trucks.

GUIDES AND OUTFITTERS

Numerous whale-watching charters operate on Vancouver Island. Among them are **Cuda Marine**, 950 Wharf St., Victoria, 250/812-6003 or 250/881-0550, e-mail cudamarine@commercial.net, www.islandnet.com/~cuda, for expeditions in Juan de Fuca Strait. **Stubbs Island Charters Ltd.**, P.O. Box 7, Telegraph Cove, BC V0N 3J0, 800/665-3066, 250/928-3185, or 250/928-3117, e-mail stubbs@north.island.net, www.stubbs-island.com, offers orca watching in Johnstone Strait and features onboard naturalists. Tours depart twice daily from the remarkable Telegraph Cove. **Seasmoke & Sea Orca Expeditions**, P.O. Box 483, Alert Bay, BC V0N 1A0, 800/668-6722 or 250/974-5225, e-mail seaorca@north.island.net, offers orca and whale watching in the Inside Passage from MV *Cetacea*, an open vessel designed for whale watching and photography, and from the sailing yacht *Tuan*. Both vessels are equipped with hydrophones; trips last from three to five hours. Alert Bay is accessible by ferry from Port McNeill.

Clavella Adventures, P.O. Box 866, Nanaimo, BC V9R 5N2, 250/753-3751, www.nanaimo.ark.com/~clavella, offers diving and cruising from the MV *Clavella*. Packages include unlimited diving, air, tanks, weight belts, meals, and shore excursions. The company offers trips to north Vancouver Island, the Gulf Islands, Haida Gwaii, and Queen Charlotte Strait.

For insights into Native culture as well as scenery and wildlife viewing, check out **Tsusiat Tour Company**, P.O. Box 191, Port Alberni, BC V97 7M7, 888/875-1833, info@westcoasttrail.com. Starting from the Nitinaht First Nation village, the tour cruises down the Nitinat Lake, through Nitinat Narrows into the Pacific, and then along the West Coast Trail. The tour is accompanied by narration by Native guides. Another Native-owned and -operated outfitter is **Ancient Voices Native Cultural Kayak Expeditions**, P.O. Box 291, Port Hardy, BC V0N 2P0, 250/949-7707. You'll get a glimpse of Native storytelling, drumming, dancing, and food, plus a four-day guided kayak journey up Quatsino Sound, with stops at Native villages and sacred sites.

Cave Treks, Box 897, Gold River, BC V0P 1G0, 250/283-7144 or 250/283-2283, gives guided tours inside the Upana Caves. For guided small-group adventure camping tours in the Carmanah, Clayoquot, Pacific Rim, and Strathcona areas, contact **Midnight Sun Adventure**

AUTHOR'S TOP PICKS: CAVING

- **Cody Cave**—*Near Ainsworth Hot Springs in the Kootenays.*
- **Nakimu Caves**—*These caves in Glacier National Park were recently opened to the public (via guided tours only).*
- **Vancouver Island**—*Cave systems include Horne Lake Caves, Little Hustan Lake Caves, and Upana Caves.*

Travel, 843 Yates St., Victoria, 800/255-5057 or 250/480-9409, e-mail midsun@islandnet.com, www.islandnet.com/-midsun/.

ECO Tours, 3198 Ilona Place, Victoria, 800/665-7463 or 250/474-7463, ecotours@oceanside.com, www.oceanside.com/oceanside/ecotours/, offers unique guided hiking and sailing trips in the Port Alberni/Barkley Sound area, Cowichan Lake, Gulf Islands, and Campbell River/Desolation Sound. The company also offers day trips involving biking, hiking, kayaking, or whale watching. Accommodation—onboard when sailing or in trailers or RVs on land-based trips—is included. **Nimmo Bay Heli-Ventures**, P.O. Box 696, Port McNeill, BC V0N 2R0, 800/837-4354 or 250/956-2000, e-mail heli@nimmobay.bc.ca, www.nimmobay.bc.ca, provides a remote luxury lodge and cabins on the BC mainland opposite Port Hardy. Guests have access to beaches, whale watching, fishing, ocean kayaking, wildlife viewing, and caving.

Literally hundreds of charters are available on Vancouver Island, from fishing charters to sailing cruises to working-boat adventures. Check locally in the yellow pages or newspapers. Among the most interesting is **G. Cook's Tours**, P.O. Box 22, Alert Bay, BC V0N 1A0, 250/974-5778. You'll cruise the Inside Passage aboard the MV *Cape Cook*, with hosts Gilbert and Vicki Cook (Gilbert is a member of the Namgis First Nation). With more than 40 years' experience in these waters, the Cooks offer excellent interpretive tours and all-inclusive packages (accommodations, gourmet meals, shore excursions).

For excursions on Alberni Inlet to the Broken Group Islands, you can't beat **Alberni Marine Transport Ltd.**, P.O. Box 188, Post Alberni, BC V9Y 7M7, 800/663-7192 or 250/723-8313 (April to September). This trip is the ideal way for kayakers to access the Broken Group Islands unit of Pacific Rim National Park Reserve. Kayaks and canoes can be loaded or rented. In summer, boats make several additional stops in Alberni Inlet. Book early!

A similar no-frills service is offered by **Nootka Sound Service Ltd.**, P.O. Box 57, Gold River, BC V0P 1G0, 250/283-2325 or 250/283-2515, www.island.net/-mvuchuck/, aboard the MV *Uchuck III*. The service begins in Gold River, proceeds west along Machalat Inlet to Nootka Sound, and stops at coastal settlements such as Tahsis, Yuquot (Friendly Cove), and Kyuquot.

CAMPING

Vancouver Island offers a dizzying choice of camping experiences. Among the provincial campgrounds accepting reservations are **Bamberton**, **Goldstream**, and **Miracle Beach**. Call 800/689-9025 or 689-9025 (from Vancouver). There are also many private campgrounds and resorts, especially in the Campbell River area.

On the southwest coast, **Juan de Fuca Provincial Park** on the Sooke Road (Highway 14) west of Victoria has 20 campsites in four separate campgrounds, plus beach camping.

Near Victoria, **Goldstream** is a lovely spot that gets very busy in summer. Large trees and private sites make it popular. The park has 159 sites suitable for every size of vehicle, plus flush toilets, hot showers, and a sani-station (sewage disposal for trailers, campers, and RVs). **Bamberton**, on Saanich Peninsula just an hour north of Victoria, is also a busy place and is popular with families. It has 47 private, shady sites situated in a Douglas fir/arbutus forest. There are flush toilets but no showers or sani-stations. The beach and access to Saanich Inlet provide safe swimming for kids.

Miracle Beach is located between Courtenay and Campbell River and offers 193 big, private drive-in sites. All the amenities are here, including a sani-station. A long, sandy beach is perfect for swimming, tidal-pool exploration, and general relaxation. Campbell River is famous for its beaches and family resorts. Check out **Campbell River Fishing Village and RV Park**, 260 South Island Hwy., Campbell River, 250/287-3630. The park has 45 sites, laundry facilites, showers, a recreation room with a television, boat rentals, fishing licenses, tackle, and fishing charters. Fees, ranging from $19 to $22, include hookups. **Elk Falls** is a provincial park and campground west of Campbell River (it's nowhere near a beach, but there's a lovely waterfall and canyon). It features 122 vehicle sites, flush toilets, and a sani-station.

Known as Little Switzerland, **Strathcona Provincial Park**, 250/954-4600, contains six of the island's seven highest peaks. You'll find terrific backcountry camping in several designated wilderness campsites, plus 161 sites in two campgrounds at Buttle Lake (with a good beach, best for families) and Ralph River.

The new development at **Telegraph Cove** includes 125 lovely, secluded campsites in a shaded campground close to the village, store, and marina. Contact Telegraph Cove Resorts Ltd., P.O. Box 1, Telegraph Cove, BC V0N 3J0, 800/200-HOOK or 250/928-3131. Sites cost from $17 to $21 per night. **Quatse River Campground**, 5050 Byng Rd., Port Hardy, 250/949-2395, has 62 sites on beautifully wooded grounds just three kilometers (five miles) from the BC Ferries terminal at Port Hardy. Amenities include flush toilets, hot showers, and a sani-station. Fees start at $14, including water. Electrical hookup costs another $4.

LODGING

A popular tourist destination as well as the provincial capital, Victoria is well supplied with a broad range of accommodations—from ritzy to spartan. At the upper end of the scale is **Ocean Pointe Resort**, 45 Songhees Rd., Victoria, 800/667-4677 or 250/360-2999. It's a lush four-star establishment on the Inner Harbour featuring all the extras—pools, sauna, health club, restaurant—and prices to match, starting at $134 and rocketing to more than $400. More reasonable is **Green Gables Inn**, 850 Blanchard St., Victoria, 800/661-4115 or 250/385-6787. It's somewhat less splashy but still conveniently located downtown, with rates from $119. A very cool and quaint spot in a residential area near downtown is **Abigail's Hotel**, 906 McClure St., Victoria, 800/561-6565 or 250/388-5363. Though it's called a hotel, this is actually a stylish bed-and-breakfast with gardens, a library, and jetted tubs. You'll find rates from $107 (low season) to $179 (high season). Another bed-and-breakfast (there are many) is **A Downtown Stroller's B&B**, 410 Government St., Victoria, 250/360-1449, with two bedrooms and private baths. It's nonsmoking, there's a two-night minimum stay, and rates start at $80.

Sooke is on the way to Port Renfrew, and it's home to numerous lovely resorts and hideaways. Check out **Point No Point**, 1505 West Coast Rd., Sooke, 250/646-2020, where you'll find suites and log cabins, fireplaces and whirlpool tubs, a one-kilometer-long private beach, and forest trails. You can enjoy lunch, tea, and dinner in the resort's restaurant. Rates begin at $85. **Sooke Harbour House**, 1528 Whiffen Spit Rd., Sooke, 250/642-3421, is a very tony inn (rates from $270) with a reputable restaurant. In Port Renfrew, **Arbutus Beach Lodge**, 5 Queesto Dr., 250/647-5458, offers beachfront rooms and one cabin. The full breakfast is free. This adult-oriented establishment is nonsmoking and offers whale watching, kayak rentals, beachcombing, and more. Rates begin at $59.

On the north side of the island, look for **Roseberry Manor Bed & Breakfast**, 810 Nimpkish Heights Rd., Port McNeill, 250/956-4788. If you like Victorian-era antiques, this is the place for you. It's a bit fussy but utterly charming. Guests get breakfast, afternoon tea, and cappuccino. Rates run $55 to $70 per night. For a true wilderness adventure, check out the **Strathcona Park Lodge and Outdoor Education Centre**, P.O. Box 2160, Campbell River, BC V9W 5C9, 250/286-3122. The center has an international reputation for teaching wilderness skills and offers outdoor summer programs for kids and families. It also offers fine food, comfortable accommodations, canoe and kayak rentals, and guided hikes in the park. Rates run from $40 to $125 for basic accommodations, $110 to $315 for a complete package.

Telegraph Cove accommodations are found in refurbished buildings on the waterfront (they offer kitchenettes, down comforters, and marina and ocean views). For reservations contact **Telegraph Cove Resorts Ltd.**, P.O. Box 1, Telegraph Cove, BC V0N 3J0, 250/928-3131 or 800/200-HOOK. Room rates run $100 to $150 per night in summer.

FOOD

Restaurants are plentiful in Victoria. For Asian food, try one of the several excellent Chinese restaurants in Chinatown. For casual dining, **Sam's Deli**, 805 Government St., 250/382-8424, has what may be the world's best date squares. The inexpensive restaurant also serves delicious shrimp and avocado sandwiches, soups (wondrous clam chowder), and specials. Sit on the front deck and watch the milling hordes on Government Street and the Inner Harbour. Don't miss **Spinnakers Brewpub**, 308 Catherine St., 250/384-2739. This is the oldest brewpub in BC (by mere hours, just ahead of the Troller in Horseshoe Bay on the mainland). Beers include a punchy ESB and a smooth-sailing stout. If you visit in December, be sure to ask for the dark and chocolatey barley wine. Food is typical pub fare—burgers, fish and chips, pizza—but of high quality, and there's lots of it. A glass of beer costs about five dollars; full meals start at eight dollars.

Sooke Harbour House, 1528 Whiffen Spit Rd., Sooke, 250/642-3421, is known as a leader in West Coast cuisine. It features fresh seafood, local ingredients, and herbs straight from the garden. Nanaimo doesn't offer much beyond suburban sprawl except for the **Dinghy Dock Marine Pub and Bistro**, 250/753-2373, located on Protection Island in Nanaimo Harbour. You can take a $4.25 ferry ride to the island, then sit right on the dock while you munch burgers or ribs and quaff cool ones.

North Vancouver Island dining can be really average. For a treat, especially after whale watching, try the **Old Saltery Pub** and the **Killer Whale Café**, located on the water's edge in the tiny village of Telegraph Cove. You'll find excellent seafood and pasta dishes, and beers brewed on site. The restaurant takes lunch orders for those on whale-watching cruises. Dinner for two runs about $50.

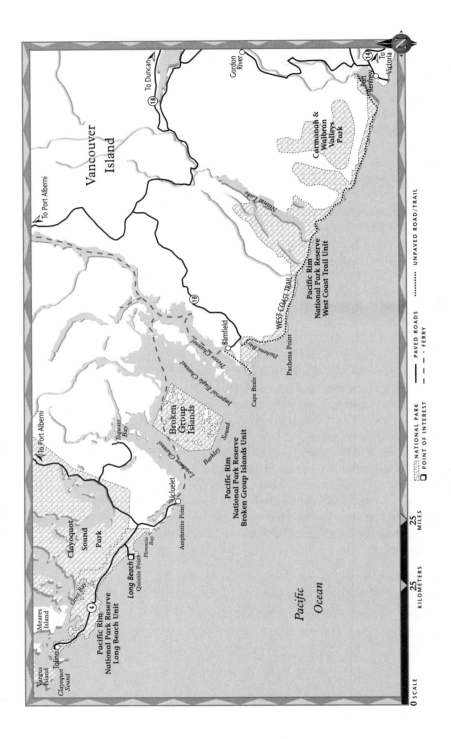

CHAPTER 4

Pacific Rim
National Park Reserve

Pacific Rim National Park Reserve is the premier ecotravel destination on Vancouver Island. It is a magical place at any time of year, an oasis of moss-laden forest giants, ferns, slugs, and salal; of roaring surf and quiet bays; of driftwood-piled beaches, tide pools, sea birds, and whales. The park offers something for everyone. Some areas are quiet and safe for families, yet there are plenty of challenging places for those in search of adventure and activity.

Established in 1970, Pacific Rim is operated as a national park but it's officially called a "national park reserve" due to unresolved Native land claims. In theory, the federal and provincial governments are negotiating with the Nuu-chah-nulth and Dididaht First Nations to resolve such issues as access, payment, and land use. In fact, talks are so slow that the bands are resorting to such tactics as charging a fee to hikers on the West Coast Trail for permission to cross aboriginal land.

There are three separate units within Pacific Rim National Park Reserve. The Long Beach Unit is the most popular and easily accessible, lying in a strip along the west coast of Vancouver Island between the towns of Tofino and Ucluelet. The West Coast Trail Unit is a thin strip of land along the coast that encompasses a 72-kilometer (45-mile) hiking trail linking the villages of Port Renfrew and

Bamfield. The Broken Group Islands Unit in Barkley Sound is a labyrinth of islands and passages, a favorite playground for kayakers, divers, and sailors.

HISTORY AND CULTURE

The aboriginal inhabitants of the Pacific Rim region of Vancouver Island include the Pacheenaht and the many bands and clans of the Nuu-chah-nulth First Nation. The coast and rain forest, although rugged, provided food and raw materials for shelter, clothing, and other necessities of life, so, prior to European contact, the region was relatively densely populated. The name Nuu-chah-nulth means "all along the mountains," an appropriate description of the many villages strung across the island's coastline with the high mountain barrier at their backs.

The Nuu-chah-nulth were the only aboriginal people of Vancouver Island to hunt whales on the open sea. Hunters prepared for the whaling expeditions by fasting, meditating, swimming in the bone-chilling ocean waters, even making short ritual dives into underwater caves. Just two or three whales each year could provide food, oil, and other riches for an entire village.

In ancient times, Japanese and Chinese boats may have drifted into Nuu-chah-nulth territories; survivors might have been taken as slaves or otherwise absorbed into Nuu-chah-nulth society. In the 1770s, Spanish and British explorers, called "people who live on a boat" by the Natives of the west coast, arrived. When Captain James Cook landed at the Nuu-chah-nulth settlement of Yuquot (Friendly Cove), he was guided around a dangerous reef by Natives shouting "Nootka, Nootka" ("go around"). Cook thought that *Nootka* was the tribal name—for 200 years the Nuu-chah-nulth have been mistakenly called Nootka.

Once Europeans discovered the rich supply of sea otters in the Nuu-chah-nulth's territorial waters, the plunder began, and the Natives were embroiled in the lust for furs—capturing, selling, and trading huge numbers of otter pelts. By the early 1800s, no sea otters remained in coastal waters. Whalers and sealers from many countries then came to exploit the area's marine life. Disease ravaged Native populations, and in 1904 American scientists and collectors removed thousands of artifacts from Yuquot, which was all but deserted at the time. A Nuu-chah-nulth whaling shrine—a complex assemblage of artifacts—currently resides at the American Museum of Natural History in New York, but the shrine has never been reassembled for display. The Mowahchat, a band of the Nuu-chah-nulth First Nation, is negotiating for the shrine's return.

Fishing and logging became the region's economic mainstays, but the only access to the west coast was by sea, in waters so difficult and dangerous that Pacific Rim became known as "the Graveyard of the Pacific." As the logging industry built access roads to the remote west coast of the island, word of the area's astonishing beauty leaked into the world at large. Squatters and artists came to Long Beach, seeking refuge and inspiration. Slowly, tourism has become an important economic factor in the area, rivaling resource exploitation. With the completion of the Island Highway (Highway 4) in 1970, Long Beach was suddenly accessible to literally millions of people in the Lower Mainland and beyond. As a result, Pacific Rim has become one of Canada's most heavily used national parks, with more than half a million visitors annually.

Despite the area's popularity, Pacific Rim is still remote—it takes effort to get there. Although several roads lead to the area, freighters deliver travelers to the Broken Group Islands, and Tofina even has an airstrip, Pacific Rim remains relatively unspoiled and isolated. Floods and winter storms still close the roads, cutting off land access to the area. And, as ever, the coast's waters are treacherous and prevent all but the most knowledgeable mariners from coming to the area by sea. Logging of old-growth forests in the region continues (outside of park boundaries), and environmentalists' efforts to stop the felling have frequently focused world attention on the ancient forests of Pacific Rim.

LAY OF THE LAND

Pacific Rim's three separate units all lie on the west coast of Vancouver Island. Regardless of which unit you choose to explore, you're never far from the sea.

Long Beach is famous for its great curving expanses of sand with rolling surf and offshore islands, the home of birds and sea lions. The West Coast Trail travels through some very rough country and gives

Lennard Island, Pacific Rim National Park Preserve

hikers an up-close look not only at the seashore but old-growth forest as well. The Broken Group Islands lie in the center of Barkley Sound, a wide notch out of the side of Vancouver Island. Rough and dangerous ocean passages separate the islands from Bamfield on the south and Ucluelet on the north.

Rain and rampant growth generally define the park's weather and vegetation, although there are pockets of surprising mini-ecosystems, especially in the Long Beach Unit. Fog is a frequent visitor to all areas of the park even in summer. In winter, when huge storms crash in from the open ocean, there is no access to either the West Coast Trail or the Broken Group Islands, but Long Beach remains open and storm watching is popular.

FLORA AND FAUNA

Pacific Rim is a birder's paradise, with pelagic seabirds, shorebirds, songbirds, and birds of prey. Bald eagles are common; so are ravens, sandpipers, gulls, an array of ducks, guillemots, cormorants, and many more. Seals and sea lions fish and frolic in the waves. Deer and bears, the occasional cougar, enormous banana slugs, and a galaxy of tide-pool creatures round out the list. Perhaps the biggest attraction, though, are whales. Orca whales frequent the waters off all three park units, and every March the world's entire population of Pacific gray whales migrates up the coast from Mexico toward Alaska, passing through Pacific Rim waters as they go.

The large undisturbed tracts of old-growth forest protected by Pacific Rim are remnants of the magnificent forest that once cloaked the entire southern end of Vancouver Island. Huge Douglas firs, red cedars, and Sitka spruce still stand within the park, although there are no known record-sized trees inside the park boundaries.

VISITOR INFORMATION

How you get to Pacific Rim National Park Reserve depends largely upon which unit you intend to explore. If you're hiking the West Coast Trail, you can start from Port Renfrew at the south end, accessible via Highway 14 (Sooke Road) from Victoria. Bus transport from Victoria to Port Renfrew is available. If you're hiking the trail from Bamfield at the north end, you can get to Bamfield via Highway 18 from Duncan on the island's east side; the highway becomes a logging road about halfway across the island. Bamfield is also accessible from Port Alberni via another logging road. The best way to get to Bamfield, though, is by taking the MV *Lady Rose* or the MV *Frances Barkley* from Port Alberni.

If you're kayaking in the Broken Group Islands, your best bet, again, is the *Lady Rose*, which makes summertime stops in the Broken Group to drop off and pick up kayakers. Strong paddlers can take a logging road from Port Alberni to Toquart Bay and paddle across the upper reaches of Loudoun Channel to get to the Broken Group. Note that this sea route is dangerous and not recommended except for expert paddlers.

Long Beach, accessible by Highway 4 (Island Highway) from Parksville, just north of Nanaimo, is the least remote of the three park units. Because this unit is easier to get to it's also the busiest of the

Pacific Rim units. For visitors to the Long Beach Unit, there are a number of visitor information sources. From May through October the Park Information Centre is open daily and has information on park activities, camping, accommodations, and more. The center is located three kilometers (nearly two miles) north of the Tofino–Ucluelet–Port Alberni junction on Highway 4. The park's main interpretive center is the Wickaninnish Centre, with exhibits, information on the park, and a restaurant. The center is located at Long Beach. For general park information, call 250/726-4212 (summer only) or 250/726-7721 (year-round) or check out the Parks Canada Web site at www.parkscanada .pch.gc.ca; or write Box 280, Ucluelet, BC V0R 3A0. For information on the West Coast Trail and Broken Group Islands, see the "Details" sections following those specific listings.

NATURE AND ADVENTURE SIGHTS: OUTSIDE THE RESERVE

Bamfield

For a true west coast experience, take the MV *Lady Rose* or the MV *Frances Barkley* from Port Alberni down Alberni Inlet to Bamfield. On both sides of tiny Bamfield Inlet near the south side of Barkley Sound, this fishing village of 250 souls swells to nearly 2,000 in the summer as hikers, paddlers, students, sportfishers, and tourists flood into town.

Bamfield is a very cool place. It's built on both sides of Bamfield Inlet, so the town's main "street" is the ocean. Boardwalks line both sides of the inlet, and since only the east side of the inlet is accessible by road, the water swarms with boats, water taxis, kayaks, and other floating transport. The village has numerous restaurants, services, accommodations, and shops. You want cappuccino? No problem. Welcome to luxury in the back of beyond.

Besides being the start (or end) of the journey for hikers on the West Coast Trail, Bamfield is the main access point to the islands of Barkley Sound, notably the Broken Group Islands. Bamfield is also a service and supply center for sail and pleasure craft cruising Barkley Sound, and a starting point for diving charters in the sound.

There are several hikes in the area—some day trips and some overnights. With the exception of the trail to Pachena Point, you'll

P. Crawford/D. Giberson

Bamfield

need a boat to access the trailheads (you can get a water taxi in town); trail maps and information are available in Bamfield. Even for a day hike you should carry fresh water and be prepared for rapid weather changes. Popular hikes include **Brady's Beach**, a half-day walk ideal for families that starts on the west side of Bamfield and wanders through a pleasant forest of red cedar, hemlock, salal, and ferns before arriving at a stretch of sandy beach and intriguing tide pools. You can also hike to **Tapaltos Bay/Cape Beale**. The lighthouse at Cape Beale was built in 1873; the original track used to haul construction materials is now the six-kilometer (four-mile) hiking trail. Although the trail is clear it can be rough and slippery depending on the weather, and is not suitable for small kids. Tapaltos Bay, a sheltered stretch of sand, is en route to the cape. At low tide you can walk across a channel from Cape Beale's rocky headland to the lighthouse, but don't get caught by rising water (use the Tofino tide tables and remember to add an hour during summer).

From the trailhead at Pachena Bay to the lighthouse at **Pachena Point**, the West Coast Trail is easy hiking on a converted roadbed and makes a great day trip for energetic hikers and families. Side trails from the main trail lead down to beaches where you can spend the day beachcombing and wondering what the rest of the world is up to. One-way distance to the light is nine kilometers (five and one-half miles). You can drive to the trailhead where there's plenty of parking (don't leave valuables in your car). Day hikers on this section of the West Coast Trail do not need a trail-use permit.

Details: Bamfield is located at the end of Highway 18, 141 kilometers (88 miles) from Duncan. It is also accessible by logging road from Port Alberni. From May to October you can take the West Coast Trail Express bus to Bamfield from Victoria and Nanaimo—see Appendix A. Contact the Bamfield Chamber of Commerce, Box 5, Bamfield, BC V0R 1B0.

Tofino

To the northwest of the park's Long Beach Unit is this hip, artsy-outdoorsy village of galleries, bookshops, whale-watching charters, and cafés. There are several beach resorts between the town and the northern boundary of the park, plus private campgrounds and many hotels and motels.

The town lies on the south side of Clayoquot Sound (pronounced KLAH-kwut). Meares Island, which lies in the sound and dominates the harbor views from downtown Tofino, was the site of a bitter dispute between conservationists and loggers in the early 1980s. Clayoquot Sound is ringed by squatters' cabins and secluded beach shacks, occupied by artists, anglers, and people seeking to escape mainstream society to live their own lives. Clayoquot Sound is also home to several First Nations villages and a very exclusive floating lodge.

Vancouver Island's only known hot springs are located 37 kilometers (23 miles) northwest of Tofino. **Hot Springs Cove** is accessible by float plane or charter boat from Tofino. The springs are protected within Maquinna Provincial Park. A visit to the springs is a great experience; you can relax in natural rock pools, watch steam rise into the treetops, and feel the hot water ease your aches and worries away. Depending on how many people are about, the springs are "au naturel" (bathing suit optional).

Details: To reach Tofino, turn right at the T-intersection, 89 kilometers (56 miles) from Port Alberni on Highway 4. Drive through the reserve to the end

C. L. Wong

Snow on the peaks above Clayoquot Sound

of the road. To visit Hot Springs Cove, book a flight with a local air charter in Tofino. Tofino Infocentre, Box 249, Tofino, BC V0R 2Z0, 250/725-3414.

Ucluelet

Situated at the end of a long, thin finger of land, the small town of Ucluelet (pronounced yoo-KEW-let) is full of fishermen who can't fish because of restrictions placed on commercial salmon fishing since 1998. It's kind of a sad place these days. The once-thriving commercial docks and fish-processing plant are now all but idle. But you can still charter a boat and head out in search of fish or whales; you can still go to the lighthouse at Amphritite Point and watch the surf pound; and you can still buy crafts in the town's shops. You can even get a meal of salmon (farm-raised) at the Canadian Princess restaurant. Ucluelet is in the process of shifting gears and in time may come to shed its hardworking fishing village image and more closely resemble its neighbor Tofino. A major new hotel may revitalize the town.

Meanwhile, Ucluelet is quieter and more down-to-earth than Tofino and is a good place to get away from the tourists of Long Beach and enjoy the tough love of the Pacific coast.

Details: At the T-intersection, 89 kilometers (56 miles) west of Port Alberni, turn left and continue eight kilometers (five miles) to Ucluelet. There are visitor infocentres at 227 Main St. (open all year) and at the T-intersection on Highway 4 (summer only). Contact the Ucluelet Chamber of Commerce, Box 428, Ucluelet, BC V0R 3A0, 250/726-4641 or 250/726-7289.

NATURE AND ADVENTURE SIGHTS: WITHIN THE RESERVE

Broken Group Islands Unit

One of Pacific Rim's three separate units is a maze of islands and waterways called the Broken Group Islands. Accessible only by boat, the Broken Group consists of about 100 islands, islets, and rocks located in the middle of Barkley Sound, a wide inlet on the west coast of Vancouver Island. The Broken Group is separated from Vancouver Island by Loudoun Channel to the northwest and Imperial Eagle and Trevor Channels to the southeast. The town of Bamfield is the "jump-off" point for adventures in the Broken Group.

Of the unit's 10,607 hectares (26,200 acres) only 1,350 hectares (3,335 acres) are land. The largest islands, Effingham, Turtle, Turret, Nettle, and Jaques, total nearly half the land base. The largest islands are clothed in spruce, hemlock, and cedar forests. The outermost islands are exposed to heavy surf, but the inner areas of the island group present a maze of sheltered waters, bays, beaches, and headlands. The Broken Group is a paradise for paddlers, sail and pleasure craft, and scuba divers. Nearly 75 percent of the boats using the islands are kayaks and canoes.

As with hiking the West Coast Trail, trip preparation and planning are vital if you're going to have a safe and enjoyable trip to the Broken Group. Knowledge of navigation, weather patterns, tides and currents, boat handling, and wilderness survival are all essential skills for anyone contemplating a trip. If you're a novice paddler but still want to experience this unique area, hook up with a tour guide/outfitter (see page 100).

P. Crawford/D. Giberson

Rainy Bay in the Broken Group Islands

Diving in the Broken Group is exceptional. Many wrecks and an incredible variety of interesting sea creatures bring the waters to life. Paddlers and campers will discover the legacy of aboriginal habitation on the islands in middens, stone fish traps, and other archaeological sites. Barkley Sound is home to a high concentration of bald eagles, along with whales, seals, sea lions, and hundreds of seabirds. The whole place has a magical "dawn-of-time" feeling, with mist and fog hanging low over the shimmering water, and eagles and ravens wheeling through the trees.

Details: *You can access the Broken Group by taking the MV Lady Rose from Port Alberni. Strong, experienced paddlers can put in at Toquart Bay and paddle eight kilometers (five miles) across the upper reaches of Loudoun Channel. Paddling across Loudoun Channel from Ucluelet or across Imperial Eagle Channel from Bamfield/Cape Beale is extremely dangerous and not recommended. There is no entry fee for the Broken Group Unit, but you may camp only in designated campsites. The nightly fee is $5 per person.*

Long Beach Unit

Prior to 1970, the only means of getting to Long Beach was a gravel logging road from Port Alberni. Despite its isolation, the area's beauty attracted artists and craftspeople, musicians, philosophers, and those seeking a tranquil, uninhibited lifestyle. With the establishment of the national park reserve came evictions from squatters' cabins and beach houses on Florencia Bay and elsewhere; even the original Wickaninnish Inn, famous for its architecture and unbeatable location right on Long Beach, was appropriated by park administration and turned into a visitors/interpretive center. Highway 4 was paved, making access to Long Beach easier (though the road is still an adventure). Today nearly 500,000 people visit Long Beach annually. Most come between mid-May and late September.

The Long Beach Unit encompasses 13,715 hectares (33,876 acres), of which about half is land. Major features within this unit include **Grice Bay**, a shallow, sheltered body of water branching from Tofino Inlet, this small bay becomes almost completely dry at low tide, exposing extensive mudflats. Grice Bay is a great bird-watching spot. During World War II, **Radar Hill** was used as a radar installation by the Royal Canadian Air Force. At 126 meters (415 feet) high, views from the hilltop include Tofino, Meares Island in Clayoquot Sound, and the Gowlland Rocks, a favorite haul-out and resting place for sea lions.

The gem at the center of the Long Beach Unit is **Long Beach** itself, a sweeping crescent of sand 10 kilometers (6 miles) long, interrupted at about the halfway mark by the rocky outcrop of **Green Point**. Long Beach is the focal point of Pacific Rim. On a sunny summer day the beach is scattered with picnic blankets, families building castles and moats in the sand, and people roaming the sand looking for shells and other treasures. The beach is open to the Pacific—next stop, Japan—and the rich, cold, offshore waters brim with life. Stroll in the moonlight, wade in the tide, ease your mind in the rhythm of waves. Green Point is a headland of basalt and quartz, and its many cracks and fissures provide homes for a kaleidoscope of marine life. Green Point campground is the only major camping facility within Pacific Rim, with drive-in and walk-in sites for forest or beach camping. Campers must obtain an overnight permit from the campground office; camping fees range from $10 to $20 per night depending upon season and services. Reservations are strongly recommended: call 800/689-9025.

The **Wickaninnish Center** (pronounced wik-a-NIN-ish) is open from mid-March until mid-October. Formerly a popular hotel, the building now houses a restaurant plus displays and exhibits on marine and rain-forest ecology as well as a bit of First Nations cultural history. Due to budget cuts, Parks Canada has not renovated or upgraded the center's displays, and the whole place is a little threadbare. A better bet for firsthand interpretive information is to take one of the self-guided nature walks or hiking trails, or sign up for a talk or beach walk with a park interpreter. Interpretive programs are also available at the Green Point campground. Guided hikes cost eight dollars per person (group and family rates are available); interpretive presentations have a nominal charge, usually two dollars per person.

Florencia Bay, also called Wreck Bay, is located southeast of Long Beach. It's another long curve of sand stretching six kilometers (three and three-quarters miles) between Quisitis and Wye Points. Florencia Bay was the site of a squatter's community during the 1960s and is still the beach of choice for those wanting to escape the throngs on Long Beach.

Details: Take Highway 4 west from Port Alberni to the T-intersection near the west coast; turn right for Long Beach. Information is available from the Park Information Center on Highway 4, three kilometers (two miles) from the junction, from the Wickaninnish Center, or by calling 250/726-4212. Day-use/parking pass is $8 per vehicle per day.

West Coast Trail Unit

The West Coast Trail is an absolutely splendid hike. A weeklong endurance test, it's both physically and mentally challenging. It provides opportunities for photography, wildlife viewing, scenery, and reverie. It could change your life. It's also exceedingly popular, perhaps excessively so. Since 1998 Parks Canada has employed strict trail-management practices to control the number of hikers that use the trail at any one time and to preserve the trail's wilderness character.

The trail's origins are rooted in tragedy. A telegraph line was strung between Victoria and the Cape Beale lighthouse, literally from tree to tree, in the 1890s, and a trail was hacked out of the dense forest parallel to it. In January 1906 the passenger steamer *Valencia* was bound from San Francisco to Victoria with 164 passengers and crew

THE SUMMER OF DISCONTENT

The forests surrounding Clayoquot Sound are the largest untouched low-elevation rain forests remaining in North America. Two forest-products companies, International Forest Products (Interfor) and Macmillan-Bloedel (MacBlo) hold tree-farming licenses for the area. When the companies prepared to clear-cut the region in 1993, protesters blocked machinery and trucks from entering the area by standing in the road. The Royal Canadian Mounted Police were called in to arrest the protesters, but no sooner was one person dragged away than someone else stepped forward as a replacement. More than 800 people, including Native elders, were arrested, and the standoff still holds the record as the largest civil-disobedience event in Canada's history.

As a result of the protests, the BC provincial government created two provincial parks in the area, Clayoquot Plateau and Clayoquot Arm. A total of 48,492 hectares (120,000 acres), including three undeveloped watersheds, is now protected. However, environmentalists say that these areas are insufficient and that the entire watershed surrounding Clayoquot Sound deserves protected status.

By 1998 logging in the area was virtually nonexistent. In 1999, however, MacBlo began to log again, in a partnership arrangement with the Nuu-chah-nulth First Nation, who claim Clayoquot Sound and its environs as their ancestral home. The company has said that it will refrain from using clear-cutting as a means of harvesting the timber. While many environmental activists commend this decision, they maintain that even selective logging practices harm the delicate and unique rain-forest environment. Nonetheless, several environmental groups, including Greenpeace, have endorsed the company's plans for selective logging in Clayoquot Sound.

on board. In bad weather the ship missed the entrance to Juan de Fuca Strait and kept heading northward along the coast of Vancouver Island. She ran aground on rocks just 30 meters (100 feet) offshore. Lifeboats filled with women and children immediately capsized in the heavy surf. Eventually a lifeboat made it to shore. The landing party found the telegraph line and was able to contact Victoria for help, 15 hours after the ship grounded. Rescue boats were launched from Bamfield but because of the dangerous surf none could approach the stricken ship. Only 38 people survived the ordeal.

After the *Valencia* disaster the provincial government upgraded the trail. In 1911 the Shipwrecked Mariner's Trail was declared a public highway, meaning that maintenance was the responsibility of the federal government. With improved marine navigation and communications the trail gradually fell into disuse and was abandoned by the government in 1954. In the 1960s the Victoria chapter of the Sierra Club started repair work on the trail and lobbied for the trail to be included as part of the national park that was then proposed for the west coast. Parks Canada took over trail upgrading work in 1973, and completed it in 1980.

Hikers contemplating an adventure on the West Coast Trail need to assess their abilities sincerely. Are you in good physical shape? Are you resourceful and experienced in the backcountry? Are you up for spending a week in the outdoors where you may encounter bears, cougars, foul weather, dangerous tides, and surf? Do you have the right gear? If you're planning to hike the West Coast Trail, get a detailed trail guide and plan your trip carefully. Guidebooks are listed in Appendix B.

The trail's northern end is at **Pachena Bay**, nine and one-half kilometers (six miles) from Bamfield. You can drive to the bay or hike the trail that starts in Bamfield. The trail continues past lighthouses, waterfalls, shipwrecks, tide pools, and magnificent, fog-shrouded forest. Ladders, logs, and hand-operated cable cars make stream crossings an adventure and help to tame the terrain. The trail finally ends at **Gordon River** near Port Renfrew.

Most hikers start from **Port Renfrew** and get the hardest part of the hike over with while they're fresh and energetic. The south part of the trail is slow and rough; it takes at least two days to walk from Gordon River to Walbran Creek. Most hikers take from five to seven days to complete the entire trek.

Details: The trail is open April 1 to October 31, and access is limited to 8,000 hikers per season. A trail-use permit is mandatory and costs $70 ($30 in April and October). Call ahead for a reservation (604/663-6000 in Vancouver, 800/663-6000 elsewhere in Canada and the United States, 604/387-1642 overseas) up to 90 days in advance or show up at either trailhead to get a permit on a first-come first-served basis (12 such permits are issued each day). You'll also pay for boat passage across the Gordon River and Nitinat Narrows (about $20 each) and may be charged a fee to cross First Nations land ($20).

Transportation companies: PBM Knight (bus to Port Renfrew from Victoria), 250/475-3010; West Coast Trail Express (bus to Bamfield from Victoria or Nanaimo), 250/477-8700; Alberni Marine Transport (MV Lady Rose to Bamfield), 800/663-7192 or 250/723-8313, Pacheenaht First Nations bus (to Port Renfrew) and hiker ferry service (Gordon River), 250/647-5521.

GUIDES AND OUTFITTERS

Numerous whale-watching charters operate on Vancouver Island; most specialize in orca whales, but the operators in Tofino and Ucluelet can also take you to watch Pacific gray whales during the annual spring migration in March. Among the local whale-watching operators are **Remote Passages**, Box 624B, Tofino, BC V0R 2Z0, 800/666-9833 or 250/725-3330; and **Seaside Adventures**, Box 178, Tofino, BC V0R 2Z0, 888/332-4252 or 250/725-2292. Both of these outfitters can also take you to Hot Springs Cove.

For scuba-diving charters, **Rendezvous Dive Ventures Ltd.**, Box 135, Port Alberni, BC V9Y 7M6, 250/720-9306, e-mail rendvous@island. net, has been in operation since 1973. They offer kayaking and guided dives in Barkley Sound. No instruction is offered—divers must be certified. Guests stay at the Rendezvous Lodge in Port Alberni.

Slipstream, P.O. Box 441, Campbell River, BC V9W 5C1, 250/287-7230, www.slipstreamadventures.com, offers guided hikes on the West Coast Trail; seven-day packages include meals and transportation.

Sea kayaking on the west coast is unparalleled and there are numerous outfitters and guiding operations available, offering services for all skill levels. Although their office is located on the mainland east of Vancouver, **Geoff Evans Kayak Centre**, Box 3097, Cultus

AUTHOR'S TOP PICKS: DIVING

- **Artificial reefs**—*Several ships have been deliberately sunk in various locations, including the* Mackenzie *and* GB Church *near Sidney on Vancouver Island, the* Chaudiere *near Sechelt, and the* Columbia *near Campbell River.*

- **Barkley Sound**—*The Broken Group and other island groups on the west coast of Vancouver Island offer terrific diving opportunities.*

- **Powell River**—*Exceptional. There is no other word.*

- **Saanich Inlet**—*An underwater park. The diving's also good in Finlayson Arm, near Victoria.*

Lake, BC V2R 5H6, 604/858-6775, e-mail gevans@uniserve.com, offers instructional kayak trips featuring interpretive guides and low-impact camping in the Gulf Islands, Broken Group Islands, and Johnstone Strait. Some experience is required for longer trips. **Tofino Sea Kayaking Company**, Box 620, Tofino, BC V0R 2Z0, 800/TOFINO-4 or 250/725-4222, e-mail paddlers@island.net, www.island.net/-paddlers, offers sea kayaking in Clayoquot Sound, courses, and rentals. The company specializes in multi-day wilderness trips and lodge-based day trips for all experience levels, as well as "Wimmin Seeking Wild" women-only expeditions. **Kingfisher Wilderness Adventures**, 1641 Lonsdale Ave., Suite 211, North Vancouver, 604/831-6180, www. kingfisher-adventures.com, is a small outfitter offering fully guided and serviced tours (they do the cooking, set up the tents, and everything but paddle your kayak) to Vargas Island, Hot Springs Cove, and Johnstone Strait. They specialize in high guide-to-client ratios. **Wild Heart Adventures**, 2774 Barnes Rd., Site H2, Nanaimo, 250/722-3683, e-mail wheart@island.net, www.island.net/-wheart also offers sea-kayaking trips for all skill levels; destinations include the northern Gulf Islands, Robson Bight (Johnstone Strait), Broken Group Islands,

Clayoquot Sound, and Nootka Sound. **Mothership Adventures**, P.O. Box 130, Victoria, BC V8W 2M6, 888/833-8887 or 250/384-8422, www.islandnet.com/-momship, combines live-aboard sailing and daily kayaking throughout the Gulf Islands and the west coast of Vancouver Island.

For excursions on Alberni Inlet to the Broken Group Islands, you can't beat **Alberni Marine Transport Ltd.** The company has two boats—the MV *Lady Rose* and the MV *Francis Barkley*, Box 188, Port Alberni, BC V9Y 7M7, 800/663-7192 (April through September) or 250/723-8313. This is the ideal way for kayakers to access the Broken Group Islands Unit of Pacific Rim National Park Reserve. Kayaks and canoes can be loaded or rented. In summer there are several additional stops in Alberni Inlet. Book early! From May to September, **Broken Island Adventures**, Box 3500, Bamfield, BC V0R 1B0, 888/728-6200, runs a sea-link service between Bamfield and Ucluelet with optional drops, pickups, and guided tours of the Broken Group Islands—ideal if you don't have a kayak. This service is an alternative way to reach Sechart Whaling Station Lodge (see Lodging).

CAMPING

The only campground in the popular Long Beach Unit of Pacific Rim National Park Reserve is **Green Point**. Open all year, it's really busy in summer; call ahead for reservations (250/726-4212). Parks Canada interpretive programs run nightly from June to September. There are 94 drive-in sites for tents, trailers, or RVs, plus 33 walk-in beach sites and 20 walk-in forest sites. Nearby in Tofino, check out **Bella Pacifica Resort and Campground**, 250/725-3400. It's open May through October and includes 160 drive-in and walk-in (beach) sites, nature trails, flush toilets, hot showers, and laundry facilities. Fees range from $20 to $27 for two people, including hookups. **Crystal Cove Beach Resort**, 250/725-4213, has 90 drive-in and beachfront wilderness sites, as well as full and partial hookups, flush toilets, hot showers, and laundry facilities. Fees vary from $22 to $35 per vehicle.

Camping on the West Coast Trail and in the Broken Group Islands is allowed in designated locations only. In the Broken Group, there are only eight islands with designated camping, and sites can be

ECO-FRIENDLY: OCEAN'S EDGE BED-AND-BREAKFAST

Bill McIntyre scrambles over the black, jagged, ocean-slick rocks on the headland below his home like a mountain goat negotiating an alpine cliff. He leads his guests to "Bill's Bench," a protected spot where he's placed a seat recovered from an old schoolbus. "Get comfortable," he says, "and watch the show." All around, enormous breakers roll in from the Pacific and smash, foaming, over the rocks, while McIntyre grins and shouts, "Isn't this amazing?"

Winter storm watching is among McIntyre's many interests, which include bird-watching, beachcombing, tide pooling, and hiking. Above all, McIntyre enjoys sharing his incredible knowledge with others, a passion developed and nurtured for more than two decades as an interpreter and outreach coordinator in Pacific Rim National Park Reserve.

Now operating a B&B in Ucluelet with his wife, Susan, McIntyre continues to exercise his unique ability to educate children and adults alike and to open the eyes, ears, and minds of west coast visitors to the incredible strength and fragility of marine ecosystems.

busy in the summer. Detailed guidebooks on hiking the West Coast Trail and paddling the Broken Group Islands clearly indicate where the campsites are located.

LODGING

The **Clayoquot Wilderness Resort** in Quait Bay, Clayoquot Sound near Tofino, 250/725-2688 or 888/333-5405, www.greatfishing.com, is, in a word, unique. Floating on a 49-meter (162-foot) barge in the sheltered waters of Quait Bay, this could be the ultimate 16-room houseboat, complete with open kitchen and stone fireplace. Activities on the surrounding 51-hectare (126-acre) rain-forest property include kayaking, fishing, guided nature tours (forest and marine, Hot Springs Cove), and mountain biking. Service is impeccable, and the food is exceptional, featuring seafood and locally or BC-grown produce, cheeses, and wine. Rates begin at $190 per night and include water transportation from Tofino. Meals are extra: $85 per person per day. Excursions and activities are also extra. The resort originally planned to operate only in summer but may extend its open season to December.

Tofino is loaded with beach resorts, hotels, motels, and bed-and-breakfasts. Among the best is **Red Crow Guest House**, 250/725-2275, on the shores of Clayoquot Sound. The lodge has its own canoe and kayaks for guest use. The lodge's owners live on the top floor (they are part owners of the Wickaninnish Inn, see below), above the three guest rooms. Breakfasts are fabulous. Rates range from $100 to $135.

Another west coast gem is **Ocean's Edge B&B**, 855 Barkley Place, Ucluelet, 250/726-7099. It includes three private rooms, baths, and scrumptious breakfasts overlooking Barkley Sound. Owners Bill and Susan McIntyre are exceptionally knowledgeable about Pacific Rim history, wildlife, and activities. Rates start at $80. At the other end of Pacific Rim is the **Wickaninnish Inn**, Osprey Lane at Chesterman Beach, Tofino, 800/333-4604 or 250/725-5100, www.island.net/-wick. Named after the original inn (now the Wickaninnish Visitor Centre at Long Beach), this all-new luxury hotel is cantilevered over the rocks at one end of Chesterman Beach. Every room has a fireplace and an ocean view. Guests may enjoy summer beachcombing and activities in the park, winter-storm watching, and spring whale watching, as well as the hotel's full-service luxury spa. Rooms start at $200 per night.

If you're staying at **Wood's End Landing**, Box 108, Bamfield, BC V0R 1B0, 250/728-3383, be sure to request one of the new cabins instead of the older Berry Patch cabin. You'll have to do your own cooking but the cabins are cozy and well equipped. The price is right at **Sechart Whaling Station Lodge**, 250/723-8313. This former whaling station is now operated in the summer by Alberni Marine (the folks who run the MV *Lady Rose*.). Access is by boat only (the *Lady Rose* or sister ship *Frances Barkley*) and the accommodations are hostel-style, starting at $30 per person. Make your reservation when you book your spot on the *Lady Rose.* To get to the lodge from Bamfield, call Broken Island Adventures (see "Guides and Outfitters").

FOOD

The **Old Country Market**, located en route to Pacific Rim National Park Reserve in the village of Coombs, offers a wide selection of local produce including cheeses, baked goods, and fresh fruit and veggies. Say hello to the goats grazing on the roof (no kidding), then stock up for camping and picnicking at Pacific Rim. Once you get to the island's west coast, dining choices are legion. The best by far is **The Pointe Restaurant** at the Wickaninnish Inn, Osprey Lane at Chesterman Beach, Tofino, 800/333-4604 or 250/725-5100, www.island.net/-wick. The restaurant's award-winning chef prepares astonishing food, especially given the isolated location. You can choose from lots of local seafood, cheeses, and produce, as well as an extensive BC wine list. The drawback is the expense, but it's worth it. The *Canadian Princess,* Peninsula Rd., Ucluelet, 250/726-7711, offers dining and accommodations in a permanently moored steamship. The local seafood is excellent, and the pub is exceptionally cozy.

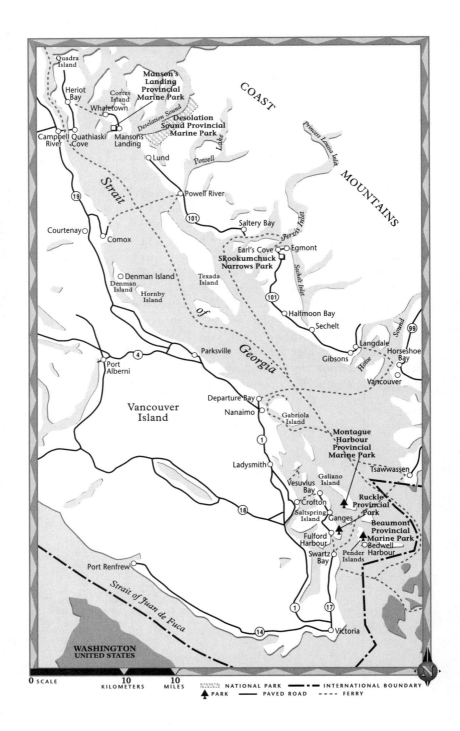

Quadra
Island

Heriot
Bay

Cortes
Island

Whaletown

**Manson's
Landing
Provincial
Marine Park**

Desolation Sound

**Desolation
Sound Provincial
Marine Park**

Campbell
River

Quathiaski
Cove

Mansons
Landing

Lund

Powell Lake

Powell

COAST

Princess Louisa Inlet

MOUNTAINS

19

Strait

Powell River

101

Courtenay

Comox

Saltery Bay

Earl's Cove

Egmont

**Skookumchuck
Narrows Park**

Jervis Inlet

Sechelt Inlet

Denman Island

Denman
Island

Hornby
Island

Texada
Island

101

Halfmoon Bay

Sechelt

of

Sound

99

Langdale

Horseshoe
Bay

Parksville

4

Georgia

Gibsons

Howe

Vancouver

Port
Alberni

Vancouver
Island

Departure Bay

Nanaimo

1

Gabriola
Island

**Montague
Harbour
Provincial
Marine Park**

Ladysmith

Tsawwassen

Vesuvius
Bay

Galiano
Island

18

Crofton

Saltspring
Island

Ganges

**Ruckle
Provincial
Park**

**Beaumont
Provincial
Marine Park**

Fulford
Harbour

Pender
Islands

Bedwell
Harbour

Swartz
Bay

Port Renfrew

Strait of Juan de Fuca

1

17

14

Victoria

**WASHINGTON
UNITED STATES**

0 SCALE   10 KILOMETERS   10 MILES

NATIONAL PARK   INTERNATIONAL BOUNDARY
PARK   PAVED ROAD   FERRY

N

CHAPTER 5

Gulf Islands and the Sunshine Coast

The Inside Passage between Vancouver Island and mainland British Columbia is scattered with islands, islets, and semi-submerged rocks. Known as the Gulf Islands, this collection of more than 200 islands provides unparalleled recreation and adventure opportunities. Some of the islands are popular and populous; others are almost deserted.

The Sunshine Coast, across Howe Sound north of Vancouver along the mainland, faces the waters of the Inside Passage and is accessible only by ferry from Vancouver, Vancouver Island, and some of the Gulf Islands. The aptly named region is an area of retirement homes and fine beaches, as well as excellent kayaking in sheltered inlets and coves, dive sites that take their place among the world's finest, long-distance paddling and hiking, and some of the best sailing on the west coast.

LAY OF THE LAND

Compared to the rough terrain of Vancouver Island's mountainous spine or the towering, steep-sided peaks of the mainland's Coast Mountains, the Gulf Islands are less rugged. But they still exhibit sheer cliffs rising from the water, narrow forested valleys, and peaks and rocky outcrops. Due to the rain shadow cast by Vancouver Island, the Gulf Islands enjoy Canada's mildest climate, with frost-free periods extending to eight months or longer. The more southerly islands are drier than those to the north. Summers in the Gulf Islands are luxurious—warm yet dry, ideal for outdoor activity. It's easy to get dehydrated in the islands' desertlike heat, and many of the islands have a shortage of fresh water. Carry your own.

Towns of the Sunshine Coast cling to the shore at the foot of the imposing Coast Mountains. While the climate is somewhat wetter than the southern Gulf Islands, the Sunshine Coast deserves its name, enjoying an average of 2,400 hours of sunshine annually. Summer days are indeed long and sunny, though heavy rain can and does occur at any time—those tall trees and lush forests aren't there for nothing! The Sunshine Coast is cut by Jervis Inlet, so travelers must take a ferry between Earl's Cove and Saltery Bay. In the northern part of the Sunshine Coast, Powell Lake is connected to the sea via the Powell River—at 500 meters (1,650 feet) long, it's the world's second-shortest river. At the north end of the Sunshine Coast lies spectacular Desolation Sound with its many islands and inlets cutting deep into the mainland coast. Major towns of the Sunshine Coast include Gibson's Landing (usually just called Gibson's), Sechelt (pronounced SEE-shelt), and Powell River.

HISTORY AND CULTURE

Several First Nations occupied the southern Gulf Islands, including Lekwammen, T'Sou-ke, and Wsanec. These peoples harvested salmon from the waters of the Inside Passage using nets. They also dug the edible bulbs of camas, picked berries, and were excellent weavers, making nets, blankets, and intricate baskets. The Shishalh and Sliammon peoples occupied the Sunshine Coast and nearby islands as far north as Desolation Sound.

The names of many of the Gulf Islands reflect early Spanish exploration of the area. Settlement of the islands by Europeans began in 1857 when pioneer farmers came to Saltspring Island. Due to the islands' mild climate, agriculture has been the major economic pursuit, followed by fishing and fish processing, whaling, logging, and sawmill operations. Except for agriculture, none of these ventures has proved to be especially lucrative, and most industrial activity on the Gulf Islands has gradually given way to tourism and retirement homes. Artists, organic farmers, and those seeking refuge from the cities have taken up residence on the Gulf Islands, giving an easygoing, neighborly, tolerant feel to island life.

This is not to say, though, that the Gulf Islands are deserted—far from it. There are towns and settlements scattered throughout the islands, and much of the land base on the larger islands is privately owned. As a result, there is a growing forest of "no trespassing" signs on many of the islands. Respect the signs and stay away from private property.

When it comes to culture and lifestyle, the Sunshine Coast resembles the Gulf Islands. It's quiet and quirky, but Joni Mitchell owns seaside property here, so the place obviously cuts the mustard for scenic seclusion. The area's mild climate and relative isolation—it takes at least one ferry to get there—have made it a haven for artists, retirees, and anyone else looking for a quiet, semirural lifestyle.

P. Crawford/D. Giberson

Arbutus tree

109

FLORA AND FAUNA

Similar ecologically to the southern end of Vancouver Island, the southern Gulf Islands' dry, mild climate has given rise to vegetation communities dominated by a mix of grasslands and open forest. Garry oak, arbutus (also known as madrone), and many species of wildflowers dot the islands, along with Douglas fir and other conifers in the moister areas. The northern Gulf Islands are wetter and more heavily forested. Arbutus is found occasionally along the Sunshine Coast, but generally this area tends to be wetter than the Gulf Islands, and therefore has heavy forest growth, especially toward the north end of the region.

Seabirds, eagles, ravens, herons, ducks—the Gulf Islands and the Sunshine Coast are a bird-watcher's paradise. Marine life is plentiful too, with whales, seals, and sea lions. Undersea life is brilliant and abundant with wolf eels, octopuses, sponges, anemones, and even small sharks. The diving at Powell River is rated among the world's best thanks to this incredible variety of animals.

VISITOR INFORMATION

Summers are busy on most of the Gulf Islands and throughout the Sunshine Coast. Campgrounds fill up quickly, as do the numerous resorts, hotels, and bed-and-breakfasts. There are no provincial campgrounds on many of the Gulf Islands, though most have private camping developments; if you're planning to camp, book ahead. Similarly, there are many excellent tour operators offering everything from whale watching to sportfishing to kayaking and diving, but their space is limited. Book ahead if you want to paddle, fish, or dive with a tour guide or outfitter.

Regular car and passenger ferry services link the Gulf Islands to one another, to Vancouver Island, and to the BC mainland. Ferry departure and arrival points are described below. Winter ferry service is less frequent than summer service; in summer, you may find yourself waiting, sometimes for hours, for a place on the smaller ferries. Call BC Ferries for information, 888/223-3779. Reservations for travel from Vancouver/Tsawwassen to the Gulf Islands can be made by calling 604/669-1211. For a fee, passengers can take their canoe, kayak, or bicycle with them onto the ferries (many kayakers take advantage of ferry services between islands).

If you'll be arriving in the islands on your personal boat or yacht, there are government wharves on all of the Gulf Islands, plus numerous private marinas. Some of the Gulf Islands are blessed with provincial marine parks. Boaters entering Canada from the United States are required to clear Canadian Customs at their first port of call. Gulf Island waters are not without their dangers—if you're cruising or sailing among the islands, be aware of tides and currents, and have the appropriate marine charts with you for locating hazards.

Hiking on most of the islands is great, especially for families or anyone who just wants to get out of the car and stretch. The hikes tend to be short and usually not too demanding. Cycling, too, is excellent. Although the islands' roadways tend to be narrow and winding, traffic is relatively light and the cycling is safe and scenic. If you're driving, be aware that cyclists are common. Take a cue from the locals— slow down, drive with caution, and enjoy the scenery. You'll get where you're bound in good time.

The islands are known for excellent saltwater fishing, plus exceptional freshwater fishing on Saltspring and Quadra Islands. The sea kayaking is also fantastic; in fact, it's so pleasant and leisurely that many outfitters offer introductory courses in these placid waters. The islands are equally renowned for scuba diving.

For detailed information, contact the Visitor Infocentre on the island you're planning to visit or Tourism Vancouver Island, #302, 45 Bastion Square, Victoria, 250/382-3551, www.islands.bc.ca.

The Sunshine Coast is served by short ferries that connect Horseshoe Bay to Langdale (across Howe Sound) and Earl's Cove to Saltery Bay (across Jervis Inlet). The ferry fare from Horseshoe Bay to Langdale includes either a return trip from Langdale to Horseshoe Bay or an onward trip across Jervis Inlet from Earl's Cove to Saltery Bay. Ferry service links Powell River to Comox on Vancouver Island. For ferry schedules and fares, contact BC Ferries at 888/223-3779 or 604/669-1211.

The Sunshine Coast is served by Highway 101 from Langdale in the south to Lund in the north, including the ferry crossing at Jervis Inlet. For detailed information on the Sunshine Coast, contact the Vancouver, Coast and Mountains Tourism Association, #204, 1755 W.

Broadway, Vancouver, 800/667-3306 or 604/739-9011, e-mail vcmtr @istar.ca, www.coastandmountains.bc.ca. There are numerous Visitor Infocentres located throughout the region—several are mentioned in this chapter.

NATURE AND ADVENTURE SIGHTS: GULF ISLANDS

Denman and Hornby Islands

Denman, with its mild climate and unhurried lifestyle, captures the essence of Gulf Island life: relaxed, to say the least. Check out the many galleries and artists' studios. Hornby is even more low-key, known for artisans working in pottery and ceramics. There are hiking, paddling, fishing and diving opportunities on both islands. Be aware that Hornby is an extremely popular summer day trip and the island can become overrun by as many as 10,000 tourists (compared to a full-time residential population of about 1,000).

Hornby's claim to fame for divers is the presence of six-gill sharks,

D. Leighton

Tribune Bay, Hornby Island

which move in the shallow waters at **Flora Inlet**, also the site of underwater caves hiding wolf eels, skates, and octopuses. The sharks, up to 6 meters (20 feet) long, normally inhabit much deeper water but, like human tourists, seem to be attracted to the warm waters of Hornby Island in the summer. Apparently the warm water makes the sharks slow and docile. Check at local dive shops for air, dive buddies, or charters.

Details: Denman Island is a 10-minute ferry ride from Buckley Bay on Vancouver Island. Ferry service to Shingle Spit on Hornby Island is from Gravelly Bay on Denman Island.

112

D. Leighton

Hornby Island

Call 250/335-0323 for a ferry schedule. Information on both islands is available from the Hornby-Denman Tourist Association, Sea Breeze Lodge, Hornby Island, BC V0R 1Z0, 250/335-2321.

Gabriola Island

Just five kilometers (three miles) east of Nanaimo off the east coast of Vancouver Island, Gabriola is home to numerous popular marinas that are particularly busy in the summer. This small island also has a variety of beaches, from sand to pebble to sandstone-shelf. Descanso Bay, the ferry terminal on Gabriola, is served by BC Ferries from downtown Nanaimo.

Details *Contact the Visitor Infocentre in Nanaimo, 2290 Bowen Rd., 250/756-0106.*

Galiano Island

A long, thin finger of land, Galiano is the driest of the Gulf Islands, with a mean annual rainfall of 60 centimeters (24 inches). Beach-

113

Tide-formed rock formations, Galiano Island

combing and sunbathing are activities of choice on this sparsely populated island. Among the island's attractions are Montague Harbour Provincial Marine Park and the seaside cliffs and well-marked hiking trails of Bodega Ridge Nature Preserve. Ferry service connects Galiano with Swartz Bay on Vancouver Island and with Tsawwassen near Vancouver.

Details: *Galiano Island Infocentre, Box 73, Galiano Island, BC V0N 1P0, 250/539-2233. The center is located on Sturdies Road near the ferry terminal.*

Pender Islands
Unlike most other Gulf Islands, North and South Pender Islands are largely accessible to the public. The majority of the islands' residents live on North Pender, which is joined to the south island by a bridge. Bedwell Harbour is a great location for canoeing, kayaking, and whale watching. **Beaumont Provincial Marine Park**, on the north side of Bedwell Harbour, is a popular site for camping, swimming, and hiking; call 250/391-2300 for information and camping reservations. Otter

Bay on North Pender Island is served by ferries from Swartz Bay on Vancouver Island and from Tsawwassen near Vancouver.

Details: Pender Island Infocentre, Box 75, Pender Island, BC V0N 2M0 (2332 Otter Bay Rd., about half a mile from the ferry terminal).

Quadra and Cortes Islands

At 276 square kilometers (107 square miles), Quadra Island is the second-largest of the Gulf Islands, and its diverse topography remains largely undisturbed, especially at the island's northern end. The convoluted shoreline has plenty of bays and coves, and the inland lakes and streams provide excellent freshwater fishing. There are several good hiking trails on the island, including **Nugedzi Lake Old Growth Forest Trail**, a well-marked path about five kilometers (three miles) in length. The trailhead is located two and one-half kilometers (one and one-half miles) past the salmon hatchery on the Hyacinthe Bay road leading to the northern part of the island.

The largest freshwater system in the Gulf Islands is Quadra's **Main Lake Chain**. The lakes offer excellent sheltered paddling with no tides or currents, and easy access to wildlife, beaches, and solitude. Put in at Village Bay Lake or Mine Lake. The length of the entire chain is perhaps seven or eight kilometers (four or five miles), but you can while away many hours just noodling around the islands and bays.

A must-see on the island is the **Kwagiulth Museum and Cultural Centre** (250/285-3733), home to more than 300 Native masks, headdresses, and other ceremonial and everyday items that were confiscated by Europeans from Native potlatch festivals in the 1920s. Native councils from the region negotiated with the various museums for repatriation of the items, resulting in the construction of the Kwagiulth Museum in the village of Cape Mudge on Quadra Island and the U'mista Cultural Heritage Centre in Alert Bay (see the entry on Alert Bay in Chapter 3).

Cortes Island lies east of Quadra Island, at the mouth of **Desolation Sound**. The sound is among the best sailing and small-craft cruising areas on the west coast (see "Sunshine Coast Destinations" below for details on Desolation Sound). Getting to Cortes involves a 45-minute ferry crossing from Quadra; as a result, Cortes is considered remote and is very quiet and peaceful.

AUTHOR'S TOP PICKS: SAILING

- **Broken Group Islands**—*This wilderness region is part of Pacific Rim National Park Reserve.*
- **Gulf Islands**—*Excellent boating and provincial marine parks accessible only by boat.*
- **Haida Gwaii (Queen Charlotte Islands)**—*Another wilderness area, complete with towering rain forests, abandoned whaling stations, and Native villages.*
- **Indian Arm, Burrard Inlet**—*This sheltered, quiet area is very popular with Vancouver-area boaters.*
- **Inside Passage**—*The sheltered waters and countless islands and islets between Vancouver Island and the mainland offer plenty of opportunities to spot whales, dolphins, and sea birds.*
- **Jervis Inlet, Desolation Sound, Princess Louisa Inlet**—*Among the many long, deep fjords on the Sunshine Coast, these three offer superb sailing and exploring opportunities, wildlife, and sheltered waters.*

Cortes's shoreline is indented by several inlets and sheltered bays, making the trip a worthwhile endeavor for paddlers. Check out Gorge Harbour, enclosed by the surrounding hills with only a narrow passage connected to the ocean; Squirrel Cove, a popular anchorage for boaters exploring Desolation Sound and the nearby mainland coast; and Manson's Landing Provincial Marine Park, which features sandy beaches and a public shellfish reserve for clams and oysters. Von Dunop Inlet nearly cuts the island in two. This long narrow finger of water provides safe anchorage and great boat-based paddling (there are no roads to the inlet).

Details: Quadra Island is a short ferry ride from downtown Campbell

River. The ferry for Cortes Island departs from Heriot Bay on Quadra. For ferry schedules call 250/286-1412. Information on both islands is available from the Visitor Infocentre in Campbell River, Box 400, Campbell River, BC V9W 5B6, 250/287-4636 (1235 Shopper's Row in Tyee Plaza).

Saltspring Island

Largest of the Gulf Islands, Saltspring covers 180 square kilometers (70 square miles). Bruce Peak, at the southern end of Saltspring, is the Gulf Islands' tallest mountain at 698 meters (2,300 feet). The two main towns on the island are Ganges and Fulford Harbour. More than half of the Gulf Islands' total population of approximately 12,000 lives on Saltspring. Many have retired to the island, but owing to Saltspring's proximity to Vancouver Island there are lots of commuters who work in Victoria, then return to their peaceful island at night. Alternative lifestyles are comfortable on Saltspring—you'll find artists and artisans, organic farmers, and even an astrologer or two.

Saltspring is diverse in every sense and aspect, from its geography that spans mountains to seacoast, to the variety of activities available. It's possible to tour the island in a day, stopping at various beaches, viewpoints, shops, and cafés, but to really "do" Saltspring you need at least a couple of days—or more if you're planning to cycle or kayak.

Ruckle Provincial Park is the largest in the Gulf Islands (480 hectares/1,185 acres) and encompasses lovely little coves and bays with views of the Gulf of Georgia and nearby islands. The park is just 10 kilometers (6 miles) from the village of Fulford Harbour. Ocean paddling opportunities on Saltspring include Fulford Harbour, Chain Islands in Ganges Harbour, Long Harbour, and Walker Hook. All consist of less then five nautical miles of mostly sheltered, hazard-free paddling. Inland, check out St. Mary Lake and Cusheon Lake for paddling and trout fishing. You're likely to see octopuses when scuba diving in Burgoyne Bay. And the extensive web of roads makes cycling on Saltspring easy (topography is steeper on the south side of the island, more rolling to the north).

Details: BC Ferries service for Saltspring Island connects Crofton to Vesuvius Bay, Swartz Bay to Fulford Harbour, and Tsawwassen to Long Harbour. Harbour Air also links Vancouver with Saltspring (see Appendix A). Contact Saltspring Island Infocentre, Box 111, Ganges, BC V0S 1E0, 250/537-4223.

Rugged coastline and Desolation Sound

K. D. Wong/Blackbird Design

NATURE AND ADVENTURE SIGHTS: SUNSHINE COAST

Desolation Sound Provincial Marine Park
BC's largest marine park is accessible only by boat. With the Coast Mountains for a backdrop, it's a glorious spot for boating and paddling in warm, sheltered waters. Because it's so easy to get here, Desolation Sound is very popular in the summer, with up to 300 watercraft populating the park in July and August. Camping is available at a number of small islands in the sound (no facilities; bring fresh water).

Details: The best access points are from Lund, 23 kilometers (14 miles) north of Powell River, or from Comox or Campbell River on the east side of Vancouver Island. Sailing charters are available in Comox and Powell River.

Egmont
This tiny village of 115 "Egmonsters" is the final supply point for yachters heading up Jervis Inlet to Princess Louisa Inlet and for

paddlers and divers heading through **Skookumchuck Narrows** and into the northern reaches of Sechelt Inlet. In the Chinook jargon, *skookum* means "strong" and *chuck* means "water"—the reference is to the powerful tidal bore that flows into and out of Sechelt Inlet over shallow rapids, creating strong and treacherous currents. Up to 900 billion liters of water (200 billion gallons) pours through the narrow opening on a rising tide. The ground literally shakes from the tremendous force of the rushing water. For those who want to see the rapids from a safe distance, a four-kilometer (two-and-one-half-mile) hiking trail leads from the Egmont access road to the rapids. Tide tables are posted at the trailhead so you can time the 45-minute hike appropriately. Best times to see the tidal bore are June and December. At low tide, look for the extra-large specimens of sea urchins, barnacles, sea anemones, and other marine life that have adapted to survive the hostile waters.

Jervis Inlet extends nearly 80 kilometers (48 miles) into the Coast Mountains and is the best means of access to the incredible **Princess Louisa Inlet**. A stretch of dangerous, shallow water, Malibu Rapids, marks the entrance to Princess Louisa Inlet. Beyond the rapids, however, the inlet is a tiny paradise for paddling—eight kilometers (four and one-half miles) of tranquil waters, moss-hung forests, and steep mountain cliffs washed by more than 60 waterfalls. At the head of the inlet is Princess Louisa Provincial Marine Park, which encompasses a towering rock face more than 1,500 meters (4,950 feet) tall and the 37-meter (122-foot) **Chatterbox Falls**.

Details: As Highway 101 approaches Earls' Cove (the ferry terminal for connections across Jervis Inlet to Saltery Bay and beyond), watch for signs indicating a right turn (east) to Egmont.

Powell River

The original pulp and paper mill that fueled settlement here, to say nothing of the destruction of the area's forests, was constructed in 1910. The mill, much expanded and improved, is now among the world's largest. The town that was built around the mill from 1910 to 1930 is now a national historic region with more than 400 well-preserved Victorian-style homes and other buildings. The city of Powell River has grown far beyond the original town and currently has a population of approximately 13,000.

Underwater mermaid statue off Powell River

P. Crawford/D. Bigerson

The city is known as "the Dive Capital of Canada," but could as easily be called "Dive Capital of the World." The offshore waters are clear (especially in winter) and the marine life is astonishing; the region is known for especially large octopuses (the world's biggest) and wolf eels. There are at least 20 excellent dive sites nearby, including shipwrecks, artificial reefs, and an underwater statue of a mermaid. Jacques Cousteau characterized the diving off Powell River as second only to diving in the Red Sea. There are numerous diving companies in town offering guided trips into the waters. If you'd prefer to dive on your own, contact the Powell River Deep Breathers Dive Club, which can hook you up with a dive buddy. The club's e-mail address is deepbreathers@hotmail.com.

The **Powell River Forest Canoe Route** begins at Lois Lake, 20 kilometers (12 miles) southeast of Powell River. It's a terrific trip with short portages joining 10 lakes over 80 kilometers (48 miles). The route can be paddled all at once or in sections, depending on how much time you have and how fit and experienced you are. There are picnic spots and Forest Service campsites along the route. Fishing is great in the lakes. The route's biggest disadvantage is its proximity to active logging, which has left clear-cut blocks visible on many mountainsides. Excellent maps of the canoe route are available at the Powell River Visitor Infocentre (see below).

Volunteers are currently completing work on the 180-kilometer (108-mile) **Sunshine Coast Trail**, between Sarah Point, which is north of Powell River, and Saltery Bay on Jervis Inlet. The trail will give hikers access to ever-diminishing old-growth forest on the north Sunshine Coast plus oceanfront and alpine hiking. It incorporates the world's first fully wheelchair-accessible hiking trail, on Inland Lake near Powell River. This paved portion of trail is 13 kilometers (eight miles) long. The volunteers hope to eventually construct huts along the entire route to facilitate long-distance hiking. At present there are three bed-and-breakfasts, one hut, one hotel, and two restaurants on or near the trail. For more information on the trail, contact the Visitor Infocentre (see "Details").

Details: Powell River is located 31 kilometers (18.5 miles) north of the Saltery Bay ferry terminal. The Visitor Infocentre is at 4690 Marine Ave., Powell River, 604/485-4701, e-mail prvb@prcn.org. BC Ferries operates between Powell River and Comox/Courtenay on Vancouver Island.

Sechelt

This artsy town is situated on a narrow neck of land barely one kilometer (one-half mile) wide. This strip of land prevents Sechelt Inlet from connecting with the Strait of Georgia; if the inlet and the strait were connected, Sechelt Peninsula would be an island.

Sechelt is a starting point for adventures and activities on **Sechelt Inlet**, the inland sea. The inlet has over 480 kilometers (290 miles) of coastline, eight provincial marine parks, and a number of marinas. There are few settlements along the inlet's shores, making this sheltered waterway an exceptional wilderness area within easy reach of Vancouver. Kayaking, canoeing, and diving are all first-rate. Sunk 35 meters (115 feet) beneath the waters of the inlet is the **HMCS** *Chaudiere* (pronounced show-dee-AIR), a decommissioned Canadian naval destroyer. The ship was gutted and deliberately sunk off Kunechin Point, six kilometers (three and one-half miles) north of Sechelt. The theory is that the ship will form an anchor for marine life, which will eventually create an artificial reef. This is an excellent dive location; dive charters are available in Sechelt.

Details: Take Highway 101 north from Langdale for 27 kilometers (17 miles). Sechelt Visitor Infocentre, Box 360, Sechelt, BC V0N 3A0, 604/885-0662.

GUIDES AND OUTFITTERS

For Gulf Island diving, contact **Clavella Adventures**, Box 866, Nanaimo, BC V9R 5N2, 250/753-4014 or 250/753-3751, www.nanaimo. ark.com/-clavella. The company offers live-aboard diving from the MV *Clavella*. The maximum group size is 10, including divers and non-divers, and packages include unlimited diving, air, tanks, weight belts, meals, and shore excursions.

The islands are wonderful for sea kayaking; in fact, many outfitters offer instructional weekend or weeklong courses in the warm, peaceful waters. Among the sea-kayak outfitters is **Geoff Evans Kayak Centre**, Box 3097, Cultus Lake, BC V2R 5H6, 604/858-6775, e-mail gevans@uniserve.com. Although the company office is on the BC mainland, Geoff Evans offers instructional kayak trips featuring interpretive guides and low-impact camping in the Gulf Islands. The largest kayak outfitter on Saltspring Island is **Sea Otter Kayaking**, 1186 North End Rd., Saltspring Island, 250/537-5678. It is located on Ganges Harbor and offer instruction, rentals, guided day and overnight tours, and special sunset, moonlight, and phosphorescent paddle trips.

Island Escapades, 118 Natalie Lane, Saltspring Island, 888/KAYAK-67 or 250/537-2537, e-mail escapades@saltspring.com, www.globalserve.net/-trplh/ie.html, offers multi-day, multi-activity Gulf Island tours including hiking, beachcombing, and kayaking. You can choose whether you want to camp or stay in bed-and-breakfasts along the way. **Wild Heart Adventures,** 2774 Barnes Rd., Site H2, Nanaimo, BC V9R 5K2, 250/722-3683, e-mail wheart@island.net, www.island.net/-wheart offers sea-kayaking trips in the north Gulf Islands for all skill levels. On the Sunshine Coast, contact **Sunshine Kayaking**, RR 4, S 12, C 18, Gibson's, BC V0N 1V0, 604/886-9760, for guided kayak trips to Princess Louisa Inlet and other destinations.

For unique guided hiking or sailing trips in the Gulf Islands, contact **ECO Tours**, 3198 Ilona Place, Victoria, 250/474-7463, e-mail ecotours@oceanside.com, www.oceanside.com/oceanside/ecotours. Accommodations are included (onboard when sailing, in trailers or RVs on land-based trips).

There are literally hundreds of boat charters available, from fishing charters to sailing cruises. Check locally in the yellow pages or newspapers. For a pleasant day on the water, including whale watching and fishing, contact **SeaCapers Charters** at Ganges Harbor on Saltspring Island, 250/537-4202. They sail to marine parks on the outer islands, visit secluded beaches, and offer both full- and half-day cruises.

When it comes to diving, **Don's Dive Shop**, 6789 Wharf St., Powell River, 800/663-6000 or 604/485-6969, e-mail donsdiving@ hotmail.com, www.prcn.org/donsdiving, is quite possibly the west coast's premier dive store. It offers boat and shore dives, charters, summer dive packages, instruction, air and equipment, dive buddies for visiting divers, and more. Also based in Powell River is **Mystic Sailing Adventures**, 4585 Marine Ave., Powell River, 604/485-6558, offering sail cruises along Desolation Sound, the Sunshine Coast, and the northern Gulf Islands, plus sailing instruction or "bareboat" charters.

CAMPING

The Gulf Islands are loaded with quaint guest homes and bed-and-breakfasts, but camping can be hard to come by. Provincial park campgrounds in the Gulf Islands accepting reservations include Montague Harbour on Galiano Island and Prior Centennial on North Pender Island. For provincial-park camping reservations, call 800/689-9025 or 689-9025 from Vancouver. There are a few private campgrounds.

On Saltspring Island, **Ruckle Provincial Park**, 250/954-4600, is great for hikers and cyclists, and includes 40 walk-in campsites on the waterfront. Private campgrounds on the island include **Cedar Beach Resort**, 1136 North End Rd., Saltspring Island, 250/537-2205. Located near Vesuvius Bay, it includes 12 shaded sites, beach activities, fishing. Fees start at $15 per vehicle. Just up the road is **Lakeside Garden Resort**, 1450 North End Rd., 250/537-5773, with 14 sites, hookups, hot showers, beach access, and boat rentals. Fees start at $18; electricity and sewage hookups are extra.

AUTHOR'S TOP PICKS: SEA KAYAKING

- **Broken Group Islands**—*This paddler's paradise, a unit of the Pacific Rim National Park Reserve, is on Barkley Sound on the west coast of Vancouver Island.*

- **Gulf Islands**—*Several marine parks in the Gulf Islands are excellent destinations for sea kayaking. Remember to bring water as many of the smaller Gulf Islands lack fresh water.*

- **Haida Gwaii (Queen Charlotte Islands)**—*Remote and beautiful, this area is best visited with a tour guide who can get access to Native sites.*

- **Sechelt Inlet**—*This sheltered arm of the sea is protected by the Sechelt Peninsula. The ocean enters and leaves the inlet through Skookumchuk Narrows. Beware of strong tidal bores.*

Montague Harbour Provincial Marine Park, Galiano Island, 250/391-2300, is a popular destination for boaters and cyclists. It has 19 vehicle sites and 21 walk-in tent sites, and is a great place for families with safe beaches and ocean swimming. On North Pender Island, **Prior Centennial** offers 17 sites at the rock-bottom price of $9.50 per night. Facilities are minimal—pit toilets, firewood, and drinking water—but there's a lovely beach close by and the sites are big and private. At **Bradsdadsland Country Camp Resort**, 1980 Shingle Spit Rd., Hornby Island, 250/335-0757, there are 25 grassy sites facing the beach and a shower house with flush toilets. Gates close at 11 at night, and no loud music is permitted in this family-oriented spot. Fees range from $16 to $19; hookups cost extra. **Hornby Island Resort**, 4305 Shingle Spit Rd., Hornby Island, 250/335-0136, has 10 campsites, laundry and shower facilities, and an on-site restaurant. Fees range from $12 to $18 per vehicle; electrical hookup costs extra.

On Denman Island, **Fillongley** is a provincial campground with

10 sites, minimal facilities, and very little privacy. But for $8.50, it's a deal. **Gorge Harbour Marina Resort** on Cortes Island, Box 89, Whaletown, 250/935-6433, has 40 sites (separate tent and RV sites), laundry facilities, showers, a boat launch, a store and restaurant, rentals (bikes, kayaks, boats, and scooters), fishing licenses and supplies, guided nature walks, charter fishing . . . whew! All this for $10 to $17, including hookups. **Heriot Bay Inn** on Quadra Island, Box 100, Heriot Bay, BC V0P 1H0, 250/285-3322, has 60 campsites, laundry facilities, showers, freezers, RV hookups, a restaurant and pub, boat rentals, fishing charters, and kayak rentals and lessons. Fees range from $10 to $16.75 including hookups. Also on Quadra, **We Wai Kai Campsite**, Box 220, Quathiaski Cove, BC V0P 1H0, 250/285-3111, has 140 sites, some shaded, some on the beach. It also has showers, laundry facilities, and a sani-station. Fees range from $15 to $17 per vehicle.

Along the Sunshine Coast there are several provincial park campgrounds, but since they're close to a large urban center—Vancouver—they fill up quickly on summer weekends. Provincial campgrounds in the area that accept reservations include Porpoise Bay and Saltery Bay. For reservations call 800/689-9025. **Porpoise Bay**, a popular spot on the shore of Sechelt Inlet, has 84 campsites, swimming, cycling (the park has four cycle-in campsites), a great put-in spot for paddlers, and a safe beach for toddlers and families. **Okeover Arm** is a kayaker's campground—a good starting point for those planning to paddle in Desolation Sound. Located at the north end of Highway 101, the campground has just five vehicle sites and four walk-in sites on the water. For paddlers, **Princess Louisa Provincial Marine Park** has several tent sites, a 12-sided picnic shelter, and pit toilets. A park ranger works the grounds June through September, and a hiking trail leads to Chatterbox Falls.

LODGING

Accommodations on the Gulf Islands vary from rustic to romantic to all-inclusive resorts. Some inns and bed-and-breakfasts are closed during the winter. Summers are busy, so phone ahead for reservations. There are numerous bed-and-breakfasts throughout the islands; for free bookings and information, contact the **Canadian Gulf Islands B&B Reservations Service**, 888/539-2930.

Hastings House, 160 Upper Ganges Rd., Saltspring Island, 800/661-9255 or 250/537-2362, is a Tudor-style country estate with formal gardens, an excellent restaurant featuring fresh herbs and local produce, and luxurious furnishings in a 1940s-era mansion. The house includes 10 unique suites, each with fireplace. Rooms are extremely expensive, ranging from $265 to $495. For something more down to earth, **Spindrift at Welbury Point**, 255 Welbury Dr., Saltspring Island, 250/537-5311, offers oceanfront cottages with fireplaces and private sand beaches. Romantic and secluded, it's for adults only and rates start at $95. The **Saltspring Island Hostel**, 640 Cusheon Lake Rd., Ganges, 250/537-4149, has both dormitory and private rooms; dorms start at $15.50, rooms at $40. The beds are comfy and the scenery is spectacular. It's a good place for families, with very friendly hosts who know all about the islands' best activities.

The **Inn on Pender Island**, 4709 Canal Rd., Pender Island, 800/550-0172 or 250/629-3353, is a year-round treat. Try one of their studio log cabins with private hot tub for $59 to $79 per night. For a complete luxury–fishing lodge experience, try **April Point Lodge** on Quadra Island, 250/285-2222. This sumptuous lodge, a great retreat even if you don't fish, operates salmon charters in the Inside Passage. Rates range from $99 to $395 depending on the size of the guest house you choose (one to six bedrooms).

The Sunshine Coast is well supplied with hotels, motels, resorts, and bed-and-breakfasts. **Desolation Resort**, 2694 Dawson Rd., Lund, 604/483-3592, fax 604/483-7942, opened in 1997, offers fully equipped cedar chalets overlooking Desolation Sound just outside the village of Lund, at the end of Highway 101. It also has canoe and kayak rentals, and the waterfront property is great for families (three-day minimum stay, open May through September). Rates range from $140 to $220. For a homey touch, try **Cranberry Comfort B&B**, 5357 McGuffie St., Powell River, 604/483-4047. In addition to three cozy rooms (the suite has its own jet bath), the B&B offers hiking, kayaking, canoeing, and sailboat charters in Desolation Sound and the surrounding area (see Mystic Sailing Adventures in "Guides and Outfitters"). The breakfasts are enormous, and special-needs diets are accommodated. Rates start at $80 per night.

FOOD

Barb's Buns, 121 McPhillips Ave., Ganges, Saltspring Island, 250/537-4491, a family-operated business for nearly 20 years, makes homemade vegetarian dishes and baked goods. It opens at six in the morning for breakfast, but is closed on Sundays. Also in Ganges and offering excellent Scandinavian cuisine for dinner is **House Picolo**, 108 Hereford Ave., 250/537-1844. Prices are moderate to expensive.

The **Sea Breeze Lodge and Restaurant**, Denman Island, 250/335-2321, has a lovely dining room serving daily buffets with fresh baked goods, soups, seafood, and beef. On Galiano Island, **La Berengerie**, Montague Harbor Rd. at Clanton Rd., 250/539-5392, is a summertime treat (closed November through March). A set four-course menu is offered each night; there's also a vegetarian-only patio café in July and August. Prices are moderate. If you're waiting for the ferry on Gabriola Island, nip in to the **White Hart Pub**, 250/247-8588, at the ferry terminal. The burgers and brews are terrific.

The village of Gibson's was the location for a long-running Canadian television series, *The Beachcombers*, and as such it became a popular tourist destination. The cameras and actors are now long gone, but the many inexpensive cafés remain. Try **Alladin's Café** (604/886-4898, Mediterranean, desserts, cappuccino), **Ali Babar's Café** (604/886-0864, Italian snacks, ice cream, cappuccino), and **Andy's Café** (604/886-3388, steaks, seafood, pasta), all of which are located right on the Sunshine Coast Highway (Highway 101). In Sechelt, check out **Café Pierrot**, 101, 5710 Teredo, 604/885-9962, for excellent home-cooked European cuisine; or the **Blue Heron Inn**, 5591 Delta, 800/818-8977 or 604/885-3847, for wonderful west coast cuisine emphasizing fresh local seafood.

In Powell River, **Beach Gardens Resort**, 7074 Westminster (Grief Point, at the south end of town), 604/485-6267, is famous for its Friday-night feasts of seafood and baron of beef; while the **Blackberry Café**, 4-7030 Alberni, 604/485-0080, is famous for fresh pasta. For delectable salmon Wellington (salmon robed in phyllo) check out the **Sea House Restaurant**, 4448 Marine, 604/485-5163. If you travel beyond Powell River on the Sunshine Coast, check out the **Backeddy Pub** in Egmont. Snack on fish and chips, sip a cool brew or two, and chat with the local divers.

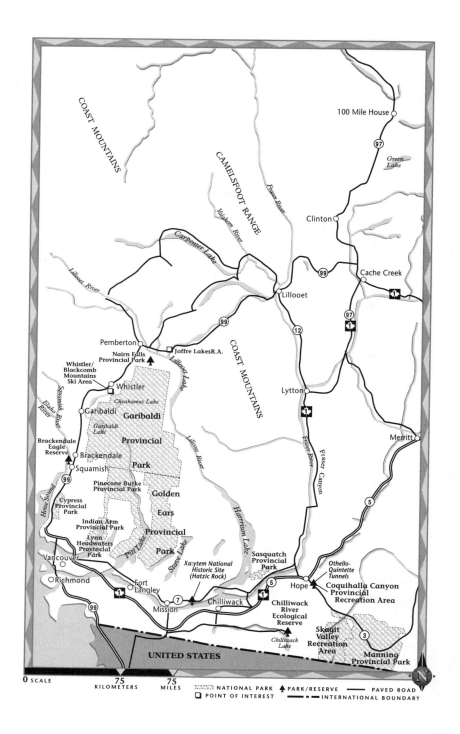

COAST MOUNTAINS

CAMELSFOOT RANGE

COAST MOUNTAINS

100 Mile House

97

Green Lake

Clinton

Carpenter Lake

Yalakom River

Fraser River

Cache Creek

99

1

Lillooet

Lillooet River

12

97

1

Pemberton

99

Joffre Lakes R.A.

Nairn Falls
Provincial Park

Whistler/
Blackcomb
Mountains
Ski Area

Whistler

Lillooet Lake

Lytton

1

Cheakamus Lake

Garibaldi

Garibaldi

Garibaldi
Lake

Merritt

Squamish River

Cheakamus River

Brackendale
Eagle
Reserve

Brackendale

Provincial

Lillooet River

Fraser River

Fraser Canyon

Squamish

99

Park

Pinecone Burke
Provincial Park

Golden

5

Cypress
Provincial
Park

Indian Arm
Provincial Park

Ears

Harrison Lake

Lynn
Headwaters
Provincial
Park

Pitt Lake

Provincial

Sasquatch
Provincial
Park

Othello-
Quintette
Tunnels

Vancouver

Stave Lake

Park

Xa:ytem National
Historic Site
(Hatzic Rock)

Hope

Coquihalla Canyon
Provincial
Recreation Area

Richmond

Fort
Langley

7

5

1

Chilliwack
River
Ecological
Reserve

Mission

Chilliwack

99

1

Chilliwack Lake

Skagit
Valley
Recreation
Area

3

Manning
Provincial Park

UNITED STATES

0 SCALE

75
KILOMETERS

75
MILES

▨ NATIONAL PARK ▲ PARK/RESERVE —— PAVED ROAD
☐ POINT OF INTEREST —▪—▪ INTERNATIONAL BOUNDARY

N

CHAPTER 6

Lower Mainland and Sea to Sky Country

Again, that word "diversity" characterizes this region. Of British Columbia's total population of 3.76 million, 1.8 million live in the Lower Mainland, thanks mainly to the concentration of people in Vancouver. The region's flat, low-lying Fraser Delta is home to both rich farmland outside of the city and urban industry within. Beyond the delta, not far outside of the city limits, are rugged and, generally, roadless mountains. Likewise, the region's recreational offerings are vast and varied. From world-class downhill skiing to exceptional cross-country skiing, from hiking amid forest giants to exploring aboriginal and archaeological sites, the opportunities for outdoor action are practically limitless. Even if you're visiting Vancouver and have only a day to spare, there are many ways to experience the area's aboriginal culture and natural ecology without so much as leaving town.

LAY OF THE LAND

The vast majority of the region is mountainous. To the north of Vancouver are the Coast Mountains, while to the east are the Cascades. Both these mountain ranges are composed of tough, erosion-resistant rock, resulting in steep-sided valleys washed by countless creeks and waterfalls. Vegetation is lush and dense. The climate is generally temperate, even in the mountains, but winter rains and snowfalls are among the heaviest in the province.

The mainland coastline is deeply incised by inlets. In the Lower Mainland area the two most prominent are Burrard Inlet and Howe Sound. Burrard gives seafaring traffic access to the port of Vancouver and is busy with cruise ships, bulk carriers, and all manner of tugs, fishing boats, recreational cruisers, and sailboats. Howe Sound angles its way up the coast, separating the Sunshine Coast peninsula from the Coast Mountains. The town of Squamish lies at the head of Howe Sound.

Major rivers and lakes in the Lower Mainland include the Fraser River, which originates in the Rocky Mountains before it winds 1,368 kilometers (855 miles) to the sea. British Columbia's longest river, the Fraser drains nearly one-quarter of the province. The Lillooet River rises in the Coast Mountains and runs southeast through Lillooet Lake and on into Harrison Lake. Harrison Lake was once an ocean inlet from the Gulf of Georgia but is now a freshwater lake, cut off from the sea by the Fraser Delta. The Elaho and Squamish Rivers empty into Howe Sound.

The Fraser River has built an enormous delta since the last Ice Age. The delta lands are composed of silt and sand scoured from the inland mountains by glaciers and carried by the Fraser. These rich, fine-grained deposits have given rise to the province's most intensive and productive agriculture. The cities of Vancouver, Richmond, Ladner, Delta, Surrey, New Westminster, and Burnaby occupy the lower portion of the Fraser Delta, where the river splits into several channels and flows into the Gulf of Georgia. The delta continues to grow at about three meters (nine feet) a year.

The rough and amazing country north of Vancouver and all the way to Whistler is known as Sea to Sky Country. In this rugged land, the Coast Mountains reveal their volcanic origins in Garibaldi Provincial Park and at Squamish. The remaining old-growth forests that blanket the area support several huge trees. Beyond Whistler is the farming community of Pemberton, home of yellow potatoes and the most succulent strawberries you'll ever taste.

The North Shore (on the north side of Burrard Inlet across from Vancouver) is mountainous and steep. The municipalities of Deep

Cove, North Vancouver, and West Vancouver are built up the mountain slopes; many residents have incredible views of Burrard Inlet and the city itself. The mountains of the North Shore, a good portion of which are protected by provincial parks, including Pinecone Burke, Indian Arm, Mount Seymour, Lynn Headwaters, and Cypress, are densely vegetated and home to an incredible diversity of wildlife.

East of Vancouver the intense urban development gradually thins, and agriculture takes over in the Fraser Delta and the fertile valley it occupies. The Coast Mountains rim the valley's north side, while the Cascades stand tall to the south and east.

HISTORY AND CULTURE

The Fraser Delta has been inhabited by aboriginal peoples since the retreat of ice-age glaciers. The Sto:lo people lived on the banks of the Fraser, harvesting fish from the river. An archaeological site at Xa:ytem National Historic Site in the Fraser Valley indicates human habitation for at least 9,500 years. Squamish and Tsleil Waututh peoples lived to the north along Howe Sound and the Squamish River. Inland, Whistler to Pemberton and beyond were the territories of the St'at'imc peoples. A form of European contact occurred in the Fraser Valley even before Europeans themselves arrived in the 1790s: Smallpox had migrated north from Mexico gradually since the 1500s, arriving to infect and devastate the Sto:lo people in the 1780s.

In 1791 the Spanish explorer Jose Maria Navarez was probably the first European to see the mouth of the Fraser; a year later, Captain George Vancouver also noticed the huge river but did not attempt to sail upstream. Instead he sailed a short distance north and entered an inlet that he named Burrard, and traded with aboriginal peoples living at what is now Stanley Park in Vancouver.

Exploration of the Fraser River was accomplished from the east by young Simon Fraser, for whom the river is named. In 1808, exploring in BC on behalf of the North West Company (NWC), Fraser thought he was on the Columbia until he reached the river's mouth and realized that he'd discovered an entirely different river. The Hudson's Bay Company established a trading post in 1827 at a location somewhat inland from the river's mouth, calling the site Fort Langley.

The European population remained sparse until 1858 when gold was discovered in the Fraser Canyon, in the mountains east of the Fraser Delta. Literally overnight thousands of gold seekers stormed into the region, using Victoria on Vancouver Island as their supply point (the settlements that later became Vancouver did not exist at the time). To maintain British control of the lower Fraser region, a Crown Colony was declared with its capital as Fort Langley. The gold rush spread inland; access and supply roads were built along the Harrison River to Lillooet and up the Fraser Canyon. When the Crown Colonies on the mainland and Vancouver Island were united in 1868, Victoria was declared capital of the new territory of British Columbia.

Not every new immigrant followed the gold rush inland. Those who remained in the Lower Mainland began to exploit the region's rich timber and mineral resources. Although Burrard Inlet offered an excellent deepwater port that welcomed ships from around the world, the timber men needed a more efficient way to get their goods to the growing markets of eastern North America. When the new country of Canada came courting in 1871, BC agreed to join the confederation (and thereby establish a Canadian nation from coast to coast) only if Canada would build a railway across the continent to link BC to the far-off east.

Little more than one hundred years ago there was no such place as Vancouver. The HBC trading post at Fort Langley was located nearly 50 kilometers (31 miles) to the east of where the city now stands. Several settlements grew around small sawmills on Burrard Inlet. Among these were Moodyville, Hastings Mill, and Gastown, a notorious saloon-filled district named for its best-known barkeep, "Gassy" Jack Deighton (his nickname referred to his loquacious habits, not to flatulence). Gastown was later officially named Granville, and Moodyville became Port Moody.

Port Moody was named the official terminus of the Canadian Pacific Railway (CPR); land speculators bought everything in sight, hoping to sell their holdings at inflated prices when the railway finally arrived. However, the government of Canada gave a huge land grant to the railway in 1881, including a chunk of bush and muskeg near Granville. When the railway was finally nearing completion in 1884, general manager W. Cornelius Van Horne declared that Granville

Vancouver marina and skyline

would be the railway's terminus—leaving Port Moody's speculators with a lot of land!

Granville was renamed to honor British Captain George Vancouver, the first European to enter Burrard Inlet nearly 100 years earlier. The city was officially incorporated in April 1886. Two months later the new city was almost completely leveled by a huge fire that was so intense that bullets exploded and glass melted. The optimistic citizens immediately rebuilt their homes and businesses—and Vancouver has never looked back. The arrival of the railway opened the door for full-scale urbanization and industrialization of the lower Fraser Delta. Growth continues today; it's estimated that the population of Vancouver will double by 2010.

Vancouver today is Canada's third-largest city. It's a cosmopolitan mix of ethnic cultures. It's a financial powerhouse, full of great restaurants, nightlife, and shopping. Despite being a big city, the lifestyle in Vancouver tends to be sporty, outdoorsy, and relaxed. Squamish and Whistler are also outdoorsy, and increasingly busy. East

133

of Vancouver, in the area's rural heartland, you have to make an effort to find ecotravel and adventure opportunities, but they're there, and they're worth finding.

FLORA AND FAUNA

Coastal temperate rain forest dominates the coastline and extends for a considerable distance inland, gradually giving way to alpine forests. Dominant tree species are hemlock, red cedar, Douglas fir, and grand fir, plus deciduous species such as big-leaf maple in the Fraser Valley. The Lower Mainland is home to some forest giants, although old-growth forest is becoming increasingly rare in the region. You can still see big trees at several easily accessible locations, including the Hollyburn Ancient Forest Loop Trail in Cypress Provincial Park, the Chilliwack River Trail in the Chilliwack River Ecological Reserve (largest known grand fir), the Skagit River Trail in the Skagit Valley Recreation Area, and the Cheakamus Lake Trail in Garibaldi Provincial Park.

The Fraser Delta lies directly in the Pacific flyway, a migratory route used by hundreds of bird species every year. The area may once have supported millions of birds. Urbanization and agriculture have obliterated the majority of the area's bogs and marshes, but vestiges remain; the Lower Mainland is still a birder's paradise. Other wildlife in the mountainous areas includes black and grizzly bears, cougars, deer, and a wide variety of small mammals.

VISITOR INFORMATION

Vancouver is a major port of entry for travelers. The city's international airport, served by numerous airlines from the United States, Asia, Europe, and other parts of Canada, is located on the western edge of the city. Taxis, city buses, and hotel shuttle services provide easy means to get into town. For airline contact information, see Appendix A.

Vancouver is the terminus of four passenger-rail services: AMTRAK, which travels to and from Seattle; BC Rail, which takes pas-

TAKE THE TRAIN, EH!

The best way to witness Sea to Sky scenery without having to battle traffic is on a train. BC Rail operates the Royal Hudson excursion steam train from North Vancouver to Squamish. The train leaves North Vancouver in mid-morning (daily Wednesday through Sunday, June through September) then chugs up the coast, arriving in Squamish by late afternoon. Passengers can sail back to Vancouver aboard the MV Britannia. *Another BC Rail train, the* Whistler Explorer, *leaves Whistler in the morning, journeys through the Coast Mountains to Kelly Lake in Fraser Canyon, then returns to Whistler in time for dinner. See Appendix A for BC Rail contact information.*

sengers from North Vancouver to the BC interior via Whistler, Pemberton, and Lillooet; VIA Rail, the only remaining transcontinental passenger rail service in Canada, linking Vancouver with Edmonton, Winnipeg, Toronto, Montreal, and others; and the Rocky Mountaineer, which offers daylight-only rail excursions to Jasper, Banff, or Calgary. For rail contact information, see Appendix A.

The region is connected to Vancouver Island and the Gulf Islands via ferry service from two major ferry terminals located at Tsawwassen, southwest of Vancouver, and at Horseshoe Bay on the North Shore. Passenger-bus service links downtown Vancouver with both ferry terminals. For ferry schedules and fares, contact BC Ferries at 888/223-3779 or 604/669-1211.

In Vancouver, passenger-only ferries operate across Burrard Inlet from downtown Vancouver to the North Shore, and across False Creek (an arm of Burrard Inlet) between the West End and Granville Island. City and regional buses operate within Vancouver and run to adjoining municipalities; a light-rail system called SkyTrain links downtown Vancouver with outlying suburbs.

Passenger bus services link all major destinations within this region. Passenger buses also run between Vancouver and Victoria, Nanaimo, Seattle, and Calgary, and to numerous destinations within BC. The bus depot is located in downtown Vancouver, in the same building where AMTRAK, VIA, and Rocky Mountaineer trains depart. See Appendix A for bus-line information.

The region's major roadways are the Trans-Canada Highway (Highway 1) and the Lougheed Highway (Highway 7), which parallel the south and north shores of the Fraser River respectively; the two roadways join at Hope. From Hope, Highway 1 continues northward through the Fraser Canyon (see Chapter 8). Highway 3, also called the Crowsnest Highway, continues eastward from Hope to Manning Provincial Park and onward, while Highway 5, the Coquihalla, links Hope to Merritt, Kamloops, and Kelowna in the interior. Highway 99, the Sea to Sky Highway, runs from North Vancouver to Whistler and Pemberton, then changes its name to Duffey Lake Road and continues on to Lillooet. The North Shore is accessible via the Lions Gate and Second Narrows Bridges; both bridges link to Highway 99 north, gateway to the Sunshine Coast (via ferries at Horseshoe Bay), Garibaldi Park, and Whistler.

To obtain all the information you could ever want on Vancouver, contact the Vancouver Visitor Infocentre, 200 Burrard St., 800/663-6000, www./travel.bc.ca/vancouver; or Tourism Vancouver, 604/683-2000, www.tourism-vancouver.org. For detailed information on the remainder of the region, contact the Vancouver Coast and Mountains Tourism Association, 1755 W. Broadway, #204, Vancouver, 800/667-3306 or 604/739-9011, vcmtr@istar.ca, www.coastandmountains.bc.ca. There are numerous Visitor Infocentres located throughout the region—several are mentioned in this chapter.

NATURE AND ADVENTURE SIGHTS: VANCOUVER

Vancouver is spectacularly situated on the western reaches of the Fraser Delta. The city is built on the delta and on several peninsulas that jut into Burrard Inlet, which separates Vancouver from the North Shore. The infamous Lions Gate Bridge, site of a continual traffic jam,

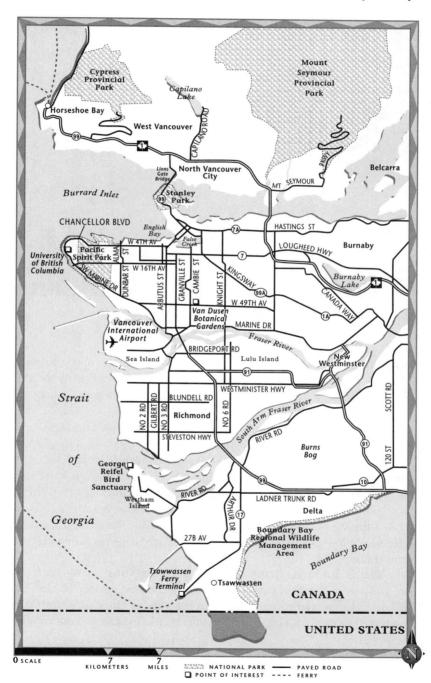

Cypress Provincial Park

Capilano Lake

Mount Seymour Provincial Park

Horseshoe Bay

West Vancouver

99

1

CAPILANO ROAD

North Vancouver City

Lions Gate Bridge

MT SEYMOUR

PKWY

Belcarra

Burrard Inlet

Stanley Park

99

CHANCELLOR BLVD

English Bay

False Creek

7A

HASTINGS ST

University of British Columbia

Pacific Spirit Park

W 4TH AV

ALMA ST

DUNBAR ST

ARBUTUS ST

GRANVILLE ST

CAMBIE ST

KNIGHT ST

7

KINGSWAY

LOUGHEED HWY

Burnaby

SW MARINE DR

W 16TH AV

99A

CANADA WAY

Burnaby Lake

1

1A

W 49TH AV

Van Dusen Botanical Gardens

MARINE DR

Fraser River

Vancouver International Airport

Sea Island

BRIDGEPORT RD

Lulu Island

New Westminster

Strait

NO 2 RD

GILBERT RD

NO 3 RD

BLUNDELL RD

Richmond

NO 6 RD

WESTMINISTER HWY

South Arm Fraser River

SCOTT RD

STEVESTON HWY

RIVER RD

Burns Bog

91

120 ST

of

George Reifel Bird Sanctuary

Westham Island

RIVER RD

ARTHUR DR

17

99

LADNER TRUNK RD

Delta

10

Georgia

27B AV

Boundary Bay Regional Wildlife Management Area

Boundary Bay

Tsawwassen Ferry Terminal

Tsawwassen

CANADA

UNITED STATES

0 SCALE

7 KILOMETERS

7 MILES

NATIONAL PARK

POINT OF INTEREST

PAVED ROAD

FERRY

N

Blackbird Design

Orca (killer whale) at the Vancouver Aquarium

spans the inlet. False Creek, an arm of Burrard Inlet, slices through the city and separates the densely populated West End from the trendy Kitsilano area. Granville Island, a popular shopping and residential development, is located in False Creek.

The city today is a cosmopolitan mix of cultures, languages, and cuisines; Asian cultures are especially well represented. The port of Vancouver is the busiest on North America's Pacific side. The city's mild climate and tolerant "live-and-let-live" attitude tend to attract society's fringe elements, particularly in the notorious East End (hint: stay away from East Hastings Street after dark). Always keep an eye on your valuables when traveling in Vancouver, and be aware that vehicles bearing out-of-province license plates are magnets for vandalism and theft.

This is not to say that Vancouver is a dangerous place—far from it. The city is consistently rated as having the best quality of life anywhere in Canada, if you can afford it. It's a city of extreme wealth and extreme poverty. As a big city, Vancouver's not exactly an eco-friendly destination, but there are some marvelous things to do and see before you head out to explore the rest of the Lower Mainland and beyond.

Vancouverites love their beaches. In summer you'll find kids, dogs, Frisbees, and picnics on the beaches of English Bay, Jericho, Spanish Banks, and others. If you're into nude sunbathing, head for Wreck Beach, a steep descent from the road that circles the University of British Columbia (UBC) campus. As a group, citizens of Vancouver are an outdoorsy bunch, with a high density of joggers, cyclists, in-line skaters, and walkers evident everywhere.

Lower Mainland Nature Legacy

This collection of municipal, regional, and provincial parks was created to preserve the remaining wilderness areas in close proximity to Vancouver, especially the area's bogs and marshlands. The legacy's parks tend to be small and isolated; nonetheless, the legacy collectively protects more than 200,000 hectares (494,000 acres). Among the legacy parks is **Boundary Bay Wildlife Management Area**, an important waterfowl habitat near the Tsawwassen ferry terminal and the Canada/U.S. boundary. Another great year-round birding spot is the **George C. Reifel Bird Sanctuary**, with observation platforms and helpful staff; in spring and autumn the variety and volume of migrating waterfowl is astonishing. **Burns Bog** is a huge area in the municipalities of Delta and Surrey, south of Vancouver—in fact, it's the largest undeveloped urban area in North America. The bog's southwest corner is the site of Vancouver's landfill (a.k.a. garbage dump), and much of the bog area itself is privately owned and inaccessible to the public, but several hiking trails are open to the public and offer a unique wilderness experience in the heart of a highly urban and industrial area. Early in 1999, tentative development plans for much of the bog were announced; a future of shopping malls, theme parks, and high-tech industry could await this forgotten corner of the city.

Details: Boundary Bay is accessible at several points; take Highway 99 south and watch for eastbound exits to Tsawwassen. Reifel Sanctuary, 5191 Robertson Rd., 604/946-6980, on Westham Island in the Fraser River, is open daily. For information on Burns Bog, contact the Burns Bog Conservation Society, 20, 11961–88 Ave., Delta, BC, 604/572-0373.

Stanley Park and the Vancouver Aquarium

One of Canada's largest urban parks, Stanley Park covers 405 hectares (1,000 acres). The land was set aside by Vancouver's first city council in 1886 and named for Canada's first governor-general, Lord Stanley (the same guy that hockey's Stanley Cup is named for). The park, located on a peninsula that juts into Burrard Inlet northwest of the city's downtown, is accessible by car (though parking is at a premium), city bus, or on foot. **English Bay**'s beaches lie on the park's west side; on the east is the **Coal Harbour** marina. The **Seawall**, a paved walking/cycling path, circles the entire peninsula. The park encompasses tranquil walkways amid forests of Douglas fir and red cedar; Lost Lagoon, a tiny, goose-infested water body; and the excellent **Vancouver Aquarium Marine Science Center**. The aquarium's exhibits include not only brilliant tropical fish and an entire wing housing an Amazonian rain forest, but displays of west coast tidal and fish life. Large open-air tanks are home to seals, sea otters (this could be the only chance you'll ever get to see one), white beluga whales, and orca whales. Whatever you may think about whales in captivity, the below-ground/underwater windows on the whale tanks give visitors an exceptional opportunity to see the leviathans up close.

Details: Stanley Park is accessible via Georgia Street or Beach Avenue; city bus 19 takes you right to the park. The aquarium is situated in the east-central part of the park. For information call 604/685-3364. Open daily.

University of British Columbia (UBC)

Pacific Spirit Regional Park, also called the UBC Endowment Lands, is 763 hectares (1,885 acres) of relatively undisturbed forested area just minutes from downtown Vancouver. The park contains trails perfect for easy hiking and cycling. The spectacular **UBC Museum of Anthropology** is a soaring, light-filled building housing an impressive collection of aboriginal artifacts including totem poles (both inside the museum and outside on the grounds), masks, cedar boxes, woven blankets, carved items, jewelry, and much more. On the grounds are life-size reconstructions of Haida houses. For anyone interested in the fascinating and complex aboriginal cultures of the North Pacific coast, this museum is a must-see.

Museum of Anthropology, University of British Columbia

Details: Pacific Spirit Regional Park is accessible from S.W. Marine Dr., W. 16th Ave., and W. 33rd Ave. The Museum of Anthropology, 6393 N.W. Marine Dr., 604/822-3825, is located on the UBC campus overlooking Burrard Inlet. Open daily (except Mondays June through September).

NATURE AND ADVENTURE SIGHTS: NORTH SHORE

Cypress Provincial Park

Encompassing 3,000 hectares (7,400 acres), Cypress Park is named for its large stands of red and yellow cedar, members of the cypress family. The park affords stunning views of Vancouver and Burrard Inlet, plus great hiking and downhill and cross-country skiing. Among the park's highlights is the **Hollyburn Ancient Forest Loop Trail**, a four-kilometer (two-and-one-half-mile) wander amid 1,000-plus-year-old yellow cedars. The trees owe their long survival to the

141

damp climate—according to one estimate there has not been a major forest fire here for two thousand years. This unique mid-elevation "snow forest" (as opposed to a low-elevation rain forest) is a true relic, and the trail is a wonderful opportunity to see a truly ancient forest with little driving or physical effort.

Details: Take either the Lions Gate or Second Narrows Bridge to the North Shore and continue west (toward Horseshoe Bay and the BC ferry terminal). Watch for signs to Cypress Bowl. Open daily; everything except downhill skiing is free. For information call 604/926-6007.

Mount Seymour Provincial Park

This park, the closest provincial park to Vancouver, encompasses 3,500 hectares (8,645 acres) of rugged mountains, dense forest, and habitat for deer, cougars, and grizzly bears. It's a great place for hiking, cross-country skiing, and mountaineering. The best hike is along the Dinkey Peak trail, which starts out steep before leveling off in forests of hemlock and cedar. At the top of the trail hikers are rewarded with views of Burrard Inlet, the city, and the Gulf Islands.

Details: Take Highway 1 north over the Second Narrows Bridge, then watch for the Seymour Parkway exit. Before the parkway enters Deep Cove, turn left (north) to Mount Seymour Provincial Park. The access road twists steeply up the mountainside.

NATURE AND ADVENTURE SIGHTS: SEA TO SKY

Garibaldi Provincial Park

Thanks to its proximity to Vancouver, Garibaldi Provincial Park is often a very busy place during the summer hiking season (the 194,600-hectare—480,000-acre—wilderness is visited by nearly 80,000 outdoor adventurers every year). Nonetheless, the park contains many spectacular natural features including everything from alpine meadows full of wildflowers to the "Black Tusk," a volcanic plug of black basalt 2,315 meters (7,600 feet) above sea level. You can climb to the top of the tusk via a rock chimney (be wary of climbers above you dislodging rocks; a helmet is advisable).

There are several ways to access the park. For the **Diamond Head** area, take the access road (the turnoff is four kilometers north of Squamish) 16 kilometers east to the parking area and trailhead; the trail is 11 kilometers long and gains 600 meters elevation. For the **Black Tusk/Garibaldi Lake** area, drive 37 kilometers north of Squamish then turn east onto a road that continues another two kilometers to the parking lot and trailhead. The trail to Garibaldi Lake is nine kilometers long and climbs 920 meters. For **Cheakamus Lake**, drive 48 kilometers north of Squamish then take a logging road eight kilometers to the trailhead. The trail is short and flat: three kilometers with no appreciable elevation change.

Details: Contact BC Parks, Garibaldi/Sunshine Coast District, Box 220, Brackendale, BC V0N 1H0, 604/898-3678.

Squamish

This small city at the head of Howe Sound has become very popular with the outdoor-adventure crowd. Rock climbers flock to **Stawamus Chief**, the world's second-largest granite monolith (after the Rock of Gibraltar) at 652 meters (2,150 feet) tall. The rock is the site of 180 climbing routes of varying degrees of difficulty. Windsurfers love the wind and water here, and bird-watchers congregate at two nearby sites, **Squamish Estuary** and Brackendale. The estuary is a wonderful place to watch for migrating shorebirds, while the **Brackendale Eagle Reserve** boasts North America's largest concentration of bald eagles. En route to Squamish on Highway 99 you'll pass right by Shannon Falls Provincial Park and 335-meter (1,105-foot) **Shannon Falls**, one of the highest waterfalls in Canada.

Details: Squamish is on Highway 99, 44 kilometers (26.5 miles) beyond Horseshoe Bay. Squamish Visitor Infocentre, 37950 Cleveland Ave., 604/892-9244. Brackendale is 10 kilometers (6 miles) north of Squamish on Highway 99; the Eagle Reserve is at the end of Government Street. To book guided walking tours during eagle season (December and January) call 604/898-3333.

Whistler

If you've come to British Columbia for recreation, Whistler is paradise. The resort is Canada's answer to Vail, Aspen, Val d'Isere, or any

Whistler

other chic recreation area you care to name. The downhill skiing at the twin peaks of **Whistler** and **Blackcomb** is among the best in North America. A combined total of 2,800 hectares (6,900 acres) of developed terrain includes more than enough skiing for any skill level. Blackcomb's vertical drop of more than 1,600 meters (1 mile) means that even if the valley-bottom village is overcast and raining, often the mountaintop is clear and the skiing is unbeatable. Cross-country and helicopter skiing, snowshoeing, snowboarding, and other activities round out the winter-recreation picture.

In summer the choices are even greater. The Whistler area has plenty of developed cycling trails (paved or rugged), horseback riding, fishing, paddling on several area lakes, and whitewater thrills on the Green and Elaho Rivers. And if you just can't get enough skiing, you can ride a chairlift and a bus up Blackcomb Mountain to ski the Horstman Glacier runs—in July.

Whistler village has more than 100 hotels and nearly 100 restaurants. The village center is closed to traffic, with parking in public and hotel-guest-only lots on the town's perimeter. Even so, accommodations within the village can be noisy when revelers roam the streets after the bars close down. For more tranquil nights, consider staying just outside the main village in a small hotel or bed-and-breakfast.

North of Whistler, Highway 99 continues through the Coast Mountains to the town of **Pemberton**, located in a verdant valley reminiscent of Switzerland. Beyond Pemberton the road becomes an adventure in itself as it makes its way 100 kilometers (60 miles) to **Lillooet** on the Fraser River, gateway to the Cariboo and Chilcotin

K. D. Wong/Blackbird Design

ECO-FRIENDLY: ECOSUMMER EXPEDITIONS

According to Ecosummer Expeditions, eco stands for Education and Challenge in the Outdoors. Teaching through experience has always been the company's focus. This outfitter was among the first to offer hands-on introductory kayak courses in the Gulf Islands and now offers fully guided sea kayaking and adventure sailing all along the coast, from the quiet orca-filled waters of Johnstone Strait to the mystical Haida villages of Haida Gwaii and beyond. Trips to Alaska and South and Central America are also part of Ecosummer's annual schedule. Ecosummer's emphasis is on finding, viewing, and photographing wildlife, but clients are also given an education in wildlife ecology, habitat preservation, outdoor-skills development, and living lightly on the land. The combination of environmental awareness and a sincere desire to share, learn, and achieve has made Ecosummer one of Canada's premier adventure-travel outfitters for a quarter-century.

districts (see Chapter 10). Grades on the road are steep, switchbacks and hairpin turns are legion, and there are numerous one-lane bridges. You'll leave behind the lush Coast Mountain forests and enter the arid reaches of the upper Fraser Canyon that lie in the rain shadow cast by the Coast Mountains. Stop to see Nairn Falls, 28 kilometers (17 miles) north of Whistler, and take another break for a quick and refreshing hike to lower Joffre Lake before continuing to Lillooet.

Details: *Whistler is a 90-minute drive from North Vancouver on Highway 99. Contact the Visitor Infocentre, Box 181, Whistler, BC V9N 2B0, 604/932-5528, www.whistler.net; or the Whistler Resort Association, 4010 Whistler Way, 800/944-7853 or 604/932-3928, www.whistler-resort.com.*

NATURE AND ADVENTURE SIGHTS: FRASER VALLEY AND HOPE

Chilliwack River Ecological Reserve

Isolated and hard to find, this tiny ecological reserve is worth the effort for the very large trees in the area, including the largest known grand fir in the world. The reserve is situated between the south end of Chilliwack Lake and the Canada-U.S. border. A wonderful trail leads from Sapper Park (a campsite popular with people fishing the lake) through the ecological reserve and its groves of red cedars, amabalis fir, and Douglas fir, to the site of a grand fir two meters in diameter and 71 meters tall. The hike is an easy nine-and-one-half-kilometer round trip with little elevation change.

Details: From Highway 1, turn right (south) on Vedder Road. Travel south on Vedder for 10 kilometers (6 miles), then turn left (east) toward Chilliwack River Provincial Park. To reach the ecological reserve, proceed along the east shore of the Chilliwack Lake, bearing right at Paleface Creek. You'll arrive at a locked gate, where you'll have to park. Hike along the lakeshore for a few kilometers. The Chilliwack River trailhead starts just south of Sapper Park.

Manning Provincial Park

Among Vancouverites' favorite playgrounds is this 65,900-hectare (163,000-acre) park. Manning was established in 1941 to preserve the forests of the Cascade Mountains. The park's southern boundary, the Canada-U.S. border, adjoins North Cascade National Park in Washington. The park's west gate is 26 kilometers (15.5 miles) east of Hope.

Manning's location straddles the wet coastal forests of hemlock and cedar as well as the drier interior Douglas fir communities. This remarkable geographic diversity permits more than 700 plant species, 200 bird species, and a host of butterflies to live within the park.

Activities in the park are many, but Manning is especially renowned for its 150 kilometers (90 miles) of cross-country ski trails. Summer is great for hiking, climbing, camping, and fishing. You can rent a horse from the stables at Manning Park Resort, or bring your own horse to explore the park's extensive network of trails. Among the park's highlights is Rhododendron Flats, where rhododendrons burst to life each June. The park's visitors center has displays explain-

AUTHOR'S TOP PICKS: CYCLING ROUTES

- *Galloping Goose* (Victoria)—*Easy gravel trail developed on an old rail bed; not exactly an adventure but you can cycle for miles and miles through lovely surroundings and loads of history.*
- *Golden Triangle*—*This loop between Lake Louise, Alberta, Radium Hot Springs, and Golden may be arduous, but the scenery is unbeatable.*
- *Gulf Islands*—*Easy to moderate cycling on paved roads; most suitable for families.*
- *Kettle Valley Railway*—*The old rail bed is easily accessible from the area's roads and offers fabulous scenic cycling. Myra Canyon is spectacular.*
- *Pacific Spirit Regional Park*—*Also called the UBC Endowment Lands, this park and its collection of easy trails is just minutes from downtown Vancouver, adjacent to the University of British Columbia.*
- *Rossland*—*Known as the mountain-bike capital of BC, Rossland includes a significant number of developed trails with names like Rabid Slug and Techno Grind.*
- *Whistler*—*There are numerous rental outlets in and around the village, plus lots of places to ride on paved, gravel or undeveloped trails that offer a range of difficulty. For the ultimate trip with none of the sweat, take a ski lift to a point high on Blackcomb Mountain, then ride down on your bike.*

ing the natural and human history of the area, and park naturalists conduct guided walks and evening talks in the summer.

Details: *Take the Trans-Canada Highway (Hwy. 1) east from Vancouver to Hope, then follow the Crowsnest Highway (Hwy. 3) toward Princeton. Park headquarters is halfway between Hope and Princeton, 68 kilometers (41 miles) from each. For information call 250/840-8836.*

Othello-Quintette Tunnels

K.D. Wong/Blackbird Design

Quintette Tunnels near Hope

These five short tunnels within the Coquihalla Canyon Provincial Recreation Area are must-sees. The Kettle Valley Railway (KVR) was constructed from Hope to the Kootenay region in southeastern BC beginning in 1910. The track spans some of BC's most difficult terrain (one notorious mile of track cost $300,000 to build—a fortune in 1914). Among the challenges to construction was the Coquihalla Gorge, where chief engineer Andrew McCullough decided to blast five tunnels straight through the granite face of the canyon.

The line officially opened for operation in 1916, but avalanches, rock slides, and cantankerous locomotives made operating the railway a financial nightmare. The KVR was closed in 1961. Today, several portions of the former rail bed have been converted to hiking and cycling trails (see Chapter 7 for more about the KVR in the Okanagan area). One trail in particular takes in the Othello–Quintette Tunnels and makes for a spectacular and unusual hike. If you decide to walk it, a flashlight is handy but not essential.

Details: From Hope, take Kawkawa Lake Road east for 15 kilometers (9 miles), then follow Othello Road to Tunnels Road. From Tunnels Road, follow the signs to the park and tunnels.

Skagit Valley Provincial Park

The Skagit River runs wild in Canada, but right across the U.S. border it's dammed for hydroelectric-power generation. The United States and Canada had agreed to allow the reservoir to flood northward into the Skagit Valley in Canada, but in the 1970s, as the dam was being built, a group of Canadian environmental activists fought to have the agreement overturned—and won, more or less. Ross Lake, the reservoir on the American side, expands across the border in late spring, then gradually recedes again throughout the year. The park is popular for camping, hiking, paddling, and fishing, and is a popular destination for cross-country skiers in winter. Skagit's eastern boundary is Manning Provincial Park, bringing the total protected area between the two parks to 93,800 hectares (232,000 acres).

The **Skagit River Trail** is a delightful 13-kilometer (8-mile) path through unspoiled groves of red cedar, Douglas fir, and rhododendron thickets (go in June to see them in bloom). It also passes a number of "culturally modified trees" (red cedars that have had strips of bark removed by aboriginal peoples). So skilled were the original inhabitants of this area at pulling bark that the trees healed and continued to thrive. It's possible to do this trail as a long day hike, but it's far more pleasant to backpack (there are several campgrounds).

Details: Take Highway 1 east to Silverhope Creek Road, then drive 35 kilometers (21 miles) east to the park. For information call 604/824-2300. The Skagit River Trail begins at the Sumallo Grove picnic area on Highway 3, 35 kilometers (21 miles) east of Hope.

Xa:ytem National Historic Site (Hatzic Rock)

A huge pyramid of rock, sacred to the Sto:lo people, was on the verge of being removed to allow development of the site when researchers discovered that the site showed signs of continuous human occupation dating back 7,500 years. As it turns out, this was the location of a village of Xat'suq' (Hatzic), or "sacred bullrush people," who lived here until the 1880s when the smallpox epidemic wiped them out. The underground dwellings excavated at this site predate the Egyptian Pyramids and Stonehenge in England. An interpretive center explains the history and significance of the site.

Details: Located on Highway 7, approximately two kilometers east of Mission. Open July–mid-September 10–4. For information call 604/820-9725.

GUIDES AND OUTFITTERS

Active Lifestyles, 1222 Doran Rd., North Vancouver, 604/984-6032, offers guided nature walks and hikes in North Vancouver. If you'd

K. .D Wong/Blackbird Design

Nairn Falls

prefer to cycle, check out **West Coaster Mountain Bike Tours**, Velo-City Cycle Tours, Inc., 604/924-0288, e-mail velocity@ direct.ca, www.velo-city.com, for bike tours on Grouse Mountain in North Vancouver.

For climbers, **Slipstream**, Box 219, Brackendale, BC V0N 1H0, 604/898-4891, rockice@slipstream adventures.com, www.slipstream adventures.com, offers multi-day climbing courses and excursions in the Coast Mountains.

If you're in Vancouver with some free time, check out **Starline Tours**, 13942-96 Ave., Surrey, 604/522-3506. They offer ecotours on the Fraser River. Tour destinations vary throughout the year depending on wildlife and bird-migration patterns; in April and May the emphasis is on sea lions.

Vancouver is home to numerous kayak outfitters offering trips to various destinations on the west coast including Vancouver Island, the Gulf Islands, Haida Gwaii (Queen Charlotte Islands), Desolation Sound, and others. **Ecomarine Ocean Kayak Centre**, 1668 Duranleau St., Vancouver, 888/4-C-KAYAK or 604/689-7575, e-mail cladner @direct.ca, www.ecomarine.com/kayak, offers day trips in Clayoquot Sound off Vancouver Island. They also offer kayak rentals and sales, an ocean kayak school with pool instruction and fieldtrips, and navigational instruction. Another good outfitter is **Great Expeditions**, 5915 West Blvd., Vancouver, 800/663-3364 or 604/257-2040, e-mail tours@greatexpeditions.com, www.greatexpeditions.com.

Ecosummer Expeditions, 5640 Hollybridge Way, Unit #130, Richmond, 800/465-8884 or 604/214-7484, www.ecosummer.com, has set the pace since 1976 as one of Canada's first ecotouring operators. The company offers sea-kayaking trips, as well as sail cruising, canoeing, rafting, heli-trekking, and marine-science camps.

Other multi-activity outfitters include **Sage Wilderness Experi-ences Ltd.**, 6017 Mountain Hwy., North Vancouver, 604/983-3108, e-mail sage@intergate.bc.ca, www.gobc.can/sage. They offer expe-ditions, learning and leadership training, and low-impact trips throughout the Lower Mainland. **GAIA Outdoor Adventures for Women**, 875 E. 31 Ave., Vancouver, 604/875-0066, www.vancouver-bc.com/gaia, has unique women-only hiking, backpacking, rock-climbing, mountain-biking, and cross-country-skiing trips. **Fresh Tracks (Canada)**, 1823 W. Fourth Ave., Vancouver, 800/667-4744, e-mail adventure@freshtracks.com, www.freshtracks.com/canadian, also has multi-day, multi-activity trips for a wide range of ability lev-els and budgets. The company offers trips in the Rockies and on Vancouver Island, from sea kayaking to ski touring.

For a unique learning experience, try **Canada West Mountain School**, 336, 1367 W. Broadway, Vancouver, 800/892-2266 or 604/737-3053, e-mail fmcbc@istar.ca, www.home.istar.ca/-fmcbc/ fmcbc.htm. The school offers winter courses (avalanche safety, ice climbing, ski touring, winter survival), summer courses (rock climb-ing, mountain rescue, wilderness survival, navigation), and courses in wilderness first aid. If you're interested in whale research, contact **Coastal Ecosystems Research Foundation**, c/o Adventure Spirit Travel Co., 1843 W. 12th Ave., Vancouver, 800/667-7799, www. zoology.ubc.ca/-megill/adspirit. The foundation conducts ecological and biological research on the BC coast and is partially supported by paying volunteers.

There are literally thousands of boat charters available through-out the region, from fishing charters to sailing cruises. One of the best charter companies is **Pacific Wave Adventures**, #25, 1486 John-son St., Coquitlam, 604/945-4035, e-mail w5enviro@home.com, offering interpretive tours of Burrard Inlet and Indian Arm. The company will also arrange other activites, from bed and breakfast stays to cycling trips.

CAMPING

Campgrounds in the Vancouver area fill up quickly on summer week-ends. Provincial campgrounds in the area that accept reservations

BOG RUBIES

The bogs of the Fraser Delta, including parts of Burns Bog, are ideal for growing cranberries. In 1998 cranberry production in the region brought in $40 million in revenue— enough to make BC the world's third-largest cranberry producer (after Minnesota and Wisconsin). A major cranberry processing plant, making juice and sauce and packaging whole berries, is located in Richmond, a municipality west of Vancouver.

include Alice Lake, Cultus Lake, Golden Ears, Manning, Porteau Cove, Rolley Lake, and Sasquatch. For reservations call 800/689-9025.

On the North Shore, **Golden Ears** accommodates more campers per year than any other campground in the area. It's located 11 kilometers (6.5 miles) north of the town of Haney on Highway 7, less than an hour from Vancouver. A total of 343 sites are available in two separate, well-treed campgrounds. Amenities include flush toilets, hot showers, a sani-station, hiking trails, and swimming.

Along the Sea to Sky Highway are several great camping spots. **Porteau Cove** is situated on gorgeous Howe Sound and includes 59 drive-in and 15 walk-in sites. **Alice Lake** near Brackendale/Squamish has 88 large and shady sites suitable for RVs, tents, or trailers. It also includes flush and pit toilets, showers, and a sani-station, and is wheelchair accessible. North of Whistler, check out **Nairn Falls**, with 88 private drive-in sites. Basic amenities, including pit toilets, drinking water, wood, and fire pits, are standard.

In **Garibaldi Provincial Park** there are 196 wilderness campsites. It's a strenuous hike up to Garibaldi Lake, but the alpine scenery is worth every grunt and groan. Cheakamus Lake is a much easier walk, but it can also be a lot busier than the Garibaldi Lake campground. For information call 604/898-3678.

East of Vancouver, camping choices include **Cultus Lake**, located

11 kilometers (6.5 miles) south of Chilliwack off Highway 1. With 297 sites in four separate campgrounds, this is among BC's largest camping facilities. All sites are big and private, and some are close to the beach. Amenities include flush toilets, hot showers, and a sani-station. **Othello Tunnels Campground**, 67851 Othello Rd., Hope, 250/869-9448, has 30 drive-in sites, a store, laundry facilities, and showers, and everything is within easy walking distance of the Othello-Quintette Tunnels.

In **Manning Provincial Park** there are four major campgrounds with drive-in sites: Hampton (98 sites), Mule Deer (49 sites), Coldspring (63 sites), and Lightning Lake/Spruce Bay (143 sites). There are also numerous backcountry (hike-in) campgrounds. For information call park headquarters, 250/840-8836.

LODGING

Vancouver offers a full range of accommodations, from ultra-expensive to pretty darn seedy. The city is a very popular destination and it can be difficult to find the style, location, or price range you want at short notice. If you know you're going to be in Vancouver, especially in summer, phone ahead for reservations. For province-wide reservations, call BC Tourism at 800/663-6000; be sure to request a copy of their excellent *Accommodation Guide*.

In Vancouver, check out the **Manor Guest House**, 345 W. 13th Ave., Vancouver, 604/876-8494. It's in a convenient location near the city hall, just outside of downtown. Breakfasts feature fresh baked goods, bottomless coffee or herbal tea, and, on Saturdays, smoked salmon. Guest rooms in this restored Edwardian home are funky and comfortable; most share bathrooms but a few are self-contained. There's also a tranquil back garden and deck. The Manor manages a second property nearby that doesn't include hot breakfasts but does have a well-stocked common kitchen in which you can make your own. Rates start at $85 per night. The best hostel in town is the **Jericho Beach Hostel**, 1515 Discovery St., 604/224-3208. Formerly a military barracks, it's clean, safe, busy, and close to the beaches, the UBC campus, and shopping. Most of the hostel's 282 beds are in dormitory-style rooms, but there are a few private rooms as well. Dorm beds cost $16 and rooms are $30 for Hostelling International members.

Among the numerous bed-and-breakfasts in the Whistler area is **Haus Heidi**, Box 354, Whistler, BC V0N 1B0, 604/932-3113. Host Trudy Rovatti-Gruetzke has lived in this delightful home north of Whistler Village for more than 20 years and welcomes guests from around the world to stay and enjoy her amazing breakfasts. Several guest rooms have their own baths and showers, and a large common room includes a fireplace and an interesting Bavarian cuckoo clock. Reservations are essential. Rates range from $69 to $99. For those on a budget, **Shoestring Lodge**, 7124 Nancy Greene Dr., 604/932-3338, has dorm rooms starting at $13 per night and private rooms for $50 to $60 per night.

While Whistler provides great downhill skiing, nordic skiers are sometimes disappointed with snow conditions in the valley. Not so at **Powder Mountain Lakeside Lodge and Mad River Nordic Centre**, P.O. Box 284, Whistler, BC V0H 1B0, 604/938-0616, located in the Callaghan Basin of the Coast Mountains, 15 kilometers (9 miles) north-west of Whistler. Guests can literally ski to the lodge during the winter (or call ahead for transportation by snowcat or helicopter). The lodge offers deluxe accommodations, all meals, and guided ski or snowshoe tours. Rates start at $150 per person per night, including all meals.

Manning Park Lodge, Box 1480, Hope, BC V0X 1L0, 250/840-8822, is located in Manning Provincial Park, 67 kilometers (40 miles) east of Hope. Comfortable cabins and chalets are close to hiking trails, horseback riding, and cross-country and downhill skiing at Gibson's Pass. Rates range from $74 to $99.

FOOD

Vancouver is a culinary paradise with lots of casual cafés, renowned restaurants, and formal dining. Ethnic food is widely available, as are organic and health foods. Whistler is likewise well supplied with restaurants.

On the North Shore, the **Raven Inn**, 1060 Deep Cove Rd., is a pub made famous by the folk-rock band Spirit of the West in their song "The Crawl." This warm neighborhood pub typifies Lower Mainland casual dining with burgers, fish and chips, and more ambitious food like escargot, salmon, and prawns. You'll also find lots of beer and good acoustic entertainment. It's a great place to eat after a day of hiking in Mount Seymour Park. **Salmon House on the Hill**, 2229 Folkstone Way, West Vancouver, 604/926-3212, has panoramic views of Vancouver and Burrard Inlet to go along with its excellent barbecued salmon. Sunday brunch is the rave of the Lower Mainland. It's open every day (except Christmas Eve and Christmas Day) for lunch and dinner. For an unbeatable heart-stopper of a breakfast (eggs, bacon, buttered toast . . . the works), check out **The Tomahawk**, 1550 Phillip Ave., North Vancouver (off Marine Dr.), 604/988-2612. The '50s-style diner serves delicious food, and their signature breakfast plate, the Yukon, is available all day.

Stop in at the **Howe Sound Inn and Brewing Company**, Squamish Town Center, 37801 Cleveland Ave., Squamish, 800/919-2537, on your way to or from Whistler. The microbrewery offers good beers, pub-style food (a.k.a. burgers), and full meals, including salmon. Another great stop on the way to Whistler is the **Roadhouse Diner** at Klahanie Inn (opposite Shannon Falls, right on Highway 99), 604/892-5312. Although the restaurant's been here forever, the menu is contemporary: Several styles of hash browns top the breakfast chart, and for dinner there's pan-fried trout with a side of maple-syrup sweet potatoes.

In Whistler, as in Vancouver, dining choices are almost innumerable. For a no-holds-barred terrific meal, go to the **Rim Rock Cafe**, 2117 Whistler Rd. (between Creekside and the main Whistler village), 604/932-5565. It's expensive, but the menu is imaginative, the food is great, and the presentation makes the price tag easier to swallow. A specialty is sea bass with a ginger and almond crust, served with black bean and mushroom sauce. Dinner for two, with wine, costs about $100. Equally pricey is the **Bearfoot Bistro**, 4121 Village Green, 604/932-3433. Stop in for a bowl of soup followed by a venison, caribou, or bison entrée, then, if you have room, go elsewhere for dessert. Dinner for two, with wine, costs about $130. If you're seeking something more affordable, try **Caramba**, 12, 4314 Main St., Village North, 604/938-1879. Entrées of roast lamb or salmon cost only $10, and the service is quick and friendly.

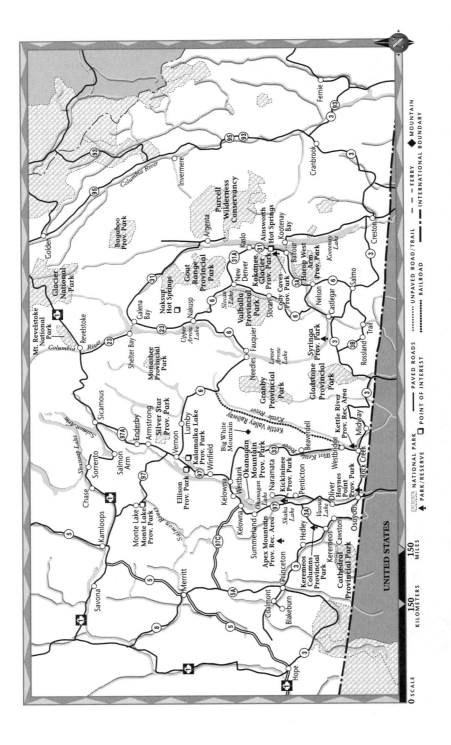

UNITED STATES

0 SCALE

150 KILOMETERS

150 MILES

▰▰▰ NATIONAL PARK
▨▨ PARK/RESERVE
▬▬▬ PAVED ROADS
▭ POINT OF INTEREST
········ UNPAVED ROAD/TRAIL
━━━━ RAILROAD
─ ─ FERRY
━·━·━ INTERNATIONAL BOUNDARY
◆ MOUNTAIN

Fernie
Cranbrook
Creston
Kimberley
Invermere
Golden

Columbia River

Purcell Wilderness Conservancy
Argenta
Kaslo
Ainsworth Hot Springs
Kootenay Bay
Kootenay Lake
Balfour
Kaslo (31A)
New Denver
Kokanee Glacier Prov. Park
Hardy West Prov. Park
Cody Caves Prov. Park
Salmo
Nelson
Castlegar
Trail
Rossland
(3B)

Bugaboo Prov. Park
Goat Range Provincial Park
Nakusp Hot Springs
Nakusp
Galena Bay
Slocan Lake
Valhalla Provincial Park
Slocan
Fauquier
Syringa Prov. Park
Gladstone Provincial Park

Mt. Revelstoke National Park
Glacier National Park
Revelstoke
Columbia River
Shelter Bay
Monashee Provincial Park
Upper Arrow Lake
Needles
Lower Arrow Lake
Granby Provincial Park
Kettle River Prov. Rec. Area
Midway
Rock Creek

Sicamous
Salmon Arm
Enderby
Armstrong
Silver Star Prov. Park
Vernon
Lumby
Kalamalka Lake Prov. Park
Big White Mountain
Kettle Valley Railway
West Kettle River
Beaverdell
Westbridge
Kettle River

Shuswap Lake
Sorrento
Chase
Salmon River
Monte Lake
Monte Lake Prov. Park
Winfield
Ellison Prov. Park
Kelowna
Westbank
Okanagan Mountain Prov. Park
Naramata
Kickininee Prov. Park
Penticton
Summerland
Apex Mountain Prov. Rec. Area

Savona
Kamloops
Merritt
Princeton
Coalmont
Blakeburn
Keremeos Columns Provincial Park
Cathedral Provincial Park
Keremeos
Cawston
Oliver
Osoyoos
Haynes Point Prov. Park
Okanagan Lake
Skaha Lake
Vaseux Lake
Hedley
Cawston

Hope

CHAPTER 7

Okanagan, Similkameen, and Kootenay Country

The Similkameen, Okanagan, and Kootenay regions occupy the southern portion of British Columbia, from the Cascade Mountains on the west to the Rocky Mountain Trench in the east. As a whole, the region is rugged and mountainous, but there are pockets of rich farmland, especially in the Okanagan Valley and the Creston area in the Kootenays. Except for the Okanagan, this region is sparsely populated.

The region's forests and mineral resources have been widely exploited; much of the region's settlement occurred in conjunction with mining for everything from gold to zinc. The Kootenays are also home to several large hydroelectric developments on the Columbia River. Despite widespread industrial development there are still incredible areas of wilderness in the Kootenays, which have survived largely because of their isolation.

Wilderness seekers will have to look long and hard to find what they're after in the Similkameen and Okanagan regions; the Kelowna area is among Canada's fastest-growing urban regions. Still, there are plenty of recreational opportunities, especially water sports, downhill skiing, cycling, wildlife viewing, and the Okanagan's greatest participation sport, winery tours.

In the Kootenays, the rugged landscape means more wilderness, especially in Goat Range, Valhalla, and Kokanee Glacier Provincial Parks and the Purcell Wilderness Conservancy. Other activities in Kootenay country include excellent mountain biking in the Rossland area, paddling on the area's lakes and reservoirs, terrific downhill skiing, and plenty of hot springs.

LAY OF THE LAND

The Cascade Mountains form the western flank of this large region while the east is the domain of the Columbia Mountains. The Columbias, in turn, are divided into several sub-ranges, notably the Monashees, Selkirks, Purcells, and Bugaboos. Between the mountain ranges are long, narrow valleys that generally lie in a north-south orientation. The largest of these is the Okanagan Valley, the most highly populated and developed part of the entire region. Many of the area's valleys are home to lakes, the largest of which are Okanagan and Kootenay Lakes. The Upper and Lower Arrow Lakes in Kootenay country are the result of dams on the Columbia River.

The broad and deep Rocky Mountain Trench separates the Columbias from the Rocky Mountains. A remarkable geographic feature visible from orbiting spacecraft, the trench is a valley that extends for 1,400 kilometers (840 miles) in BC alone, from the Liard River in the far north to the Canada/U.S. border and beyond. For much of its length, the Rocky Mountain Trench is occupied by the Columbia River, which rises in the Kootenays and flows north around the Selkirk Mountains. At that point the Columbia makes an about-face and starts its southward journey, passing back through the Kootenay region and crossing the border into Washington.

The Similkameen and Okanagan Valleys lie in a rain shadow cast by the Cascade Mountains and are among Canada's driest areas. In fact, the lower reaches of the Similkameen and Okanagan constitute the northern end of the Great Basin Desert (Canada's only true desert), which stretches across the international boundary from Washington. The rain-shadow effect becomes less pronounced toward the northern end of the Okanagan. In the Kootenays, the high Columbia Mountains create their own miniature interior rain forest. The Rocky Mountain Trench tends to be semiarid.

South Okanagan Valley

One of BC's forgotten corners, the Similkameen was once swarming with prospectors and dotted with isolated mining towns. Now it's ranching and farming country. Heavily irrigated fields stand out like emeralds against the backdrop of soft, dun-colored hills, and the fast-flowing Similkameen River hugs the U.S. border from the Cascades to Osoyoos, where it turns south into Washington. Few travelers stop as they zip along Highway 3 between Princeton and Penticton, but there are some surprising geographical features and wilderness areas worth visiting, and plenty of intriguing back roads and ghost towns.

The Okanagan Valley runs for 160 kilometers (96 miles) from the Canada/U.S. border in the south to the city of Vernon in the north. At its widest point it's only 19 kilometers (11.5 miles) across. Okanagan Lake occupies most of the valley floor, meaning that arable and habitable land is at a premium. Homes, farms, and vineyards perch on narrow benches and terraces above the sparkling lake.

Increasing urban and residential development is rapidly changing the face of this former rural holiday spot. The Okanagan accounts for just 3 percent of BC's total land base, but 8 percent of the province's population lives here, attracted by long and hot summers, mild winters, and a casual, outdoorsy lifestyle. There are at least 19 golf courses throughout the valley, plus beaches, resorts, and no end of tourist-oriented activities like go-cart parks and waterslides. If you're bound for the Okanagan and looking for wilderness or even a scrap of native vegetation, bring your microscope—wild places remain in the Okanagan, but they're small, isolated, and threatened.

Kootenay Country is a region of steep-sided mountains, narrow valleys, and long lakes (many of them are reservoirs held back by large dams). Because the Columbia Mountains are high, considerable moisture falls in parts of this region, making for lush vegetation and fantastic powder skiing. Because of the difficult topography—many parallel valleys separated by high, steep mountains—access to Kootenay Country is actually easier from the south than from any other direction. As a result, the region as a whole remains relatively undiscovered, with lots of backcountry and wilderness to explore.

The southeast corner of the region, centered around the city of Creston, is warm enough to grow fruit and cereal crops such as wheat. In fact, Creston boasts BC's only grain elevators (huge storage bins that load grain into railcars) outside of the remarkable Peace River district in the province's northeast.

FLORA AND FAUNA

From desert to rain forest, this broad interior region again exhibits BC's remarkable diversity. The Similkameen and Okanagan are characterized by communities of ponderosa pine and Douglas fir with undergrowth of sagebrush and bunchgrass. To the east the Columbia Mountains force eastward-moving weather systems to rise and shed moisture, thereby creating an interior rain forest that is more diverse (in terms of plant species) than the coastal rain forests. Many of the same trees found along the coast also thrive in the wet belt of the Columbias—red cedar, hemlock, and large Douglas fir.

The desert areas of the lower Okanagan and Similkameen are home to rattlesnakes, bighorn sheep, coyotes, and deer. The region's large lakes harbor a large population of waterfowl; both the Okanagan and Kootenay areas are excellent for bird-watching.

HISTORY AND CULTURE

When the Ice Age glaciers melted away from the Okanagan, they left in their wake an enormous lake. They also left a thick deposit of fine silt, sand, and clay. In the thousands of years since, the water level has declined to form today's Okanagan Lake and several smaller bodies of water, and the rich soil deposits have become the foundation for the fertile land in the valley today.

The valley's aboriginal occupants were the Okanagan peoples, who lived as far east as Slocan Lake in the Kootenays. From there to the Rocky Mountain Trench and beyond to the Rocky Mountains lived the remarkable Ktunaxa (Kootenay). Like the Haida language of Haida Gwaii (Queen Charlotte Islands), the Ktunaxa language is unrelated to any other aboriginal language group, perhaps a testament to the isolation of this rugged and mountainous region.

Food was relatively scarce in the mountains and valleys, as compared with the rich abundance enjoyed by coastal peoples. The Okanagan and Ktunaxa were nomadic, moving from place to place in pursuit of game. In the winter the Okanagan tribes would settle in villages of underground pit houses. The Ktunaxa often traveled east through the Rocky Mountains to hunt bison on the high plains.

The first white explorer passed through the region in 1807 when David Thompson, in search of furs and Native trading partners for his employer, the North West Company, befriended both the Ktunaxa and the Okanagan. The Fraser River gold rush of 1858 resulted in an influx of whites heading north through the Okanagan territories, bringing missionaries, cattle ranching, agriculture, permanent settlement, and disease in their wake. By 1875 tensions hit the boiling point. The Okanagan and their Secwepemc allies to the north held a council of war, but their intent dissolved amid promises from the government that questions of land ownership and access to traditional lifestyles would be resolved—promises that remain unfulfilled to this day.

Lakes and rivers were used as the major transportation routes through the region, and paddle wheelers plied their waters until rails

Fruit orchard, Okanagan Valley

and roads were built. One of the first roads, the rough Dewdeney Trail, was completed in 1865 to connect the Kootenay region with the west coast (today's Highway 3 follows much of the same route). And the Kettle Valley Railway, built through the Similkameen, lower Okanagan, and Kootenay areas, began operating in 1916.

The Okanagan's excellent soils, combined with the valley's dry, sunny climate, attracted European settlement. Today the Okanagan and Similkameen supply much of the province with its fruit, especially peaches, cherries, apricots, apples, pears, and grapes. The mild climate and casual lifestyle have also attracted retirees to the region.

Mining has been the major industrial activity in the Kootenays. Lead, silver, gold, and other minerals have been extensively exploited in the past, though present mining activity has slowed almost to a standstill. The exception is the globe's largest lead-zinc smelting complex at Trail. To create a supply of electricity for BC, and for sale to the United States, both the Columbia and Kootenay Rivers were dammed in the 1960s and 1970s.

▲ Vancouver–Victoria ferry (© D. Leighton)

▲ Rafting on the Tatshenshini River (K.D. Wong/Blackbird Designs)

▼ Rogers Pass, Glacier National Park (Blackbird Designs)

▼ Native carving traditions have been revived. (K.D. Wong/Blackbird Designs)

▲ The town of Rossland in the Kootenay region (© D. Leighton)

▼ Black bears are common throughout British Columbia. (© D. Leighton)

▲ Rocky Mountain wildflowers
(P. Crawford/D. Giberson)

▲ A totem pole at the 'Ksan
village in Hazelton
(K.D. Wong/Blackbird Designs)

▼ Powell River offers world-class diving. (P. Crawford/D. Giberson)

▲ Mount Revelstoke National Park (© D. Leighton)

▼ 'Ksan, a restored Native settlement in Hazelton (K.D. Wong/Blackbird Designs)

▲ Mountain goat in the Rockies (© D. Leighton)

▼ The town of Kaslo on Kootenay Lake (© D. Leighton)

▼ Haida Gwaii rain forest (Holly Quan)

▲ Kayaking in Barkley Sound, Pacific Rim National Park Reserve
(P. Crawford/D. Giberson)

▼ Pacific coast sea lions (K.D. Wong/Blackbird Designs)

▲ Visitors at the Ninstints village in Gwaii Haanas National Park Reserve (Holly Quan)

VISITOR INFORMATION

Getting to the Similkameen, Okanagan, and Kootenay region is best accomplished by car. A major road in the area is the Coquihalla Highway (Highway 5). It extends east from Hope to the interior town of Merritt, then splits; the northern branch provides access to Kamloops, and the southern branch goes straight to Kelowna in the heart of the Okanagan Valley. Another primary road is the Crowsnest Highway (Highway 3), which snakes across the southern edge of the province between Hope and the Kootenays, passing through the Similkameen and Okanagan Valleys en route. One of the highest public roads in Canada, Highway 3 climbs to Kootenay Pass and an altitude of 1,774 meters (5,854 feet).

Other major roadways include Highway 6, which crosses most of the Kootenay region from east to west, connecting the northern Okanagan with the Kootenay settlements of Nakusp and New Denver; Highway 23, which runs north from Nakusp to connect with the Trans-Canada Highway at Revelstoke (see Chapter 9); and Highway 97, which travels northward through the entire length of the Okanagan Valley. In the Kootenay region, a tangle of roads provides a network of connections between the area's major towns of Castlegar, Trail, Rossland, and Nelson. Access to the Kootenays is actually easier from the south than from any other direction. U.S. visitors have a choice of seven border crossings from Washington and Idaho.

The area is also served by several regional airlines, and commercial airports are located at Kelowna and Castlegar. There are several smaller airstrips throughout the region. Bus lines, too, operate between all major towns and cities in the Similkameen, Okanagan, and Kootenays, and link the region with Vancouver, Calgary, and other destinations. There is no passenger-rail service in the area at present.

A system of ferries operates in the Kootenays to provide access across the reservoirs created by the large hydro dams. The inland ferries are free and operate every day, all year. Major ferry routes connect Balfour to Kootenay Bay across Kootenay Lake (connecting Highways 31 and 3A), Needles to Fauquier across Lower Arrow Lake (Highway 6), and Shelter Bay to Galena Bay across Upper Arrow Lake (Highway 23).

For detailed information on the region and its transportation options, contact the Thompson-Okanagan Tourism Association, 1332

Water St., Kelowna, e-mail osta@awinc.com, www.travel.bc.ca/region/ok. For information on the Kootenays, contact the BC Rockies Tourism Association, P.O. Box 10, Kimberley, BC V1A 2Y5, 250/427-4838, bcrockies@cyberlink.bc.ca, www.travel.bc.ca/region.rockies. Visitor Infocentres are located throughout the entire region.

NATURE AND ADVENTURE SIGHTS: SIMILKAMEEN

Cathedral Provincial Park

High above the arid valley floor is this wonderland of lakes, forests, and 32 kilometers (19 miles) of well-maintained hiking trails. The base area is at Quiniscoe Lake (one of the five Cathedral Lakes), site of several campgrounds and Cathedral Lakes Lodge. The private lodge offers excellent accommodations and food, and access to the area's fine hiking trails. There are also 70 walk-in wilderness campsites in the park. Campers must be completely self-sufficient, as there are no facilities in the park (except the lodge).

The five Cathedral Lakes shimmer like a string of gems, each in a unique setting, each a different color. Hiking trails lead to bizarre rock formations such as Stone City (scattered house-sized boulders interspersed with tiny, fragile alpine flowers), Macabre Tower, and Grimface Mountain. Mountain goats and bighorn sheep are common.

First-time visitors are encouraged to call Cathedral Lakes Lodge and arrange for transportation; there is a road into the park but it's closed to private vehicles. The lodge's taxi is free for registered guests and is available for a fee to campers. Alternatively, you can choose to hike in. The trail is 16 kilometers (10 miles) long and takes six to seven hours to walk. It's hot and dry, so bring plenty of water.

Nearby, but not within the park, are the **Keremeos Columns**. These vertical towers of basalt are the result of volcanic activity nearly 30 million years ago. The formation is 100 meters (330 feet) long and up to 30 meters (100 feet) high. The desert site can be reached via a hot and dry five-kilometer (three-mile) hike. Carry lots of water and wear a hat. To get to the trailhead take Highway 3A north from Keremeos four kilometers (two and one-half miles), then turn right at the cemetery and drive 400 meters (a quarter-mile) to a locked gate where the trail begins.

PACIFIC RATTLESNAKE

British Columbia's only poisonous snake is the timid Pacific rattlesnake, found in the southern Okanagan and Similkameen. The adult Pacific rattler is tan-brown and can grow to one and one-half meters (five feet) in length, though 80 centimeters (2.5 feet) is the average. The snake doesn't necessarily rattle before striking, and when it does strike, its bite can be dangerous. When hiking in dry or rocky areas, particularly during the summer, pay attention to where you put your hands, what you step on, and where you sit. In the winter there's a lot less to worry about—the Pacific hibernates underground when the weather gets cold and doesn't reappear until March or April.

Details: Drive east from Hope on Highway 3. Turn south (right) onto Ashnola River Road, 63 kilometers (38 miles) east of Princeton. Continue for 21 kilometers (12.5 miles). If you've booked a ride with Cathedral Lakes Lodge's taxi, park in the lot; call 250/226-7560 to book a room or a taxi ride. If you're not taking the taxi, continue another two kilometers (one mile) along Ashnola Road to the trailhead at Lakeview Creek. For more information, contact the Okanagan District Office, BC Parks, Box 399, Summerland, BC V0H 1Z0, 250/494-6500.

Princeton

Princeton, located in the foothills of the Cascade Mountains, is a good fuel and rest stop for those traveling between Vancouver and the interior. The area is renowned for its excellent fishing—"a lake a day as long as you stay" is the pitch to tourists. The **Yellow Pine Ecological Reserve** is a small patch of undisturbed ponderosa forest right on Highway 3, three kilometers (two miles) west of Princeton, and is a pleasant rest stop. For ghost towns, travel the historic stagecoach route, now called the Coalmont-Tulameen Road, just west of Princeton. You'll encounter the abandoned coal-mining town of **Blakeburn**, **Coalmont** (a few residents remain and the hotel is still operating), and **Granite City**, a gold-mining settlement that was BC's third-largest town between 1885 and 1888.

The **Mascot Mine**, 35 kilometers (21 miles) east of Princeton, was part of a gold-mining enterprise on Nickel Plate Mountain dating back to 1904. The mine buildings have been restored as a museum. The road leading up to the mine museum, known locally as "Corkscrew Road," is steep and winding. Make sure your vehicle is in good condition before you take on this challenge. Views from the road are spectacular.

Details: Princeton is 135 kilometers (81 miles) east of Hope on Highway 3. Contact the Princeton Chamber of Commerce, Box 540, Princeton, BC V0X 1W0, 250/295-3103. For the Coalmont-Tulameen Road, take Tulameen Avenue out of Princeton. For Mascot Mine, take Highway 3 east for 43 kilometers (26 miles). "Corkscrew Road" leaves Highway 3 approximately four kilometers east of Hedley.

NATURE AND ADVENTURE SIGHTS: OKANAGAN

Kettle Valley Railway (KVR)

The KVR was built between 1910 and 1914 through some of BC's toughest terrain. The original track went from Hope to Osoyoos, turned up the Okanagan Valley to Kelowna, then dropped back down the Kettle Valley to the town of Midway (the onward route to Castlegar in the Kootenays was operated by the Columbia & Western Railway). Reputed to be the world's most expensive railway, the KVR operated until 1960 when it was abandoned due to exorbitant maintenance costs—train wrecks, rockslides, and avalanches plagued the route.

After the line was closed, the tracks were lifted but the rail bed, tunnels, and trestles were left in place. Today the rail bed is, for the most part, open to the public, and is being restored by volunteer societies for use by cyclists, horseback riders, and hikers. There are no official facilities along the trail, but there are numerous access points and the route passes close to several campgrounds, restaurants, pubs,

166

and wineries. Bike shops in Penticton and Kelowna rent bikes and other equipment and sell good maps of the route.

While the route is relatively easy and family-friendly, it's not without its challenges. In some places the rail bed has been plowed under or is otherwise impassable. There are also creek crossings, detours, tunnels, trestles, and other hazards. The trestles are especially dangerous. Although many of them have been restored, and handrails have been built to make them safer, people do fall from them on occasion. Always use caution as you cross a trestle, and never approach the edge of one with no railing. As for the tunnels, bring a good flashlight or headlamp and walk your bike. If there's a barricade at the entrance to a tunnel, stay out.

The best way to cycle the Okanagan section of the KVR is from east to west (from Midway to Penticton or Osoyoos). Here's a quick rundown of what you'll find along the way: At the start in Midway is **Midway Station**, a heritage building now operated as a museum. Before you go, drop in at the museum for an explanation of the railway's construction and operation. About 68 kilometers (41 miles) from Midway, you'll come to **Beaverdell Station**. The station building itself is gone but the nearby settlement of Beaverdell boasts BC's oldest continuously operated hotel and pub, a good place to stop for the night. **Hydraulic Lake**, at 121 kilometers (72.5 miles) from Midway and with two campgrounds (see "Camping" and "Lodging"), is a good place to rest on the second night.

Myra Canyon, which can be reached from Kelowna (via the Myra Forest Service Road), is popular as a day trip. The Myra Canyon Trestle Restoration Society is refurbishing this section's trestles to bring them up to BC Parks' standards for safety. While it's just 10 kilometers (six miles) long, the section contains 18 trestles and two tunnels.

Chute Lake, at the 171-kilometer mark (102.5 mile), is another good overnight stop (see "Camping" and "Lodging"). From the lake the KVR passes several vineyards, including Lang Vineyards in the settlement of Arawana and Hillside Cellars in the village of Naramata. Finally, the route enters **Penticton**, the Okanagan's second-largest city. Its many hotels and restaurants make it a good end-of-the-road destination for KVR cyclists.

A short section of the KVR spur line northwest of **Summerland** (north of Penticton on Highway 97) has been restored and is used by the Kettle Valley Steam Railway Heritage Society for excursions on a 1924 Shay steam locomotive. For information and bookings, contact the society at 250/494-8422, fax 250/494-8452, e-mail kvr@img.net.

Details: Contact the Okanagan-Similkameen Parks Society, P.O. Box 787, Summerland, BC V0H 1Z0; or the Visitor Infocentres in Penticton (185 Lakeshore Dr., 250/493-4055), Summerland (Box 1075, Summerland, BC V0H 1Z0, 250/494-2686), or Kelowna (544 Harvey Ave., 800/663-4345). For detailed route descriptions, see Dan and Sandra Langford's excellent book, Cycling the Kettle Valley Railway, *widely available in BC bookstores (see Appendix B).*

Osoyoos

This resort town has a Spanish feel—many buildings are finished with white stucco and red roof tiles. **Osoyoos Oxbows Fish and Wildlife Management Reserve** is a preserved fragment of desertlike habitat including a subsection called the Haynes' Lease Ecological Reserve (also known as the Pocket Desert), a remnant of the Okanagan Valley as it existed prior to the introduction of irrigation and farming. At first glance the landscape here appears to be barren and harsh, but closer inspection reveals many unique—and rare—plants and animals. Due to the delicate nature of the desert ecology, camping and other potentially harmful activities are disallowed within the ecological reserve. If you visit the Pocket Desert, leave your dog at home and tread carefully over the fragile landscape.

Details: Osoyoos is on Highway 3, four kilometers north of the Canada/U.S. border and 112 kilometers (67 miles) east of Hope. The Osoyoos Oxbows Reserve is seven and one-half kilometers north of Osoyoos on Highway 97; watch for signs for Road 22 on the right (east) side of the highway. For the Pocket Desert, continue on Road 22 for one kilometer beyond the Oxbows Reserve and park at the abandoned farmstead. For information call the Osoyoos Desert Centre at 250/495-2470 or 877/899-0897.

Vaseux Lake

Shallow and marshy, Vaseux Lake (*vaseux,* pronounced va-SOO, is the French word for "muddy") is among Canada's best birding sites. In fact, some of the species found here, such as the white-headed woodpecker, exist nowhere else in Canada. More common waterfowl include herons, geese, swans, and ducks. The Vaseux Wildlife Centre maintains trails and bird-watching blinds, and there's a small campground nearby. Bring a canoe for a quiet morning paddle, the best time to see birds and other wildlife.

Details: Vaseux Lake and the Vaseux Wildlife Centre are located 14.5 kilometers (9 miles) north of Oliver on Highway 97. For information on the Wildlife Centre call Vaseux Lake Provincial Park, 250/494-6500.

NATURE AND ADVENTURE SIGHTS: KOOTENAY COUNTRY

Arrow Lakes Waterway

The Columbia River is North America's fourth-longest waterway. Two-thirds of its drainage basin, which exceeds 155,000 square kilometers (60,450 square miles), lies within BC. The river rises in the Purcell range and flows north, then makes an about-face around the northern end of the Selkirk range to flow south through the Kootenay region and on into Washington State.

D. Leighton

Vaseux Lake

169

GHOST TOWNS

Along Highway 31A between the towns of Kaslo and New Denver are several ghost towns that date from the late 1890s. The best of them is Sandon, which lies five kilometers (three miles) south of the highway (watch for the access road just west of Three Forks). Established in 1892 and built around the silver-mining industry, Sandon once had 24 hotels, just as many saloons, and a population of 5,000. Today a handful of people still live in Sandon, amid the ruins of the old buildings. A small museum is open daily from mid-June to mid-September.

In 1961 the government of British Columbia signed a treaty with the United States that resulted in the construction of several major dams on the Columbia in BC. The Hugh Keenleyside Dam, located near Castlegar, holds back the Columbia's flow to create the Upper and Lower Arrow Lakes, which extend for more than 230 kilometers (138 miles) north to the city of Revelstoke. The reservoir's water level is controlled by the dam and can fluctuate up to 20 meters (66 feet) between its springtime highs and autumn lows. The fishing and paddling are great, and there are lots of places to beach a canoe or kayak for impromptu camping. A good put-in point is Syringa Provincial Park, 19 kilometers (11 miles) northwest of Castlegar on Highway 3A.

Details: Castlegar is on Highway 3, 170 kilometers (102 miles) east of Rock Creek. Contact the Castlegar Chamber of Commerce and Travel Infocentre, 1995-Sixth Ave., Castlegar, 250/356-6313. For information about the Arrow Lakes Waterway, contact Scottie's Marina, 250/365-3267, or Syringa Park Marina, 250/365-5472.

Cody Caves

Except for the installation of a few ladders, nothing much about the caves in this 63-hectare (155.5-acre) provincial park has changed since they were discovered a century ago. The caves extend for more than a kilometer (half-mile) underground and include stalagmites, stalactites, soda straws, moon milk, and more. If you're venturing into the caves (access is by guided tour only), take a rope, flashlight, sturdy footwear, a helmet, and rain gear.

Details: *Access to Cody Caves is from Highway 31 north of Balfour. A rough 12-kilometer (seven-mile) road leads from Highway 31 to the trailhead, with a 20-minute walk to the caves. To book a tour, call HiAdventure Corporation, 250/353-7425.*

Goat Range Provincial Park

Established in 1995, 88,000-hectare (217,000-acre) Goat Range Provincial Park is nearly roadless and utterly remote. There are no facilities and BC Parks intends to keep things that way in order to discourage all but the most dedicated and self-reliant of backcountry adventurers. Access is difficult (a four-wheel-drive vehicle is a good idea), but well worth the effort. If you do manage to get into the backcountry, you may be rewarded with a glimpse of a rare white grizzly.

Topographic maps are a must for all the Kootenay Country wilderness parks (also see Kokanee Glacier, Purcell Wilderness, and Valhalla, below). To obtain maps, contact the local BC Parks office at RR 3, Nelson, BC V1L 5P6, 250/825-4421; or Maps BC, Third Floor, 1802 Douglas St., Victoria, 250/387-1441. The city of Nelson, located 41 kilometers (24.5 miles) north of Castlegar on Highway 3A, is a good starting point for trips into the parks. The city is the largest urban center in the Kootenays, with a population of around 10,000, and is recognized for its preserved and restored heritage buildings as well as excellent mountain biking and downhill skiing. Contact the Nelson Visitor Infocentre at 225 Hall St., 250/352-3433.

Details: *Goat Range Provincial Park is 83 kilometers (52 miles) north of Kaslo. Drive north on Highway 31 (Trout Lake Rd.), which is paved as far as Howser. For more information, call 250/825-3500.*

Kokanee Glacier Provincial Park

With high meadows, huge mountains, 30 alpine lakes, and a maze of trails, Kokanee Glacier Provincial Park is easily one of BC's finest

AUTHOR'S TOP PICKS: DOWNHILL SKIING

- **Kootenays**—*Red Mountain (Rossland) and Whitewater (Nelson) offer incredibly deep, soft snow at small, intimate, and friendly ski hills.*

- **Okanagan Valley**—*Three major ski resorts (Silver Star, Big White, Apex) plus estate wineries, brewpubs, shopping, and nightlife.*

- **Sun Peaks**—*Newly expanded and improved, north of Kamloops.*

- **Whistler/Blackcomb**—*Whistler is consistently rated as North America's best place to ski. It's extremely expensive—but you only live once.*

hiking experiences. There are no facilities in this wilderness park, so hikers must be prepared to fend for themselves.

Details: From Balfour, drive north on Highway 31. For more information call 250/825-4421.

Kootenay Country Hot Springs

Among the developed hot springs in the area is **Ainsworth Hot Springs**, located on Highway 31, 49 kilometers (29 miles) northeast of Nelson. The water holds the highest mineral concentration of any hot spring in Canada but lacks the typical sulfur smell. The hottest pool, at 45 degrees Celsius (113 degrees Fahrenheit), features a well-lit, U-shaped cave half-filled with water; bathers can wade a few meters into the mountain to the hot spring's source. There is an adjacent hotel and dining room. For reservations at the hotel, call 800/668-1171 or 250/229-4212. At **Nakusp Hot Springs,** the pools are owned by the town of Nakusp and are open daily. Water temperatures range from 38 to 41 degrees Celsius (100.4 to 105.8 degrees Fahrenheit), and there are showers, lockers, change rooms, and a small campground nearby. The springs are located 16 kilometers (10 miles) northeast of Nakusp.

Details: For information contact Box 1268, Ainsworth Hot Springs, BC, VOG 1A0, 250/229-4212 or 800/668-1171, and Box 280, Nakusp, BC, VOG 1RO, 250/265-4528.

Purcell Wilderness Conservancy

The only way to get in and out of this 199,000-hectare (491,000-acre) protected area is on foot. The only established trail in the wilderness is the 61-kilometer (36.5-mile) **Earl Grey Pass Trail**, a fabulous three-day route that traverses the Purcell Mountains to the town of Invermere in the Columbia River Valley. The path is rugged, to say the least, and includes several creek crossings by cable car.

Details: From Kaslo, drive 30 kilometers (18 miles) north on Highway 31 to Lardeau. Cross the Duncan River and head south five kilometers (three miles) to the tiny settlement of Argenta. The west trailhead is located four kilometers past the Argenta post office. For more information call 250/422-3212.

Rossland

This busy, friendly, and very outdoors-oriented town of 4,000 is perched at an elevation of more than 1,000 meters (3,300 feet). Beginning in 1890, over $3 million in gold was removed from the mountain slopes north of town. In fact, for the first 16 years of the twentieth century, half of BC's gold came from the Rossland area. Of the more than 100 gold claims staked in Rossland's vicinity, the Le Roi Gold Mine proved to be the most lucrative. Many of the town's heritage buildings dating from the gold era have been restored; a walking-tour map is available at the Visitor Infocentre.

Because of the area's topography—you can't walk too far in Rossland without going either uphill or downhill—the town and the local region are known for two sports that take great advantage of slopes and gravity: mountain biking and downhill skiing. **Red Mountain**, the local downhill ski hill, has produced a couple of world-champion skiers: Nancy Greene and Kerrin Lee-Gartner. The hill is small, friendly, and easy to negotiate, yet it's also big enough to satisfy the powder-hungry among us. The Kootenays are known for powder snow and lots of it, and Red Mountain is no exception. Cross-country skiing is also available on adjacent Granite Mountain or at a number of nearby provincial parks.

As for summer, Rossland has become the self-declared "Mountain Bike Capital of Canada." There are at least a dozen developed trails (totaling over 100 kilometers/60 miles) in the area, suitable for all levels of experience and fitness. Many trails start right in the center of town and radiate into the surrounding alpine country. Relatively easy trails include Railgrade and Midnight Loop, both of which take less than two hours to complete. Smuggler's Loop and 007 are more challenging. Rubberhead, Rabid Slug, and Techno Grind are steep, experts-only trails.

Details: From Castlegar, take Highway 22 south for 26 kilometers (15.5 miles) to Trail. Rossland is on Highway 3B, 10 kilometers (6 miles) west of Trail. The Rossland Visitor Infocentre, 250/362-7722 (summer only), is located in the Rossland Historical Museum at the junction of Highways 22 and 3B. During winter contact the Rossland Chamber of Commerce, Box 1385, Rossland, BC V0G 1Y0, 250/362-5666. For information on Red Mountain, including ski and accommodations packages, call 250/362-7384. For bike rentals and information, check out Chico's Bike Shack and Tours, 250/362-5788.

Valhalla Provincial Park

This wilderness park encompasses the gorgeous Valhalla Range and the western shore of Slocan Lake, and is a veritable treasure for experienced backcountry hikers and campers. The major attraction is a network of excellent hiking trails—the Evans Creek/Beatrice Lake trail, for example, runs the entire length of the park from north to south.

Details: Drive west from Kaslo on Highway 31A. At New Denver, turn south on Highway 6 and continue to Slocan. For park information, call 250/825-3500.

GUIDES AND OUTFITTERS

Revolution Adventure Tours, P.O. Box 179, Nelson, BC V1L 5P9, 800/301-8858 or 250/354-1566, e-mail revotour@bc.sympatico.ca,

Valhalla Provincial Park

www.adventure-experts.com, offers day, multi-day, and customized pedal and paddle tours in the Kootenays as well as guided walking tours of historic sites. All gear is supplied, the trips are fully escorted, meals are provided, and accommodations are included on overnight trips. **Okanagan Bicycle Tours**, 800/991-3233 or 250/766-4086, offers supported cycle tours of the Kettle Valley Railway. **Osprey Tours**, Suite 6, 373 Baker St., Nelson, 800/301-8858 or 250/352-2699, e-mail osprey@netidea.com, www.adventure-experts.com, is a multisport outfitter offering Kootenay adventures such as cycling, bird-watching, hiking, whitewater kayaking, horseback riding, llama trekking, fishing, skiing, and snowboarding. Climbers should check out **Northern Lights Alpine Recreation**, Box 399, Invermere, BC V0A 1K0, 250/342-6042. The company offers guided climbing in the Purcell Mountains for all experience levels. They also conduct rescue seminars and lead hiking treks (individually arranged to suit the skill level and ambitions of the group).

175

TOURS AND TASTINGS

Many estate wineries in the Okanagan offer tasting and retail departments. You can occasionally take tours of the winemaking facilities as well, usually by appointment or at set times. For a handy booklet describing winery locations, contact the Thompson-Okanagan Tourism Association, 1332 Water St., Kelowna, 800/567-2275, and request a copy of "Tours of Abundance."

Two annual events spotlight winemaking in the Okanagan. The Okanagan Wine Festival's spring event, during April and May, welcomes the new season. (This is a terrific time to see the Okanagan's huge fruit orchards in full bloom—the air is sweet and literally hums with bees!) The autumn festival, held in October, is among North America's top food and wine events, with tastings, gala dinners, tours, and more.

Brewery tours are also available at several Okanagan locations, including the Tin Whistle Brewery in Penticton and the Okanagan Spring regional brewery and Old Schoolhouse brewpub, both in Kelowna.

CAMPING

Throughout the Okanagan and Kootenay regions there are numerous private campgrounds to supplement the campgrounds in provincial parks. Parks in the area that accept reservations include Bear Creek, Ellison, Fintry, Haynes Point, Okanagan Lake, Otter (Okanagan/ Similkameen) and Champion Lakes, and Kokanee Creek. For information and reservations call 800/689-9025.

In the Okanagan area, **Bear Creek Campground**, Box 399, Summerland, BC V0H 1Z0, 250/494-6500, is located nine kilometers (five and one-half miles) west of Kelowna. Beaches, canyons, and waterfalls are all part of the local scenery. The campground has 122 sites suitable for RVs, trailers, or tents, plus a boatload of amenities such as flush toilets, showers, a sani-station, and wheelchair access. It's open March through November; fees are charged April through October.

A nice private campground 13 kilometers (8 miles) south of Kelowna is the **West Bay Beach Resort**, 3745 West Bay Rd., Westbank, 250/768-3004. The campground's main feature is a large beach on Okanagan Lake. Activities include tennis, volleyball, and indoor games such as table tennis and billiards. Amenities include laundry facilities, a store, and fire pits on the beach. It's open April through October.

Among the campgrounds along the Kettle Valley Railway cycle route are McCullough Lake Resort and Chute Lake Resort. **McCullough Lake Resort and Campground**, 250/491-8804 or 205/862-7834, is located at Hydraulic Lake and has showers, flush toilets, and other amenities. (See "Lodging" for information on the resort's cabins.) **Chute Lake Resort**, 250/493-3535, has 24 drive-in sites and electrical hookups, showers, a sani-station, washrooms, laundry facilities, and a store. Campsites range from $10 to $20 with nominal extra charges for electric, sewer, and water hookups. (See "Lodging" for information on the resort's cabins.)

If you're exploring the desertlike areas in the vicinity of Osoyoos, check out **Haynes Point Campground**. Flush and pit toilets are the only amenities, but the 41 sites are located on a spit reaching into Osoyoos Lake, so half the sites have direct access to the beach. The lake is warm and suitable for swimming in the summer. A summer interpretive program offers insight on the area's ecology and wildlife. Nearby, **Vaseux Lake Campground** is a small (12 sites) provincial campground situated on shallow Vaseux Lake. The lake is excellent for paddling, fishing, and bird-watching. For information on both these campgrounds, contact BC Parks, Box 399, Summerland, BC V0H 1Z0, 250/494-6500.

In the Kootenay region, **Kokanee Creek** is an excellent provincial campground located 19 kilometers (11.5 miles) east of Nelson on Highway 3. The campground, set on the shore of Kootenay Lake, offering water-based activities such as swimming, boating, and fishing, and includes 132 private and wooded campsites for RVs, tents, and trailers. For information contact BC Parks, RR 3, Site 8, Comp 5,

Nelson, BC V1L 5P6, 250/825-3500. The West Kootenay Visitor Centre, offering useful information and interesting interpretive programs, is close by. **Rossland Lions Park**, 932 Black Bear Dr., Rossland, 250/362-5043, is a private campground with 18 sites featuring full hookups, flush toilets, showers, a sani-station, firewood, and more. It's located two blocks from the center of Rossland.

LODGING

The Okanagan region has long been a summer holiday destination for Canadians, so there is a wide range of accommodation styles and prices. The Kootenay region is more sparsely populated and the range of accommodations is more limited. In both areas it's wise to phone ahead for reservations, especially during the busy summer months.

Cathedral Lakes Lodge, RR 1, Cawston, BC V0X 1C0, 888/255-4453 or 250/226-7560, www.cathedral-lakes-lodge.com, is a fully equipped lodge with chalet and cabins. Located on Quiniscoe Lake within the boundaries of Cathedral Provincial Park, it is capable of accommodating 40 people and is open May through October. Rates, from $115 to $190, include a 16-kilometer (10-mile) jeep ride from the lodge's parking lot to the lodge itself, as well as all meals. Living quarters are a bit rustic (shared bathrooms), but the welcome is friendly and the meals are hearty.

If you're exploring the unusual landforms and wildlife of the Similkameen and southern Okanagan, check out the **Login Bed-and-Breakfast**, C1 Site 27, Hwy. 3, RR 1, Keremeos, BC V0X 1N0, 250/499-2781, e-mail loginbnb@keremeos.com. They welcome both people and their horses. The scenery here is absolutely breathtaking, and the bighorn sheep . . . well, you'll see. Another way to avoid the busy hotels of Osoyoos is by staying at one of the three guest rooms at the **Haynes Point Lakeside Guest House**, 3619 Jasmine Dr., Osoyoos, 250/495-7443. The owners are familiar with the area and have put together guides to both the local birds and nearby wineries (at least 10 wineries are within a half-hour drive).

There are several hotels and resorts along the Kettle Valley Railway bike route. The **Beaverdell Hotel**, c/o Box 40, Beaverdell, BC V0H 1A0, 250/484-5513, built in 1901, is, shall we say, funky. British

Vineyard in the south of Okanagan

Columbia's oldest continuously operated hotel and pub, it's located in the town of Beaverdell, on Highway 33. The hotel's double bunk beds (equipped with cozy down duvets), shared bathrooms, and pub-style food come at a dirt-cheap rate ($30 to $35 per night), but with only four rooms, reservations are a must. **Chute Lake Resort**, Site 16, Comp 16, RR 1, Naramata, BC V0H 1N0, 250/493-3535, has six cabins with kitchen facilities and wood stoves, as well as another eight rooms in the lodge. Bedding costs extra, but you're welcome to use your sleeping bag. Guests may eat their meals in the lodge's intimate dining room, which is furnished with a jukebox and lots of KVR memorabilia. **McCullough Lake Resort and Campground**, Site 13C, Apt. 8, RR 5, Kelowna, BC V1X 4K4, 250/491-8804 or 205/862-7834, offers rustic cabins overlooking Hydraulic Lake. The cabins come with kitchens and wood stoves, but linens are not supplied.

Travelers wandering the Kootenay region should try the **Ram's Head Inn**, Red Mountain Rd., Rossland, 250/362-9577, a cozy bed-and-breakfast lodge with ski-to-your-door convenience at the foot of

Red Mountain. Thanks to the fact that it has only 14 rooms, the inn is quite intimate and offers exceptional service. Big breakfasts include selections like lemon poppy-seed pancakes, fresh fruit, and yogurt. If you visit in summer the staff will tell you where to go for the best mountain biking.

In Nelson, the **Dancing Bear Inn Hostel**, 171 Baker St., Nelson, 250/352-7573, is a bit unusual but comes at an unbeatable price. The inn is more like a bed-and-breakfast than a traditional sweep-the-floors-before-you-leave kind of hostel. The rooms are small but the beds have down duvets, and there's a comfy common room with a fireplace and library. Rates start at $17 for Hostelling International members.

FOOD

In the Similkameen region, the **Grist Mill Tea Room**, RR 1, Upper Bench Rd., Keremeos, 250/499-2888, is a heritage site with a restored mill. The working flour mill features a 3.5-meter (12-foot) waterwheel and costumed interpreters performing milling activities just as they would have in 1877 when the mill was built. The tea room serves baked goods and other items made from flour and organically grown veggies. An admission fee is charged for access to the mill and grounds, including the tea room.

If you're skiing in the Okanagan, don't miss the **Gunbarrel Saloon**, 800/387-2739, at Apex Alpine ski resort, 32 kilometers (19 miles) southwest of Penticton on Green Mountain Road. The moderately priced full-service restaurant and bar is located in the resort's on-hill "village." The menu—ranging from lamb with poppy-seed crust to seared yellowfin tuna to a selection of splendid desserts—is surprising and eclectic. Also near Penticton, in the town of Naramata, is the **Country Squire**, 3950 First St., Naramata, 250/496-5416. The restaurant takes a unique approach to service: You choose from several entrées when you make your dinner reservation, then, when you get there, the host presents you with a card outlining the courses you'll be served. The food and wine is excellent, and everything comes at a flat rate of $39.50 per person.

In the town of Rossland, **Gold Rush Books and Espresso**, 2063 Washington St., 250/362-5333, and **Elmers Corner Cafe**, Second Ave.

and Washington St., 250/362-5266, are both casual-dining spots. They're so casual, in fact, that you can drop in immediately after a mountain-bike ride and nobody will even notice. The Gold Rush, open every day, serves fancy coffee and tea, baked goods, soups, and sandwiches. Elmers caters to lunch and dinner crowds until nine in the evening every day but Tuesday. Check out their Thursday pasta special, a steal at less than $10.

The accommodations at **Ainsworth Hot Springs Resort**, 800/668-1171, may be spartan (the pool's the attraction, not the concrete-block hotel), but the hotel's dining room is worth a stop, especially for dinner. The menu features European-style cuisine with several delicious pastas, a good wine list, and scrumptious desserts. The restaurant is open daily.

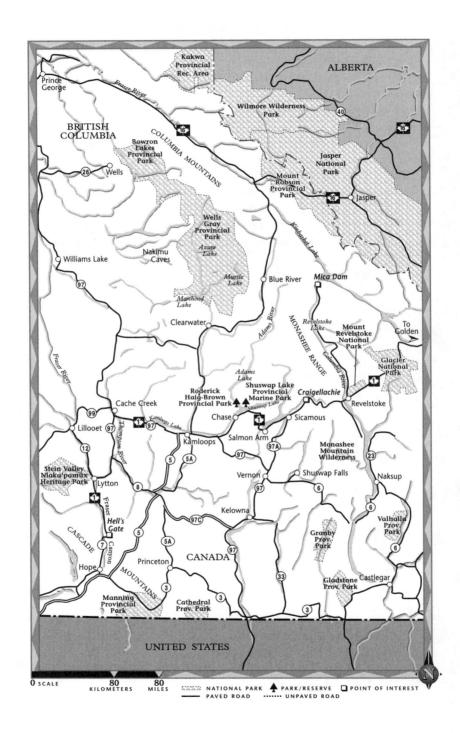

ALBERTA

BRITISH
COLUMBIA

Kakwa
Provincial
Rec. Area

Wilmore Wilderness
Park

Prince
George

Fraser River

COLUMBIA MOUNTAINS

Bowron
Lakes
Provincial
Park

Jasper
National
Park

Mount
Robson
Provincial
Park

Jasper

Wells

Williams Lake

Wells
Gray
Provincial
Park

*Azure
Lake*

Nakimu
Caves

*Murtle
Lake*

Blue River

Mica Dam

Kinbasket Lake

*Manhood
Lake*

Clearwater

Adams River

*Revelstoke
Lake*

MONASHEE RANGE

Mount
Revelstoke
National
Park

To
Golden

Glacier
National
Park

Columbia River

*Adams
Lake*

Roderick
Haig-Brown
Provincial Park

Shuswap Lake
Provincial
Marine Park

Craigellachie

Cache Creek

Thompson River

Kamloops Lake

Chase

Shuswap Lake

Sicamous

Revelstoke

Lillooet

Fraser River

Kamloops

Salmon Arm

Monashee
Mountain
Wilderness

Stein Valley
Nlaka'pamux
Heritage Park

Lytton

Vernon

Shuswap Falls

Naksup

Hell's
Gate

Kelowna

CASCADE

Fraser River

Canyon

Hope

MOUNTAINS

Princeton

CANADA

Granby
Prov.
Park

Valhalla
Prov.
Park

Gladstone
Prov. Park

Castlegar

Manning
Provincial
Park

Cathedral
Prov. Park

UNITED STATES

N

0 SCALE   80   80
      KILOMETERS MILES   ▨▨▨ NATIONAL PARK ▲ PARK/RESERVE ☐ POINT OF INTEREST
                           ──── PAVED ROAD   ······ UNPAVED ROAD

CHAPTER 8

High Country

British Columbia's High Country is a crescent-shaped slice of lofty peaks encompassing portions of the Coast and Cascade Mountains, the dry Interior Plateau, and the Columbia Mountains. The area is home to two national parks: Mount Revelstoke and Glacier. It also accommodates the Stein Valley Nlaka'pamux Heritage Park and two exceptional provincial parks, Wells Gray and Roderick Haig-Brown. Its hiking and skiing opportunities are phenomenal, and its wildlife, even along its well-traveled highways, is abundant. But perhaps just as important as the corridor's natural splendor is its historical significance: It's home to the Canadian Pacific Railway, which, when completed in 1880s, connected British Columbia with the rest of Canada to the east.

LAY OF THE LAND

The Coast Mountains form the western boundary of this large region. The Fraser Canyon separates the Coast Mountains from the Cascade Mountains to the east. Still farther east is the high and rolling Interior Plateau, followed by the Columbia Mountains, which include the rounded Monashees and the steep-sided and towering Selkirks. Major rivers are the Fraser and Stein in the west; the Thompson system in the interior; and the Columbia in the east. The Fraser River rises in the Rockies near Mount Robson, then flows west across the province before turning south. Many lakes and reservoirs are found in the area: Kamloops, Murtle, Adams, Shuswap, Revelstoke, and Kinbasket Lakes are a few of the largest.

The region's abundant mountain ranges and water systems make for a similarly remarkable climate. As moisture-laden storms move eastward from the Pacific, they must first climb over the Coast and Cascade Mountains. By the time the storms clear the high peaks and drop down to the Interior Plateau, much of their moisture has been spent. East of the plateau, however, storms must again gain altitude to jump the Columbia Mountains, again dumping loads of rain and snow. The Columbia Mountains in turn cast a rain shadow over the Rocky Mountain Trench, which remains relatively dry.

HISTORY AND CULTURE

Fraser Canyon and the land around it are the homeland of the Nlaka'-pamux (ng-kla-KAP-muh) peoples. Secwepemc (SHE-wep-m) peoples lived along the Thompson River, in the Kamloops area and as far east as the Rocky Mountains, where their territory overlapped that of the Ktunaxa and Kinbasket. The oldest archaeological sites show evidence of human habitation for 7,500 years.

Life must have been difficult for the first inhabitants of this harsh, rugged land. They were largely nomadic during summers, following game through the mountain valleys and traversing high passes to trade or battle with neighboring tribes and clans. In winter they settled in large villages to share preserved meat, tell stories, and make tools and clothing. For those whose territories included the salmon rivers (the Fraser, Thompson, and Adams), protein needs were met by the rich salmon runs. Other aboriginals of the interior hunted moose, deer, elk, and bear, and harvested edible and medicinal plants from the forests.

The interior peoples' first contact with Europeans came by way of the eastern fur trade. The Hudson's Bay Company and its rival, the North West Company, firmly established in the east and across the prairies, sent scouts and explorers into the mountains to claim territory and determine the abundance of fur-bearing animals. In time the

SNOW WARS

As you drive the Trans-Canada Highway through Rogers Pass, you may wonder about those odd concrete installations on the roadside that look like huge toadstools. They're gun platforms. The world's most extensive avalanche-control operation takes place here every winter when the Canadian armed forces fire missiles into the mountains to trigger avalanches. They close the highway, fire away, then clear the resulting avalanches from the roadway.

interior was further populated by ranchers, missionaries, and miners. Eventually—especially when the gold rush swept up the Fraser and on to the northern rivers—the smallpox and influenza these settlers brought with them devastated the Native population.

In 1871 the British Crown Colony of British Columbia agreed to become a province of Canada if the Canadian government built a railway north of the Great Lakes, across the plains and through the mountains to the Pacific. Early surveys indicated that the most favorable route for the railway was through Jasper and the relatively low Yellowhead Pass, but the Canadian government had an ulterior motive: Building a railway close to the 49th parallel would establish a firm and undeniable Canadian presence and would thwart any attempts at expansion by the United States. With nation-building a top priority, a southern route had to be found.

Imposing Kicking Horse Pass was chosen as the railway's route through the Rocky Mountains, and the equally impossible Fraser Canyon was picked as the gateway from the interior to the Pacific. But even with the east and west ends building toward one another, there was still no known route through the awesome Selkirk Mountains. Major A. B. Rogers finally found a promising pass, and, in November 1885, the Canadian Pacific Railway was completed when the last spike was driven at Craigellachie west of Revelstoke.

BRITISH COLUMBIA

Today logging is the major industrial pursuit in High Country. The Interior Plateau is ranch country, and irrigation makes farming possible in the Thompson Valley around Kamloops. Hydroelectric developments on the Columbia River have created two enormous reservoirs in the High Country and deliver power to much of the province. Tourism is on the rise, too. Scenery, outdoor activities, and abundant wildlife draw visitors from around the world.

FLORA AND FAUNA

Wildlife is abundant throughout the region. Deer, moose, elk, bighorn sheep, mountain goats, coyotes, and black bears are common. Grizzly bears, wolves, and cougars are less common, but can be found in the backcountry. Bird life in the region is not as concentrated as in coastal areas, but there are plenty of good birding spots.

Thanks to the rain shadow cast by the Coast and Cascade Mountains, the Interior Plateau's vegetation resembles that of a desert—sagebrush and bunchgrass, scrubby willows along riverbanks, ponderosa pines in sheltered draws and on north-facing slopes. Farther east, the Selkirk Mountains create a significant wet belt that supports the province's highest concentration and greatest selection of plant species. Cedars and Douglas firs, smaller and younger than their relatives on the coast, loom over the Selkirk's valleys and fast-flowing streams.

VISITOR INFORMATION

Principal towns and cities are (from west to east) Hope, Cache Creek, Kamloops, Salmon Arm, and Revelstoke, all of which are on the Trans-Canada Highway (Highway 1), the region's primary transportation artery. From Hope, the Coquihalla Highway (Highway 5) leads to Kamloops via the town of Merritt. North of Kamloops, Highway 5 continues to Clearwater and Blue River (both towns provide access to Wells Gray Provincial Park) before joining the Yellowhead Highway (Highway 16), which runs east to Mount Robson Provincial Park and the town of Jasper in Alberta. From Cache Creek, Highway 97 leads northwest into the Cariboo-Chilcotin region (see Chapter 10). From

Salmon Arm, a town on Shuswap Lake, Highway 97B leads south into the Okanagan (see Chapter 7).

Passenger buses connect all major towns, and two railways serve the region. The area's only major airport is in Kamloops. (See Appendix A for transportation information.) Regular passenger-train service, operated by VIA Rail, connects Jasper (and points to the east including Edmonton, Winnipeg, Toronto, and Montreal) to Tete Jaune Cache, then continues south along the North Thompson River to Kamloops, west to Cache Creek, and south again through the Fraser Canyon before eventually emerging from the mountains at Hope and continuing to Vancouver. A more spectacular (and historic) route begins in Banff, crosses the Rocky Mountains, then follows the Kicking Horse River and climbs to Rogers Pass before dropping down to Kamloops and continuing to Vancouver via Fraser Canyon. For more information about High Country, contact High Country Tourism, #2, 1490 Pearson Place, Kamloops, BC V1S 1J9, 800/567-2275 or 250/372-7770.

NATURE AND ADVENTURE SIGHTS

Fraser Canyon

Among Canada's most scenic drives is the stretch between Hope and Cache Creek, a distance of 193 kilometers (116 miles). The Trans-Canada Highway twists and turns, dives through tunnels, and flies, via lofty bridges, over the boiling, silt-heavy Fraser River. There are few places to safely pull off the busy two-lane road and admire the view. The best place to stop is at **Hell's Gate**, from which it's possible to take a three-minute tram ride over the river.

At **Lytton** the Fraser continues north while the highway (and both railroads) follows the Thompson River east. At the confluence of the green Thompson and the gray Fraser, clear and muddy waters move down the channel side-by-side for nearly a kilometer before they mix. Lytton, among Canada's hottest, driest places, is also gateway to the Stein Valley, the site of a 1980s ecological battle that pitted aboriginals and environmentalists against loggers. The valley eventually won protection as the **Stein Valley Nlaka'pamux Heritage Park** in 1995.

Today the park is managed by both BC Parks and the Nlaka'pamux First Nation, and is a great place for hiking. One short and pleasant trail leads to the Stein River, a perfect spot to enjoy a picnic and see aboriginal pictographs. More adventurous (and experienced) hikers can tackle the 75-kilometer (45-mile) **Stein Heritage Trail**, which leads to the Stein's headwaters and takes about nine days to complete. To reach the park from Lytton, take Highway 12 north for two kilometers (about one mile) to the self-operating reaction ferry that crosses the Fraser River (the ferry can carry two vehicles and is activated by the river's current; no service during high water). After you cross the river, continue four and one-half kilometers (three miles) to a parking lot and trailhead. There may be a nominal admission fee.

Details: *The Trans-Canada Highway enters the Fraser Canyon just north of Hope. Hell's Gate is 54 kilometers (32.5 miles) north of Hope. The tram operates daily April through October; call 604/867-9277 for details. Lytton is 111.5 kilometers (67 miles) north of Hope. For Stein Valley Nlaka'pamux Heritage Park, contact the Nlaka'pamux tribal office, 250/455-2304, or BC Parks, Thompson River District, 1210 McGill Rd., Kamloops, 250/851-3000.*

Glacier National Park

Glacier National Park protects 136,500 hectares (337,000 acres) of interior rain forest and more than 400 glaciers and ice fields. The mountains are very similar in appearance to Hawaiian volcanoes, with near-vertical slopes and lush, mixed-wood forests. Alpine wildflower meadows host grizzly bears, mountain goats, and marmot, while the wooded slopes hide caribou and black bears.

For a terrific introduction to the park and its ecology, visit the **Glacier National Park Information Centre**, where interactive displays explain rail construction and the ongoing "snow wars" (see sidebar on page 185). When you're ready to stretch your legs, hike the easy 1.2-kilometer **Abandoned Rails Trail** to the 1,382-meter summit of Rogers Pass. A significantly more ambitious day hike with astonishing views of Rogers Pass is the **Avalanche Crest Trail**, which gains 795 meters over its four-kilometer length.

Among the park's most unusual attractions are the **Nakimu Caves**. Charles Deutschmann was out looking for gold in the Selkirk Range, high above the Canadian Pacific Railway, when he "discovered" a network of underground chasms and chambers known to the Secwepemc as Nakimu, or "grumbling spirit." The caves form as water dissolves limestone layers deep within the harder, erosion-resistant volcanic rock. The mineral-laden water evaporates slowly, gradually depositing calcium carbonate in fantastic and unusual forms. The sound of water—rushing, falling, dripping—is constant everywhere inside the caves. Nearly six kilometers (three and three-quarter miles) of the caves' system has been explored, to a depth of 269 meters (887 feet) below the cave mouth. Public entry to the caves is now permitted through lottery only, and winners must go with a guide. For an application, contact Glacier National Park, Backcountry Manager, Box 350, Revelstoke, BC V0E 2S0, 250/837-7500.

Details: The park is located on the Trans-Canada Highway, 49 kilometers (29 miles) east of Revelstoke. The park information center, 250/837-6274, is located at Rogers Pass on the west side of the highway, adjacent to Glacier Lodge. Park entry $4 per adult. Campgrounds $13 per vehicle per night; backcountry sites $6 per person per night; backcountry huts $10 to $20 per night. Contact Glacier National Park, Box 350, Revelstoke, BC V0E 2S0, 250/837-7500.

K. D. Wong/Blackbird Design

Trans-Canada Highway from Avalanche Crest, Glacier National Park

Kamloops

There's not much to recommend the city of Kamloops (the name is derived from a Secwepemc word meaning "where the rivers meet") except that it's a major transportation crossroads, and you can hardly avoid the place. Kamloops is BC's fifth-largest city by population (77,000) and its largest in terms of area (31,000 hectares or 76,600 acres). Smack in the middle of the southern interior, Kamloops makes a good stopover if you're headed from Vancouver to the Rockies or to the north via Wells Gray Provincial Park.

While you're in the neighborhood, check out **Secwepemc Heritage Park and Museum** for a glimpse of Secwepemc culture. The park, on Secwepemc lands, includes an archaeological dig site at an ancient winter village. Visitors to the park can also enjoy aboriginal songs, dances, and storytelling, plus salmon barbecues, crafts demonstrations, and, each August, a major powwow.

Details: Kamloops is on the Trans-Canada Highway, 80 kilometers (48 miles) east of Cache Creek. Secwepemc Heritage Park, 250/828-9801, is on the banks of the South Thompson River at 355 Yellowhead Highway. Open June through September daily; weekdays only the rest of the year. Adults $6, children and seniors $4.

Mount Revelstoke National Park

The park protects more than 26,000 hectares (64,000 acres) of wilderness in the Monashee Mountains, including the 1,830-meter (6,039-foot) summit of Mount Revelstoke, which can be reached via the Summit Parkway. The alpine mountaintop is cloaked with wildflowers all summer long. Other highlights of the park are the Giant Cedars Trail, which follows boardwalks and pathways amid a grove of 800-year-old red cedars; and the Skunk Cabbage Trail, which enters a marshy area adjacent to the Illecillewaet (il-a-SILL-a-wut) River for a view of wildflowers, birds, and wetland life. Both trails are short and relatively easy to walk.

Among the park's more challenging hiking trails are Standard Basin, a 21-kilometer (13-mile) round trip through alpine meadows; and Martha Creek, a challenging nine-kilometer (six-mile) trek through forests and meadows. There are no serviced campgrounds within the park, but there is backcountry camping at several locations.

Details: Park entry $4 per adult. Backcountry camping $10 per person for a cabin; $6 per person for tent sites. Due to avalanche danger, registration for backcountry ski touring is mandatory from November to April. For more information contact Box 350, Revelstoke, BC V0E 2S0, 250/837-7500.

Revelstoke

Located at the foot of the Selkirk Range, Revelstoke serves as a base camp for fantastic backcountry adventure. The hiking is great and the paddling on nearby Revelstoke Lake or the Columbia River is sublime, but at heart this is a ski town. The area receives an average of more than 1,600 centimeters (630 inches) of snowfall annually. Further charm comes in the form of Victorian-era buildings, tall trees, and a pedestrian-friendly village square. Check out the **Revelstoke Railway Museum**, 719 Track St. W., 250/837-6060, for all the intriguing details about the Canadian Pacific Railway.

Details: Contact the Revelstoke Visitor Infocentre, Box 490, Revelstoke, BC V0E 2S0, 250/837-5345 or 250/837-3522, e-mail cocrev@junction.net.

Mount Revelstoke National Park

Roderick Haig-Brown Provincial Park

This small park (less than 1,000 hectares/2,500 acres) has a dispro-portionate impact on the province's salmon population. The park encompasses the Adams River, among the world's most productive salmon streams. Each year, sockeye and other salmon species swim upriver from the Pacific, a journey of 485 kilometers (290 miles) that takes about three weeks. Once the exhausted salmon arrive in the Adams River they spawn, die, and are eaten by eagles and bears. Major runs occur every four years; the next big run is expected in 2002. The park maintains several observation areas, and naturalist programs are offered during the October salmon runs.

Details: Nine kilometers east of Chase on the Trans-Canada Highway. Turn left (north) and cross the Squilax Bridge over the Little River, then drive another five kilometers. For information, call 250/851-3000.

Shuswap Lake

This oddly shaped lake has more than 1,000 kilometers (600 miles) of shoreline. The Trans-Canada Highway passes along the lake's busy south shore, lined with water slides, golf courses, fruit stands, farms, marinas, hotels, and shopping malls. But the beauty of Shuswap Lake is its relatively unpopulated north shore, and its long reach into remote portions of the Monashee Mountain wilderness.

The best way to access the north shore is by houseboat. The town of Sicamous (SIC-a-moos) calls itself "the Houseboat Capital of Canada." Several outfitters rent these buoyant holiday trailers by the day or week. Throw your groceries in the cooler, slap on the sunscreen, take a quick operations course from the outfitter, and you're bound for the high seas—or at least for the other side of the lake. You can land at one of the many beaches within **Shuswap Lake Provincial Marine Park**.

Details: Sicamous is on the Trans-Canada Highway, 137 kilometers (82 miles) east of Kamloops. The Visitor Infocentre, Box 346, Sicamous, BC V0E 2V0, 250/836-3313, maintains a directory of houseboat outfitters.

Wells Gray Provincial Park

Encompassing more than half a million hectares (1.3 million acres), Wells Gray Provincial Park is a BC gem. The attractions within the

Columbia River

park—including peaks, glaciers, remote lakes, stunning waterfalls, wildlife, flowers, extinct volcanoes, lava flows, mineral springs, and more—would occupy an explorer for a lifetime.

There are four drive-in campgrounds within the park, 25 wilderness camping areas, a renowned backcountry lodge, and a guest ranch. Trails, for hiking or ski touring, range from short nature jaunts to extended backcountry trips. Opportunities for paddling and fishing abound. **Murtle Lake** is North America's largest "paddlers-only" lake (no motorized boats).

The park's **Helmcken Falls**, at 137 meters (452 feet), is among Canada's tallest waterfalls. Its source, the Murtle River, plunges over a rock lip and straight into a waiting cauldron below. From the parking lot it's just a short stroll to a good view of the falls.

Details: Take Highway 5 north from Kamloops for 122 kilometers (73 miles) to the town of Clearwater, then drive 35 kilometers (21 miles) up a steep access road to Wells Gray Provincial Park. For park information contact BC Parks, Box 4516, RR 2, Clearwater, BC V0E 1N0, 250/587-6150.

To get to Murtle Lake, drive 105 kilometers (63 miles) northeast of Clear-

193

water on Highway 5, then drive west from Blue River on a 26-kilometer (15.5-mile) access road. When the road ends, portage your canoe and gear another two and one-half kilometers (one and one-half miles) to the lake. Purchase a canoe permit at the BC Parks office in the settlement of Blue River.

GUIDES AND OUTFITTERS

The most popular adventure activity in the Shuswap region is houseboating, and the destination of choice is the town of Sicamous. **Sun 'N' Fun Houseboat Vacations**, P.O. Box 68, Sicamous, BC V0E 2V0, 800/663-4028 or 250/836-2282 even rents houseboats with hot tubs on board. Another long-established houseboat outfitter is **Three Buoys Houseboat Vacations**, P.O. Box 709, Sicamous, BC V0E 2V0, 800/663-2333 or 250/836-2403. Rates can be as low as $99 per person in low season (early spring and late autumn).

For an exceptional bike tour, call **Summit Cycle Tours**, Box 2647, Revelstoke, BC V0E 2S0, 250/837-3734. They'll drive you to the top of Mount Revelstoke, take you exploring through the alpine wildflower meadows, then set you free for a smooth, 27-kilometer downhill.

For multi-activity and lodge-based adventures, **Golden Alpine Holidays**, P.O. Box 1050, Golden, BC V0A 1H0, 250/344-7273, offers hiking and ski touring between three alpine lodges in the Esplanade Range of the Selkirk Mountains north of Golden. In Wells Gray Provincial Park, **Wells Gray Backcountry Chalets**, Box 188B, Clearwater, BC V0E 1N0, 888/SKI-TREK or 250/587-6444, offers hut-to-hut hiking or ski touring between three rustic huts located within the park. Multi-day packages including hiking and canoeing. For something a little less rustic (downright luxurious in fact) try **Mike Wiegele Heli-Ski Resort**, Box 159, Blue River, BC V0E 1J0, 800/661-9170 or 250/673-8381, www.wiegele.com. In winter this is the place to be for world-famous heli-skiing (Mike pioneered the sport in the 1960s); in summer the company offers accommodations and activities ranging from heli-hiking to fly-in fly-fishing to trail riding. **Kumsheen Raft Adventures**, Box 30, Lytton, BC V0K 1Z0, 800/663-6667 or 250/455-2296, offers rafting trips on the Thompson and Fraser Rivers, as well as rappelling, rock climbing, mountain biking, horseback riding, and kayaking.

Helmcken Falls, Wells Gray Provincial Park

CAMPING

Drive-in campgrounds are scattered throughout the region. Summers are busy and reservations are advised. The Shuswap Lake area is especially well supplied with private campgrounds. For information, contact the High Country Tourism Association (see Appendix B).

Jade Springs Park, Box 449, Lytton, BC V0K 1Z0, 250/455-6662, has 40 sites and is open from March to November. Amenities include flush toilets, hot showers, a restaurant and store, and laundry facilities. Whitewater rafting is nearby. Fees range from $10 to $15 for two people; electricity costs extra. The **Kumsheen Rafting Centre**, Box 30, Lytton, BC V0K 1Z0, 800/663-6667 or 250/455-2296, has 50 sites and amenities such as hot showers, flush toilets, a coffee bar, and a hot tub. They also have hiking trails, rent mountain bikes, and lead whitewater-rafting trips. Fees are $20 per site for two people

Shuswap Lake Provincial Campground, 800/689-9025, has 271 sites suitable for tents and RVs. Facilities include flush toilets, hot

AUTHOR'S TOP PICKS: NORDIC SKIING

- **Garibaldi Park**—*A long ski season with abundant snow (over 20 meters/66 feet) and fabulous scenery, all just a short trip from Vancouver.*

- **Glacier National Park**—*Steep slopes and incredible snow accumulations make this a favorite spot for telemark skiing.*

- **Manning Park**—*A labyrinth of trails of varying length and difficulty within easy reach of Vancouver (you can even take the bus).*

- **Rocky Mountains**—*Top spots for wilderness touring are at Lake O'Hara and Mount Assiniboine. The only way to get to Lake O'Hara is on skis, but you can take a helicopter to Mount Assiniboine.*

- **Wells Gray**—*The Clearwater Valley area has 80 kilometers (50 miles) of tracked trails. Among these is a 14-kilometer (9-mile) trip to frozen Helmcken Falls.*

showers, and a sani-station. Due to its handy location at Squilax on Shuswap Lake, this campground is busy all summer; there is virtually never an empty spot. **Glen Echo Resort and Campground** in Salmon Arm, 250/832-6268, has 60 beachfront or wooded campsites, flush toilets, showers, a private beach on Shuswap Lake, a boat launch, and swimming. Fees range from $19 to $22. Nearby **Hidden Valley Campground and RV Park**, 250/832-6159, has 70 sites, laundry facilities, and showers. Fees range from $14 to $19.

There are three campgrounds in **Glacier National Park** (see "Nature and Adventure Sights"), including Mountain Creek (250 sites), Loop Brook (20 sites), and Illecillewaet (59 sites). Of these, Mountain Creek has flush toilets but no showers or sani-station. The other two have pit toilets. For more luxury, **Canyon Hot Springs**

Resort, Box 2400, Revelstoke, BC V0E 2S0, 250/837-2420, is a sumptuous private campground featuring hot pools, showers, laundry facilities, and a cafeteria. It's open from mid-May through September 30. Rates range from $18 to $25 per vehicle.

Wells Gray Provincial Park (see "Nature and Adventure Sights") has hundreds of backcountry campsites as well as three drive-in campgrounds accessible from the town of Clearwater off Highway 5: Dawson Falls (10 sites), Clearwater Lake (32 sites), and Falls Creek (41 sites).

LODGING

In Wells Gray Provincial Park, try **Helmcken Falls Lodge**, Wells Gray Park, P.O. Box 239, Clearwater, BC V0E 1N0, 250/674-3657, helmfall @mail.wellsgray.net, www.profiles.net/helmcken. The lodge, built in 1949, was recently upgraded and now has a wonderful dining room. Guests can enjoy hiking, canoeing, and horseback riding.

The rustic but comfortable **Durrand Glacier Chalet**, c/o Selkirk Mountain Experience, Box 2998, Revelstoke, BC V0E 2S0, 250/837-2381, located 40 kilometers (24 miles) northeast of Revelstoke, is a mountain lodge offering mountaineering, ski touring, telemark skiing, and more. In winter it's especially enticing, as the snowfall is so great that the ski season doesn't let up until July. In summer the hiking is outstanding. Access is via a short helicopter ride from Revelstoke.

For heli-hiking, high-alpine ski touring, immense meals, and all-inclusive packages, check out Canadian Mountain Holidays' lodges in the Purcells, including **Bugaboo Lodge** and **Bobbie Burns Lodge**. You can contact CMH at P.O. Box 1660, Banff, Alberta T0L 0C0, 800/661-0252. Packages include helicopter access to the lodges, three or four heli-drops per day (for hiking or skiing), guides, meals, accommodations, and clothing (parka, hiking boots, and backpacks). As is true with most inclusive packages, the rates are expensive: about $575 per person for two nights, or $1,690 per person for a week.

Purcell Lodge, ABC Wilderness Adventures, Box 1829, Golden, BC V0A 1H0, 250/344-2639, located on the eastern boundary of Glacier National Park, has no road access. Instead, guests must hike or fly in via helicopter from Golden. Despite its remote location, the lodge

AUTHOR'S TOP PICKS: WHITE-WATER RAFTING

- *Chilko and Chilcotin Rivers*—Many people think the Chilko River between Chilko Lake and Alexis Creek is among Canada's best paddle or raft trips. The Chilcotin is also good, and relatively bug-free due to the dry surroundings in the upper Fraser Canyon area.

- *Illecillewaet River*—Several outfitters in Revelstoke offer trips down this fast, cold, and absolutely gorgeous river.

- *Kicking Horse River*—This scenic trip near Golden is guaranteed to get your heart racing. Full-day and half-day trips are available from Golden and Lake Louise, Alberta.

- *Lower Mainland*—The Chilliwack and Fraser Rivers are popular adventure sites for kayakers and rafters seeking white water. Outfitters also run motorized rafts through Hell's Gate on the Fraser.

- *Thompson River*—Trips start from Spence's Bridge and include rapids with names such as Devil's Kitchen and Jaws of Death.

- *Whistler Area*—The Squamish, Green, and Elaho Rivers provide roller-coaster thrills.

includes amenities such as hot showers and flush toilets. Rates start at $130 per person per night in the winter and climb to as high as $215 per person per night during summer.

FOOD

In the Shuswap area, summers are prime time for fresh-picked fruits and veggies, available from several large roadside fruit stands. If you're camping, load up with fruit, veggies (even fresh corn), locally made cheese and dairy products, and fish.

Restaurants throughout High Country tend to be less than exciting, geared mostly to fast food for passing travelers, but there are a few exceptions. Kamloops is home to several neighborhood pubs, including **Duffy's Tavern** (1797 Pacific Way, 250/372-5453)—a local watering hole for students and young professionals that serves decent food, more than your average pub grub. **The Fox n Hounds** (20 Sahali Centre, 945 W. Columbia St., 250/374-9425) is a charming and comfortable place where you'll find burgers, soups, salads, and daily specials.

In Salmon Arm, check out the **Chocolate Bean** (250 Alexander St., 250/832-6681) for soups, sandwiches, muffins, cookies, and the cappuccino clan. Up the street, **Schwartzie's Bagel Noshery** (371 Alexander St., 250/804-0263) features a variety of enormous bagels and "schmears"—cream cheese and an assortment of other luscious toppings. Also in Salmon Arm—located right on the Trans-Canada Highway—is **Nutter's Bulk & Natural Foods** (Centenoka Park Mall, 250/833-0144), with plenty of locally produced fresh fruit and veggies in season, plus nuts, grains, preserves, and juices. Stock up for your camping trips.

Among the better bets in Revelstoke is **Alphaus** (600 Second St. W., 250/837-6380) for Bavarian-style lunches and dinners (schnitzel and sausages), plus a good hearty breakfast. Revelstoke is home to numerous cafés and delis; among them are **Blue Beary Patch Café** (212 Mackenzie Ave., 250/837-5500) and **Chalet Bakery & Deli** (555 Victoria Rd., 250/837-4556). Both are good choices for light lunches and fresh baked goods.

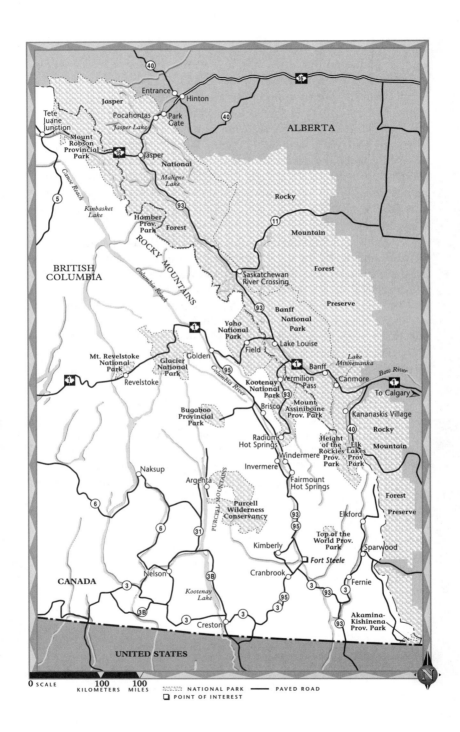

Entrance
Hinton
Jasper
Tete Juane Junction
Pocahontas
Park Gate
Jasper Lake
ALBERTA
Mount Robson Provincial Park
Jasper
National
Malighe Lake
Kinbasket Lake
Hamber Prov. Park
Forest
ROCKY MOUNTAINS
Rocky
BRITISH COLUMBIA
Columbia Reach
Canoe Reach
Mountain
Saskatchewan River Crossing
Forest
Banff
Yoho National Park
National
Preserve
Park
Mt. Revelstoke National Park
Golden
Field
Lake Louise
Glacier National Park
Banff
Lake Minnewanka
Revelstoke
Columbia River
Kootenay National Park
Vermilion Pass
Canmore
Bow River
To Calgary
Bugaboo Provincial Park
Brisco
Mount Assiniboine Prov. Park
Kananaskis Village
Rocky
Radium Hot Springs
Height of the Rockies Prov. Park
Elk Lakes Prov. Park
Mountain
Naksup
Invermere
Windermere
Argenta
Fairmount Hot Springs
PURCELL MOUNTAINS
Forest
Purcell Wilderness Conservancy
Preserve
Elkford
Top of the World Prov. Park
Sparwood
Kimberly
Nelson
Fort Steele
Cranbrook
Fernie
CANADA
Kootenay Lake
Akamina-Kishinena Prov. Park
Creston
UNITED STATES

0 SCALE   100 KILOMETERS   100 MILES   ░░░ NATIONAL PARK   —— PAVED ROAD
▢ POINT OF INTEREST

N

CHAPTER 9

Rocky Mountains

The Rocky Mountains are a high, nearly impenetrable wall of rock running from the Canada/U.S. border north, angling from southeast to northwest and forming the spine of the North American continent. The range is also home to exceptional scenery, wildlife, and Canada's four most popular national parks: Yoho, Kootenay, Jasper, and Banff (the latter two are in Alberta; the four combined are a UNESCO World Heritage Site). Famous as an ecotravel and adventure destination, with everything from hiking and skiing to camping, fishing, and whitewater rafting, the Rockies are truly spectacular. The one drawback? People. Lots of people. But don't let the threat of crowded trails keep you away. The Rocky Mountains are huge—you can always find some quiet corner to get away from it all.

LAY OF THE LAND

Geologically speaking, the Rocky Mountains are young—it's taken a mere 750 million years for them to attain their present form. The Canadian Rockies lie in successive, roughly parallel ranges and are almost entirely composed of sedimentary rock—sandstone, limestone, and shale—formed from the slow deposit of materials at the bottoms of ancient lakes and seas. As eastward-moving crustal plates crashed into the westward-moving North American plate, these formerly flat-lying marine sediments were pushed and crowded together, lifting, folding, breaking, and thrusting up to form the Rockies. Subsequent glaciation has also left its mark in U-shaped valleys, sharp ridges, hanging valleys, and cirques that even today harbor glaciers, ice fields, and snow that never melts.

Between the Columbia Mountains and Rocky Mountains lies the remarkable Rocky Mountain Trench, a wide, flat-bottomed valley. The Columbia River rises from Columbia Lake, flows north up the Trench, makes a hairpin turn around the northern end of the Selkirk Mountains, then flows south again. That portion of the trench occupied by the Columbia River is called the Columbia Valley.

The Rocky Mountains are the backbone of North America. Some of Canada's highest peaks are in the Rockies, including Mount Robson, a massive pyramid reaching more than 3,900 meters (13,000 feet) into the air. The range is home to enormous glaciers; roaring waterfalls; short, fast rivers; and lakes exhibiting a peculiar blue-green color, the result of suspended rock particles in the water. British Columbia's longest river, the Fraser, rises in the Rocky Mountains near Mount Robson and flows westward, turning south at a point near the geographic center of the province then west again at Hope for its final plunge toward the sea.

The Rockies tend to be wetter on their west side than on their east, as Pacific weather systems lose most of their moisture before they can clear the massive ridge. Generally speaking, the range's summers are warm and dry, although subject to thunderstorms, and its winters are intensely cold with moderate snowfall.

HISTORY AND CULTURE

Original inhabitants of the western Rocky Mountains included the Ktunaxa and Kinbasket in the south, the Secwepemc in the lower north, and the Dakelh in the far north. Aboriginal peoples who lived on the east side of the Rockies crossed to the west side of the range to hunt, trade, or raid their enemies. The Ktunaxa often migrated east over the high passes to hunt bison on the plains.

The first Europeans in the region came from the east with the fur trade. Among the original traders to extensively explore the range was David Thompson, an employee with the North West Company who mapped the area and established several trading posts in the early 1800s. Later, between 1857 and 1859, an expedition led by John Palliser explored much of the southern Rockies on behalf of the British government. In the process, Palliser and his men gave English names to many of the region's peaks and lakes.

Westward-moving construction of the Canadian Pacific Railway finally reached the Rockies in 1883, opening the range to exploitation for logging, mining, and, of course, tourism. The CPR's general manager, W. Cornelius Van Horne, was determined to bring visitors from around the world to witness the magnificent Rocky Mountain scenery. To encourage tourism, the CPR built a string of luxury hotels in the mountains and hired Swiss guides to safely conduct mountaineering expeditions. The CPR also played a vital role in the establishment of Canada's first national park, Banff, in 1885.

The railway had its troubles, though. The descent from Kicking Horse Pass at the top of the Continental Divide to the town of Field, a stretch of terrifyingly steep rail known as the Big Hill, catapulted many a locomotive off the rails and into oblivion. The railway solved the problem by building the remarkable Spiral Tunnels, which corkscrew their way through Cathedral Mountain and Mount Ogden to reduce the murderous grade to a manageable slope. Still, the track requires an engineer's care and attention to navigate safely.

Today tourism continues to be the area's leading economic force. Other major industries are logging and coal mining in the southeastern areas of BC, especially in the Elk Valley.

FLORA AND FAUNA

The Rockies are *the* place to see wildlife in BC. Wild critters are everywhere—deer, moose, elk, bighorn sheep, mountain goats, and caribou; coyotes, wolves, wolverines, black bears, grizzly bears, cougars; squirrels, marmot, and pika. The variety of bird life found in the Rockies is not as extensive as that in coastal areas of BC, but there are still plenty of songbirds, eagles, ducks, and wading birds, especially in the Columbia

Bighorn sheep ram

Valley between Radium and Golden, where the river meanders through low-lying marshes.

The forests of the Rocky Mountains are not lush, but what they lack in productivity they make up for in area. The mountain slopes are carpeted with lodgepole pine, white and Engelmann spruce, and subalpine fir. Alpine larch grows in high alpine areas and is Canada's only deciduous conifer; in September, larch needles turn a brilliant gold—a stunning sight against a backdrop of blue sky and early snow. The range is also renowned for its wildflowers, especially in open meadows above tree line and along tumbling mountain streams.

VISITOR INFORMATION

The Trans-Canada Highway (Highway 1) roughly parallels the CPR mainline from east to west and serves the region's largest settlement, Golden. The tiny town of Field, also on Highway 1, is located within Yoho National Park just west of the Continental Divide. From the city of Golden, Highway 93/95 leads south through the Columbia Valley, providing access to numerous provincial parks and Kootenay National Park, at Radium Hot Springs. Farther south, the highway joins the Crowsnest Highway (Highway 3). Highway 3 loops eastward up the Elk Valley past the town of Fernie then continues over Crowsnest Pass into Alberta. Highway 3 also extends westward into the Kootenay region (see Chapter 7). The Yellowhead Highway (Highway 16) traverses Yellowhead Pass west of Jasper, Alberta, and passes through Mount Robson Provincial Park before continuing westward to Prince George and Prince Rupert (see Chapter 11).

All major destinations within the Rockies, including the Columbia and Elk Valleys, are connected by passenger-bus service. There is small airstrip at Golden. There is no regular passenger-rail service in the southern Rocky Mountain region, but the excursion train Rocky Mountaineer passes through twice weekly as it connects Vancouver, Kamloops, Banff, and Calgary. Regular passenger-rail service is operated by VIA Rail, which offers connections to Vancouver, Kamloops, and Jasper. See Appendix A for contact information.

For more visitor information contact BC Rockies Tourism, P.O. Box 10, Kimberley, BC V1A 2Y5, 250/427-4838, www.travel.bc.ca /region/rockies.

NATURE AND ADVENTURE SIGHTS: COLUMBIA VALLEY

Bugaboo Provincial Park

The solid granite spires of the Bugaboo Range of the Purcell Mountains literally stand on end. Thanks to incredible tectonic forces, once flat-lying rock strata now rise perpendicular to the sky. The peaks provide challenging mountaineering for expert climbers, and spectacular scenery for hikers and backcountry skiers. The park's access road passes through the **Columbia Wildlife Area**, a great place for birding.

Details: From Golden, take Highway 95 south 132 kilometers (79 miles) to Brisco. Turn west on Brisco Road and continue for one and one-half kilometers (one mile) to the Columbia Wildlife Area and 48 kilometers (29 miles) to Bugaboo Provincial Park. Beware of logging trucks on the narrow access road. The park has walk-in camping. For information call 250/422-4200.

Golden

If you don't mind rubbing shoulders with the local loggers, this small city at the confluence of the Kicking Horse and Columbia Rivers is a great place to begin a rafting expedition. Several whitewater-rafting outfitters offer trips on the Kicking Horse, a fast and narrow flume of water that's milky green with glacial silt. The river cuts through two canyons—the lower canyon lies just east of Golden; the upper is farther east in Yoho National Park.

Details: Golden is located on the Trans-Canada Highway, 61.5 kilometers (37 miles) east of Glacier National Park. For information, contact Box 1320, Golden, BC V0A 1H0, 250/344-7215.

Purcell Wilderness Conservancy

This is not, strictly speaking, a Rocky Mountain destination (it lies in the Purcell Range of the Columbia Mountains), but you can access the Purcell Wilderness Conservancy from the Columbia Valley. The 199,000-plus-hectare (491,000-plus-acre) conservation area has no motorized access—visitors must come and go on foot. The only development in the area of any kind is the 61-kilometer (37-mile) **Earl Grey Pass Trail**, a fabulous three-day wilderness route that starts from the town of Invermere in the Columbia Valley and traverses the Purcell Mountains to the town of Argenta in the Kootenay region north of Nelson (see Chapter 7). The trail is rugged, to say the least, and includes several creek crossings by cable car.

Details: From Golden, take Highway 93/95 south 121 kilometers (73 miles) to the Invermere access road. Turn west and drive four kilometers (two and one-half miles) to the town of Invermere. From Invermere, take the Toby Creek logging road west for 32 kilometers (12 miles) to the trailhead for the Earl Gray Pass Trail. Keep an eye out for logging and ore trucks. For more information contact BC Parks, Box 118, Wasa, BC V0B 2K0, 250/422-3212.

Radium Hot Springs

These alpine springs, named for the naturally high (but still safe) level of radioactivity found in the water, include two pools. One is hot, at 39 degrees Celsius (102 degrees Fahrenheit); the other is warm, at 29 degrees Celsius (84 degrees Fahrenheit). The hot pool is especially nice in winter when clouds of steam rise to the sky and snowflakes hiss and melt into the water. The pools are just inside the west entrance of **Kootenay National Park** and are operated by Parks Canada. The nearby town of Radium has hotels, restaurants, golf, and services.

Details: The springs, just east of Highway 95, 104 kilometers (62 miles) south of Golden, and are open daily. Park permits $5 adults; pool fee $5 adults (reduced rates for kids, seniors, and families). Call 250/347-9485 for more information.

AUTHOR'S TOP PICKS: CLASSIC CLIMBS

- *Anderson River Group—The Coquihalla Highway gives easy access to this group of granite peaks, including Steinbok Peak, Chamois Peak, Yak Peak, and Zopkios Ridge. Many first ascents in the area were accomplished as recently as the 1980s.*

- *Bugaboo Mountains—Seventy-million-year-old granite spires make for scenic and challenging climbing in Bugaboo Glacier Provincial Park and Alpine Recreation Area west of Radium.*

- *Mount Golden Hinde—At 2,200 meters (7,219 feet) in height, this is Vancouver Island's highest point.*

- *Rocky Mountains—There is accessible high-peak climbing throughout the region, especially in Yoho and Kootenay National Parks and Mount Robson and Mount Assiniboine Provincial Parks.*

- *Stawamus Chief—The world's second-largest granite monolith (after Gibraltar) is located at Squamish and is the site of 280 climbing routes.*

NATURE AND ADVENTURE SIGHTS: ROCKY MOUNTAINS

Akamina-Kishinena Provincial Park

Declared in 1995, this protected corner is as far south and east as you can go without leaving BC. The park has some impressive neighbors: On the east side of the Continental Divide, in Alberta, is Waterton Lakes National Park; south of the Canada/U.S. border, in Montana, is Glacier National Park (together the two national parks are a UNESCO World Heritage Site). Offering magnificent solitude in an extremely remote part of the province, Akamina-Kishinena's main features are the beautiful Akamina and Kishinena ridges, long bands of rock composed of argillite, sandstone, and limestone in green, red, buff, and white. Visitors can enjoy ridgeline hiking, wilderness camping, and a variety of interesting—and sometimes rare—vegetation. Thanks to its isolation, the park is home to a large population of grizzlies. There are no facilities.

Details: Take the Crowsnest Highway (Highway 3) east over Crowsnest Pass and into Alberta. Turn south on Highway 6 to Waterton Lakes National Park. From Waterton, take the Akamina Parkway (Cameron Lake Rd.) to the trailhead for Akamina Pass. Akamina-Kishinena Provincial Park lies west of the pass. A ranger station on the BC side of the pass is staffed June through September. Camping is permitted at Akamina Meadows. For information call 250/422-3212.

Elk Valley

The Crowsnest Highway (Highway 3) snakes across the southern edge of the province through the lower Okanagan and Kootenay regions. It then turns north through the Elk Valley before climbing to the Continental Divide at Crowsnest Pass.

One of the main highlights within the Elk Valley is **Fernie**, a town full of adventurers who moved here for the laid-back atmosphere and exceptional outdoor opportunities. Established as a coal-mining and railroading town, Fernie today is known for its nearby downhill ski resort, which in turn is known for deep powder snow. Increasingly, Fernie is also becoming a summer destination for hiking, white-water rafting, and mountain biking. Island Lake, 10 kilometers (6 miles) north of Fernie, is a great place for lodge-based hiking, biking, and cross-country and telemark skiing in wide-open powder bowls.

North of Fernie are **Elk Lakes** and **Height of the Rockies Provincial Parks**. These two parks fit together like puzzle pieces at the southern extremity of an enormous protected area more than 600 kilometers (360 miles) long. The mountain scenery, including 3,300-meter (11,000-foot) peaks, tumbling waterfalls, and beautiful lakes of brilliant jade and turquoise, is exceptional. Wildlife, such as deer, elk, moose, bears, and small mammals and birds, is nearly as abundant as the wildflowers. For backpacking, day hiking, and ski touring, these two lovely provincial parks are unbeatable.

Details: *Fernie is located on Highway 3, 67 kilometers (40 miles) north of the Canada/U.S. border. Contact the Fernie Chamber of Commerce, Hwy. 3 and Dicken Rd., Fernie, 250/423-6868.*

For Elk Lakes and Height of the Rockies Provincial Parks, continue north on Highway 3 to Sparwood, then turn north onto Highway 43 and drive another 32 kilometers (19 miles) to Elkford. The Elk Lakes Forestry Road continues north to Elk Lakes Provincial Park. In wet weather and winter you'll need a four-wheel-drive vehicle. For information and maps, contact BC Parks, 250/422-4200.

Kootenay National Park

One of Canada's four Rocky Mountain national parks, Kootenay is a long and narrow J-shaped area bisected along its entire length by the Banff-Windermere Parkway (Highway 93). It encompasses glaciers, racing rivers, hot springs, important Native sites, and excellent hiking, as well as a plethora of wildlife, especially elk. Kootenay's ecology is so varied that both cacti and glaciers are found within its boundaries.

Highlights within the park include **Radium Hot Springs** (the pools are just inside the park; see page 208 for details). Aboriginal people gathered at the steaming pools and used the Kootenay River valley as a north-south travel corridor for thousands of years. There is a large campground at **Macleod Meadows** on the Kootenay River, 26.5 kilometers (16 miles) east of the town of Radium. The eight-kilometer (five-mile) **Simpson Trail** leads to the roadless Mount Assiniboine Provincial Park (see next entry).

The sacred aboriginal site of **Paint Pots**, located 56.5 kilometers (34 miles) beyond the campground, are a short walk from the highway. The deposits of natural red ochre, in shades of umber, orange, tangerine, and brick red, were used as dyes by Native peoples. Several of the park's spectacular backcountry hiking trails begin at the Paint Pots. Just down the road is **Marble Canyon**, a narrow cleft in the soft limestone cut by fast-flowing glacier meltwater. In places the canyon is just a few meters wide but up to 39 meters (129 feet) deep.

Details: *From Golden, take Highway 95 south for 104 kilometers (62 miles) to Radium Hot Springs, then turn east on Highway 93, the Banff-Windermere Parkway. Park entry fee $5 per adult. Campground fees $13–$21 per vehicle. Backcountry camping fees $6 per person; backcountry reservations*

Mount Robson, the highest peak in the Canadian Rockies

K. D. Wong/Blackbird Design

recommended in summer. Permits are available from the warden's office in Radium Hot Springs. For more information, contact Kootenay National Park, Box 220, Radium Hot Springs, BC V0A 1M0, 250/347-9505 (June–Sept.) or 250/347-9615 (year-round).

Mount Assiniboine Provincial Park

This park, nestled between Banff and Kootenay National Parks, is accessible only by foot or helicopter from the town of Canmore, just east of Banff. Three-sided Mount Assiniboine, at 3,618 meters (11,867 feet) in height, is often referred to as "Canada's Matterhorn" and is the park's main attraction, drawing climbers, hikers, and backcountry skiers. A rustic lodge and several cabins sit at the mountain's foot, as do more than 60 kilometers (36 miles) of hiking trails.

Details: There are no roads into the park. Access from the west is via the Simpson Trail, which starts in Kootenay National Park. The trail leads eight kilometers (five miles) to the park boundary and another 32 kilometers

212

(19 miles) to Assiniboine Lodge. It is also possible to hike in from several points in Alberta, but the best way in is via helicopter. For flight information contact Canadian Helicopters, 403/678-2207.

Mount Robson Provincial Park

For eastbound travelers on the Yellowhead Highway, the isolated, glacier-clad peak of Mount Robson is a visual spectacle: At 3,954 meters (13,042 feet), this enormous pyramid is the highest mountain in the Canadian Rockies. An enormous massif that creates its own weather (it's unusual to see the peak free of clouds), Robson literally towers over neighboring mountains. There is a decent spot for viewing the peak along Highway 16 (the park's information center is located at the viewpoint parking lot), but the way to truly experience the mountain is through a two-day trek to **Berg Lake** on its northwest flank.

The park is the birthplace of BC's longest river, the Fraser. Rising from the glaciers and creeks on the west side of the park, the river enters Fraser Lake then dumps over **Rearguard Falls** (just west of Mount Robson Provincial Park, on the Yellowhead Highway) before continuing more than 1,300 kilometers (800 miles) to the Pacific Ocean. The falls act as the final obstacle for salmon migrating upriver—by the time the fish get this far they're too exhausted to jump the falls.

Details: From Kamloops, take Highway 5 north 338 kilometers (203 miles) to the Yellowhead Highway (Highway 16). Turn east and drive 14 kilometers (8.5 miles) to the park's west entrance. The Mount Robson viewpoint and park information center are located two kilometers (one and one-half miles) from the west entrance. The trailhead for Berg Lake is located two kilometers (one and one-half miles) from the viewpoint, along a paved access road. Contact BC Parks, Box 579, Valemount, BC V0E 2Z0, 250/566-4325.

Yoho National Park

Yoho, a Native expression of awe or wonder, the aboriginal equivalent of "Wow," is a fitting name for this incredible 131,300-hectare (324,300-acre) park. The Kicking Horse River rises from Wapta Lake near the Continental Divide and carves its way through the mountains to join the Columbia River at Golden; en route, it has gouged two deep canyons that make for bone-crunching whitewater rafting.

ECO-FRIENDLY: ALPENGLOW AVIATION

Ann and Steve Neill founded their modest, two-person air-charter and flightseeing operation in Golden, based on their experience flying small aircraft for ski trips in New Zealand and assisting mountain-climbing expeditions in Alaska. Steve Neill combines his love of the Rocky Mountain back-country with meticulous attention to safety, making Alpenglow Aviation among the safest flightseeing operators in the business. His enthusiasm for the stunning scenery is infectious, and his knowledge of the mountains is extensive.

Neill's fleet includes Cessna 180, 185, 206, and de Havilland Beaver aircraft. "We want to provide an alternative to mass tourism sightseeing tours on the crowded highways in the national parks," says Neill. "I take people comfortably and safely to areas that are impossible to access any other way."

Neill also provides charter air support for independent ski-touring trips on the Columbia and Clemenceau Icefields, including drop-off, pickup, and flyover safety checks. Safety is his stock-in-trade. He knows that air travel is not just an exceptional tool for dramatic sightseeing but also a lifeline in the wilderness.

Many of the park's highlights are clustered near the eastern boundary. **Emerald Lake** is great for canoeing, hiking, or, if you'd prefer to relax, for sipping wine at the sumptuous lodge on its shore. The town of **Field** is another good base from which to explore the park. Nearby you'll find the winding road to **Yoho Valley** and **Takakkaw Falls**, Canada's third-highest waterfall at 384 meters (1,267 feet). From the falls, several excellent hiking trails extend into the wilderness of the upper valley. Field is also the home of the Yoho-Burgess Shale Foundation, the only sanctioned organization permitted to lead hikes to the famous **Burgess Shale**. The limestone outcrop, set high on Wapta Mountain, is a fossil bed of global importance and the final resting place for many soft-bodied animals from the Cambrian era.

For excellent high-alpine hiking, check out **Lake O'Hara**. Trails lead from the dark-green spruce and pine that surround the lake up into alpine meadows offering spectacular views of towering dolomite and limestone spires. A wonderful lodge and cabins stand on the lake's shore, and there are campsites nearby. In summer you can take a bus up the nine-kilometer (five-and-one-half-mile) access road, or you can hike in; in winter, the only way to get to the lake is on skis.

Details: *Park admission $5. Camping fees $12–$17 per vehicle per night. Backcountry campsites $6 per person per night. Backcountry permits are available at the warden's office in Field. For more information, contact the Yoho Infocentre, Field, BC V0A 1G0, 250/343-6324.*

For information on Emerald Lake Lodge and Lake O'Hara Lodge, see "Lodging." To make a reservation for a guided hike to the Burgess Shale, contact Yoho-Burgess Shale Foundation, Box 148, Field, BC V0A 1G0, 250/343-6480.

K. D. Wong/Blackbird Design

Burgess Shale

215

GUIDES AND OUTFITTERS

In Golden the number-one adventure is white-water rafting, especially on the roaring Kicking Horse River. There are numerous white-water outfitters in town—the competition is fierce. One reputable outfitter is **Whitewater Voyageurs**, Box 1983, Golden, BC V0A 1H0, 800/667-7238 or 250/344-7335. The company offers half-day, full-day, and two-day Kicking Horse River trips through rapids with names like Man Eater and Terminator, as well as scenic float trips (no white-water) on the nearby Blaeberry River. **Wild Water Adventures**, based in Lake Louise, Alberta, also operates on the Kicking Horse; contact them at Box 25, Lake Louise, AB T0L 1E0, 888/771-9453 or 403/522-2211. River rafting is also popular in Fernie. **Canyon Raft Company**, Box 1953, Fernie, BC V0B 1M0, 888/423-7226 or 250/423-7226, offers full-day, half-day, or "Fast Blast" trips on the Elk River.

For an offbeat treat, try flightseeing. **Alpenglow Aviation**, Box 4031, Golden, BC V0A 1H0, 888/244-7117 or 250/344-7117, offers Cessna flights to the Bugaboo Mountains and Glacier National Park, a tour of the Rockies' icefields and waterfalls along the Continental Divide, or a trip through Rogers Pass and over Revelstoke.

Another unique way to experience the mountains is by llama trekking—you do the walking, your llama carries the bags. **Strider Adventures** is based in Prince George but offers llama trips to several Rocky Mountain destinations. For information, contact RR 1, Site 24, Comp 7, Prince George, BC V2N 2H8, 800/665-7752 or 250/963-9542, www.pgweb.com/strider.

The good folks at **Kapristo Lodge**, located just south of Golden, P.O. Box 90, Golden, BC V0A 1H0, 250/344-6048, will arrange just about anything to

Wildflowers in Kootenay National Park

tickle your fancy, from fishing, horseback riding, and white-water rafting, to snowmobiling and skiing.

CAMPING

Macleod Meadows, in Kootenay National Park, Box 220, Radium Hot Springs, BC V0A 1M0, 250/347-9505 (June through September) or 250/347-9615 (year-round), is a large campground with 98 sites and a sani-station. It's a great put-in spot for paddling on the Kootenay River. Wildlife is abundant (this is their backyard—be sure to run a clean camp and put your food away; you don't want to tempt the bears).

In addition to its splendid backcountry camping, **Yoho National Park** includes a total of 262 drive-in campsites and two easily accessible walk-in campgrounds. RV campgrounds include Chancellor Peak and Hoodoo Creek, neither of which have facilities. For information contact Yoho National Park, 250/343-6324.

Mount Robson Provincial Park contains 176 campsites in three separate campgrounds, plus wilderness camping at Berg Lake. For reservations call 800/689-9025 or 250/566-4325. The largest campground is the 125-site **Robson Meadows**, located at the west entrance to the park on Highway 16. It includes flush toilets and hot showers and is wheelchair accessible. It's also close to the park's information center and the hiking trails to Berg Lake.

LODGING

Island Lake Lodge, Island Lake Mountain Tours, Cedar Valley Rd., Fernie, 888/4CATSKI or 250/423-3700, e-mail islandlk@elkvalley.net, located in the Lizard Range west of Fernie, specializes in family packages with emphasis on activities and learning opportunities for kids. You can drive to the lodge in summer, but in winter they'll send a snowcat (a tracked vehicle similar to the grooming machines used at downhill ski resorts) out to fetch you. Inclusive packages (accommodation, meals, and activities) are available. Rates start at $280 per room, including meals.

Mount Assiniboine Lodge, Box 8128, Canmore, AB T1W 2T8, 403/678-2883, www.canadianrockies.net/assiniboine, is very popular both for summer hiking and winter ski touring. The lodge was constructed 60 years ago by the Canadian Pacific Railway to accommodate adventurers who came to the Rockies by train. Snuggled into the hills at an elevation of 2,170 meters (7,118 feet), it is Canada's highest alpine lodge. Access is by hiking, skiing (expert skiers only), or helicopter. Rates—$125 per person for a lodge room, $150 per person for a cabin— include all meals and guiding services. Helicopter transportation is extra: $90 per person each way.

Storm Mountain Lodge, Box 760, Banff, Alberta T0L 0C0, 403/762-4155, at Vermilion Pass in Kootenay National Park, was built in the 1920s by the Canadian Pacific Railway. Now privately owned and operated, the establishment includes log cabins with fireplaces and private baths. There is excellent hiking in the area. Call for rates. Farther south but still within the park is **Kootenay Park Lodge**, Box 1390, Banff, Alberta T0L 0C0, 403/762-9196. It features rustic but cozy log cabins with fireplaces, a main lodge with a restaurant, a gas station, laundry facilities, and a gift shop. Rates range from $80 to $100.

For utter luxury in the Yoho National Park wilderness, **Emerald Lake Lodge,** Box 10, Field, BC V0A 1G0, 800/663-6336 or 250/343-6321, is the place to be. The lodge includes a collection of townhouse-style cabins with fireplaces, down duvets, and balconies overlooking Emerald Lake. The food served in the lodge's restaurant is exquisite. Room-only rates range from $115 to $205 per person per night. Also within Yoho National Park is **Lake O'Hara Lodge**, Box 55, Lake Louise, Alberta T0L 1E0, 403/343-6418 (summer) or 403/678-4110 (winter), www.canadianrockies.net/lakeohara. Accommodations are in the main lodge building or in one of several lakeside cabins. Meals are exceptional; they'll even pack you a lunch if you plan to hike to the nearby alpine meadows. Summer rates range from $220 to $341 per person per day and include all meals and transportation to the lodge from the Trans-Canada Highway.

If you're passing through and need a place to lay your head, check out **Sisters & Beans**, 1122 10th Ave. S., Golden, 250/344-2443, a very enjoyable café (see "Food") and bed-and-breakfast in Golden. The rooms are small but comfy, with twin beds and private showers. The breakfasts are delicious. Rates range from $55 to $70. In Field, check out the **Wildflower Guesthouse**, 303 Kicking Horse Ave., 250/343-6707. It may be small—there's only one suite—but it's wonderful. The room includes a private entrance, fireplace, full kitchen, bath, and a fluffy down comforter on a queen bed. And it costs just $55 per night. The town of Fernie includes a similar establishment, the **Wildflower B&B**, 12 Parkland Dr., Fernie, 250/423-6484, offering king- and queen-size beds, private or shared baths, fireplaces, and Jacuzzi-style tubs. Rates range from $65 to $100. In Radium, one of the many motels and resorts is the **Apple Tree Inn of Radium Hot Springs**, 4999 Hwy. 93, Radium, 250/347-0011. This family-friendly establishment offers one- and two-bedroom suites with kitchens and gas barbecues. Rates range from $45 to $99.

FOOD

Several restaurants in the Rocky Mountain region stand out. In Golden, at **Sisters & Beans**, 1122 10th Ave. S., 250/344-2443, three European women serve up simple yet excellent home-cooked food. Daily specials usually include a hearty pasta, and the soups are always nourishing. Two can dine very well for about $30.

If you're journeying to or from Earl Grey Pass Trail and the Purcell Wilderness Conservancy, stop in Invermere to check out **Strands Old House Restaurant**, 818 12th St., Invermere, 250/342-6344. Strands offers succulent lamb dishes and, for early birds, a great deal: If you arrive between five and a quarter after six in the evening you'll get a three-course meal for $12.

The excellent dining room at **Emerald Lake Lodge** serves "Rocky Mountains cuisine" for breakfast, lunch, and dinner. Game dishes, such as homemade sausages of venison and bison, are the stars of the menu. Desserts, too, are luscious, and the wine list is extensive. The only drawback is the price—dinner for two can cost up to $100. If you're looking for something less pricey, **Cilantro's**, a separate café located adjacent to the lodge, features pizza, pasta, and salads at about half the price.

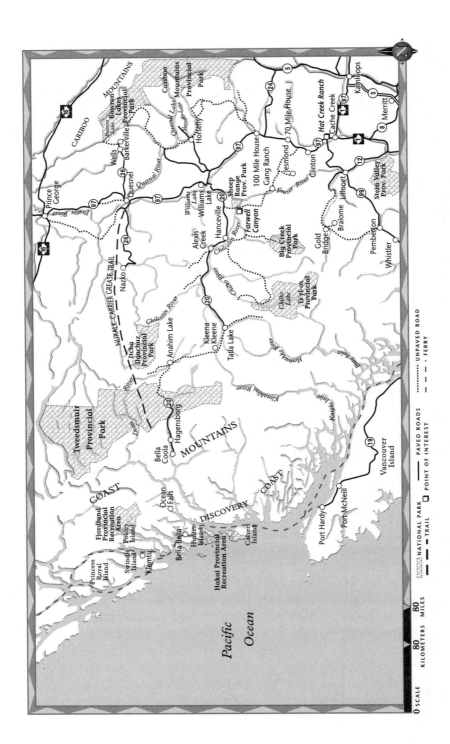

SCALE

0   80   KILOMETERS
    80   MILES

Pacific
Ocean

COAST

DISCOVERY

COAST

MOUNTAINS

Tweedsmuir
Provincial
Park

CARIBOO

MOUNTAINS

Cariboo
Mountains
Provincial
Park

CARIBOO

Prince
George

Fraser River

Quesnel River

Wells
Barkerville Provincial
Park

Bowron
Lakes
Provincial
Park

Quesnel

Nazko

NUXALK-CARRIER GREASE TRAIL

Itcha
Ilgachuz
Provincial
Park

Chilcotin River

Anahim Lake

Dean River

Bella
Coola

Hagensborg

Ocean
Falls

Fiordland
Provincial
Recreation
Area

Pooley
Island

Swindle
Island

Klemtu

Princess
Royal
Island

Bella Bella

Hunter
Island

Hakai Provincial
Recreation Area

Calvert
Island

Port Hardy

Port McNeill

Vancouver
Island

Kleena
Kleene

Tatla Lake

Klinaklini River

Knight Inlet

Homathko River

Bute Inlet

Alexis
Creek

Williams
Lake

Williams
Lake

Hanceville

Farwell
Canyon

Chilcotin River

Big Creek
Provincial
Park

Chilko River

Chilko
Lake

Ts'yl-os
Provincial
Park

Sheep
Range
Prov. Park

Hotsenj

Mahood Lake

Quesnel Lake

100 Mile House

Gang Ranch

Fraser River

70 Mile House

Jesmond

Clinton

Lillooet

Gold
Bridge

Bralorne

Pemberton

Whistler

Stein Valley
Prov. Park

Cache Creek

Hat Creek Ranch

Kamloops

Merritt

LEGEND

▨ NATIONAL PARK
▨ PROVINCIAL PARK
─── PAVED ROADS
········· UNPAVED ROAD
─ ─ ─ TRAIL
- - - FERRY
□ POINT OF INTEREST

5
24
97
20
26
12
8
5
97
99
19

CHAPTER 10

Cariboo-Chilcotin and the Discovery Coast

This region's splendid isolation and stunning scenery make it a true adventure-travel destination. You'll get all the spectacular scenery of the High Country mountains, plus north coast destinations and First Nations culture as rich as anything you'll find on Vancouver Island— but without the crowds. The Cariboo-Chilcotin is hard to get to, period. Horses, boats, and floatplanes are the transportation modes of choice in this rugged territory. In spite of its remoteness, however, this region is quickly being "discovered" and is among the hottest destination zones in the entire province. The region is jointly named for the Cariboo Mountains and the Tsilhqot'in (Chilcotin) Plateau.

LAY OF THE LAND

The Cariboo-Chilcotin region encompasses the entire north-central portion of British Columbia, from the First Nations coastal settlements of Bella Coola and Bella Bella, across the near-roadless wilderness of Tweedsmuir Provincial Park, into the ranching country around Williams Lake, and east to touch the northern boundary of Wells Gray Provincial Park.

The western reaches of this region include ocean inlets, fjords, and islands; this area, between the northern end of Vancouver Island and the southern extremes of Haida Gwaii (Queen Charlotte Islands), is the only place on BC's mainland coast exposed to the open force of the Pacific Ocean. The Coast Mountains rise straight and tall from the sea, clothed in dense forests of hemlock and spruce. This region has been dubbed the Discovery Coast by BC Tourism; among environmentalists, it's referred to as the Great Bear Rain Forest.

The mountains, containing numerous swift rivers and large lakes, extend inland to meet the rolling Interior Plateau west of the town of Williams Lake. The mountains cast an intense rain shadow, so that parts of the plateau are extremely dry. To the east of Williams Lake, the plateau gradually rises to meet the Cariboo Mountains, home of many excellent fishing and paddling lakes.

The Fraser River passes through this region from north to south; the town of Quesnel and many of the region's major ranches are on the river's banks. Tributaries to the Fraser include the Chilcotin, which in turn is fed by many streams and rivers flowing from the Coast Mountains. The Dean, Klinaklini, and Homathko Rivers rise in the mountains and flow westward to the sea. On the region's eastern side, the Quesnel, Horsefly, and Bowron Lakes all drain into the Fraser. At 530 meters (1,750 feet) deep, Quesnel is the deepest lake in BC and the second-deepest lake in North America.

HISTORY AND CULTURE

The Nuxalk, a tribe that inhabited the sheltered waterways and islands of the coast, created a culturally rich heritage similar to those of the Kwakwaka'wakw to the south and west and the mighty Haida and Tsimshian to the north. Thriving villages with multifamily cedar-plank houses, totem poles, carved canoes, and all the hallmarks of the North Pacific aboriginal tribes flourished here until the arrival of smallpox, salmon canneries, and logging.

The Nuxalk traded with the neighboring inland nations of the Tsilhqot'in and Dakelh peoples. The Tsilhqot'in (Chilcotin) occupied a small pocket of territory between the Fraser River and the Coast Mountains. Fierce defenders of their culture and territory, the

SPIRIT BEAR SANCTUARY

Nearly one bear in seven on Princess Royal Island is a white "spirit" bear. A bear sanctuary is proposed for a portion of Princess Royal Island, along with nearby Swindle and Campania Islands and portions of the mainland. However, the same area is in danger of being logged in the near future. Clear-cutting the old-growth forests would destroy habitat for black, Kermode, and grizzly bears currently inhabiting the area. For information on the current status of the proposed park, visit the Valhalla Wilderness Society Web site at www.alpine.net/-williams/spirithome.html.

Tsilhqot'in allowed the Hudson's Bay Company to establish a single trading post on the Chilko River in 1829, but by 1844 the fort was abandoned. The gold rush of the 1860s brought Europeans, Americans, and Asians to the region. The remarkable Tsilhqot'in War—the only armed uprising of First Nations peoples to occur west of the Rockies and north of the 49th Parallel—began in 1861 and culminated in the loss of several Native and white lives in 1864. The war was quelled with the arrest and execution of several Natives (an action later judged to have been unjustified). Today the Tsilhqot'in territory remains firmly aboriginal in character; the only non-Native settlements in the area are Anahim Lake and Alexis Creek.

To the north and east are the traditional territories of the Dakelh, called Carrier by Europeans. Living in a land filled with lakes and rivers, the Dakelh were great travelers, especially by canoe. They were also renowned traders, and established a permanent trade route to the coast now known as the Nuxalk-Carrier Grease Trail (the long-distance hiking/horseback trail is officially called the Alexander Mackenzie Heritage Trail). Westbound goods, including obsidian (a hard volcanic rock used for making tools), furs, and meat, were traded for salmon and *oolichan* oil (the "grease" for which the trail is named), which the Dakelh depended on as a source of fat and energy for the long, harsh winters.

Alexander Mackenzie, employed by the North West Company to find a trade route to the Pacific, was the first European to cross North America. He was guided to the coast by the Dakelh, and arrived at Dean Channel near present-day Bella Coola in July 1793. Nearly a century later, gold seekers flooded up the Fraser and into the heart of the Cariboo-Chilcotin region. Unfortunately, with them came disease, and the Native populations were devastated. A by-product of the gold rush was the hastily built Cariboo Wagon Road, which extended up the Fraser from Lillooet to Barkerville. Many of the region's present-day community names, such as 70 Mile House and 100 Mile House, bear witness to the roadhouses established along this route.

Today this region is true frontier country, occupied by individuals as rugged as the land they call home. Very large and remote cattle ranches, some dating from the 1890s or earlier, now sprawl over much of the Fraser Canyon and the eastern slopes of the Coast Mountains. Logging and mining, too, have left their marks on the area. Tourist and adventure destinations include Tweedsmuir and Ts'yl-os Provincial Parks, Bowron Lakes, and the many guest ranches of the region. On the coast, the southern reaches of Kitlope Provincial Park and the Fjordland and Hakai Provincial Recreation Areas provide unparalleled waters for paddlers and other boaters.

FLORA AND FAUNA

Coastal forests are, for the most part, very dense and diverse; however, thanks to cooler climate conditions, their trees don't reach the proportions of the ancient old-growth giants found on Vancouver Island's west coast. Once too remote for serious exploitation by the forest-products industry, the region, known as the Great Bear Rain Forest, is now threatened by large-scale mechanized logging, and an intense battle between environmental and Native groups, the forest-products industry, and the BC government is underway. For information on the Great Bear Rain Forest preservation campaign, see the Greenpeace Web site at www.greenpeace.org.

Just inland from the coast, dry conditions have given rise to tough grasses, sagebrush, and pockets of poplar and pine. East of the dry belt, the Interior Plateau was once carpeted by a near-continuous forest of lodgepole pine and white spruce; over the years, however, it has been largely denuded by spruce budworms and pine beetles. Logging is also heavy in this region and has contributed to the deforestation. The Cariboo Mountains are home to evergreen forests and meadows bursting with flowers.

Bull elk

Wildlife in the area includes wolves, grizzly and black bears, mountain goats, bighorn sheep, deer, elk, and moose, plus plenty of small mammals such as river otters and beavers. Coyotes are common, especially in the rolling ranch country of the Fraser Canyon dry belt. Bald eagles and osprey are common along the coast, while the interior is home to migrating waterfowl (ducks, geese, herons, loons) and songbirds. Trumpeter swans and rare white pelicans are summer residents of the Chilcotin area.

Among the region's most famous and elusive inhabitants are the Kermode or "spirit" bears. Found primarily on Princess Royal Island, these rare, white-coated black bears are genetically different than their black and brown cousins. Native and environmental groups are working to have Princess Royal Island, Pooley Island, and the adjacent mainland coast declared a park or sanctuary in order to guarantee the survival of Kermode bears.

VISITOR INFORMATION

There are just two major roads linking the Cariboo-Chilcotin to the outside world. One is the Cariboo Highway (Highway 97), which

225

traverses the region from south to north, connecting Cache Creek on the Trans-Canada Highway with Prince George to the north; most of the highway uses the same route as the old Cariboo Road built during the gold rush. Towns along Highway 97 include 70 Mile House, 100 Mile House, Williams Lake (the largest town in the entire region), and Quesnel. Highway 24, the "Fishing Road," leads east from Highway 97. This secondary road provides access to many small lakes and fishing resorts and connects with Highway 5 south of Wells Gray Provincial Park. Highway 26 leads east from Quesnel to Wells, Barkerville, and Bowron Lakes Provincial Park.

From Williams Lake, Highway 20 (Freedom Road) is the region's other major road. It winds west through tiny settlements such as Hanceville, Alexis Creek, Tatla Lake, Kleena Kleene, and Anahim Lake before crossing Tweedsmuir Provincial Park and ending in Bella Coola. The terrain through which this road travels is so extreme that it was originally thought that no road could be built here. But residents of Bella Coola and the Chilcotin area knew better, and in 1950 they took it upon themselves to complete the 60-kilometer (36-mile) gap through the Coast Mountains.

Regional airlines serve Williams Lake, Quesnel, Bella Coola, and several smaller communities (see Appendix A for detailed information). One of the best ways—and often the only way—to reach remote areas of this region is by charter plane. Most settlements, especially along Highway 20, have airstrips or lakes where floatplanes can land. You can easily charter a plane for a quick flight over the Coast Mountains or for access to remote areas of Tweedsmuir or other parks.

BC Rail serves the region from North Vancouver, up the coast through Whistler, then inland through Pemberton, Lillooet, and Williams Lake. It then continues north to Quesnel and Prince George, where connections are available to Prince Rupert, Jasper, Edmonton, and points in eastern Canada (see Appendix A for detailed information).

BC Ferries recently began offering service to Bella Coola through what they call the Discovery Coast Passage. The vehicle and passenger ferry *Queen of Chilliwack* connects Port Hardy on Vancouver Island with Bella Coola on the mainland's north coast, and includes offshore island stops at places like Ocean Falls and Bella Bella.

For detailed information on all travel issues, contact Cariboo Country Tourism, 266 Oliver St., P.O. Box 4900, Williams Lake, BC V2G 2V8, 250/392-2226, fax 250/392-2838, e-mail cariboo@netshop. net, www.travel.bc.ca/region/cariboo.

NATURE AND ADVENTURE SIGHTS: CARIBOO

Barkerville Historic Town

Highway 26 (a secondary road) leads east from Quesnal to Barkerville, a restored gold rush–era village from the 1860s that is now a "living museum" with costumed interpreters. There are more than 40 restored buildings in the town, including a theater, bakery, and restaurants. Slide shows are staged during the off-season, and in the winter there is excellent cross-country skiing in the area.

Details: Barkerville is located 88 kilometers (53 miles) east of Highway 97 on Highway 26. For information contact Box 19, Barkerville, BC V0K 1B0,

K. D. Wong/Blackbird Design

Cariboo Country

227

250/994-3332. The living museum is open year-round, but most activities take place June through September. The admission fee is $5.50.

Bowron Lakes Provincial Park

Bowron Lakes Provincial Park is home to one of BC's best extended canoe routes. The 116-kilometer (70-mile) Bowron Lakes route follows a circular path across six major lakes with short portages between waterways. The route is well serviced with over 100 wilderness campsites; many campgrounds have cooking shelters and hiking trails. Wildlife includes a dense population of black bear, plus deer, moose, and caribou. You can bring your own canoe and gear, rent equipment in Quesnel or at Bowron Lake, or travel the route in luxury with an outfitter (see "Guides and Outfitters").

Details: The park is located 109 kilometers (65.5 miles) east of Highway 97 on Highway 26. For information contact BC Parks, 281 First Ave. N., Williams Lake, 250/992-3111. Reservations for the canoe route are mandatory for groups of six or more. All paddlers must purchase a backcountry permit at the park office.

Clinton-Area Guest Ranches

Some are historic, some are operating cattle ranches, some are specifically conceived and run as tourist destinations offering multi-day guided trail rides and pack trips into the spectacular backcountry. Regardless, guest ranches offer a glimpse into the true lifestyles of those that survive on this austerely beautiful land. Many ranches are located in the Clinton area, "the Guest Ranch Capital of Canada." For details on guest ranches, tour packages, and accommodations see "Guides and Outfitters".

The famous **Gang Ranch**, once the largest cattle ranch in North America, is located 100 kilometers (62 miles) west of Highway 97 along the rugged and narrow Meadow Lake Road. Started in the 1860s, the ranch today encompasses 400,000 hectares (988,000 acres). Gang Ranch is no longer a guest ranch, but accommodations are available (you're pretty much on your own—don't expect them to lend you a horse or bring you breakfast). Contact the ranch at Gang Ranch Post Office, BC V0K 1N0, 250/459-7923.

Hat Creek Ranch is a historic site that includes a restored road-

Relaxing at the Gang Ranch

house, blacksmith's shop, stables, and many other buildings, all of which were constructed between 1863 and 1915 to provide a convenient stopping point for travelers on the old Cariboo Wagon Road from Lillooet. Guided tours of the buildings are available. To get there, take Highway 97 north from Cache Creek for 11 kilometers (6.5 miles). The ranch is located at the junction of Highways 97 and 99 and is open daily May through September from 10 to 6. Admission is five dollars. Call 250/457-9722 for information.

   Details: *Clinton is located 40 kilometers (24 miles) north of Cache Creek on Highway 97. Contact the Clinton and District Chamber of Commerce, 1522 Cariboo Hwy., Clinton, 250/459-2640.*

Lillooet

Located at the foot of the Coast Mountains, Lillooet marks the western boundary of the interior dry belt. From here, Highway 99 threads a spectacular line way up and over the Coast Mountains to Pemberton and Whistler. For travelers coming from the coast, this small town makes a good rest stop before continuing south to Cache Creek or north to Williams Lake. The area is laced with back roads; if you have a four-wheel-drive vehicle and don't mind getting a little lost, head out and explore the stark and beautiful Fraser Canyon and the rolling hill country that surrounds it.

Details: Lillooet is located 86 kilometers (51.5 miles) north of Cache Creek. Contact the Lillooet Visitor Infocentre, Box 441, Lillooet, BC V0K 1V0, 250/256-4308.

Quesnel

In 1793, as Alexander Mackenzie traveled downstream on the Fraser River, seeking a trade route to the Pacific, he was persuaded by the Dakelh people to follow their ancient overland trail instead. His decision proved to be a good one, and he reached Dean Channel later that year. Mackenzie's path is now a hiking trail, but at about 420 kilometers (250 miles) in length, it's no cakewalk. Much of the **Nuxalk-Carrier Grease Trail**, also known as the Alexander Mackenzie Heritage Trail, is remote and not serviced. You can, however, hike or ride on horseback for portions of the trail, especially in Tweedsmuir Provincial Park. The trailhead is 60 kilometers (36 miles) north of Quesnel (kwa-NELL) and ends at Burnt Bridge on Highway 20 just west of Tweedsmuir Provincial Park. From here the highway itself is the route to the ocean.

Hiking the entire length of the trail takes 18 to 21 days to complete and requires food drops at prearranged points along the way. The trail cuts through several First Nations reservations and ancestral lands; if you plan to hike the whole thing, you should contact the appropriate band offices for permission before you go (see Cheryl Coull's book, *A Traveller's Guide to Aboriginal B.C.*).

Details: Quesnel is located 119 kilometers (71 miles) north of Williams Lake on Highway 97. Contact the Quesnal Visitor Infocentre, 800/992-4922 or 250/992-8716.

Williams Lake

With a population of approximately 11,000, this town is the region's largest settlement. Williams Lake embraces cowboys, loggers, Natives,

Chilko Lake

bush pilots, and anyone looking for wilderness. It's also the gateway to numerous remote roads that wind through the backcountry, and is the starting point for adventures along Highway 20. The local claim to fame is the annual rodeo, the **Williams Lake Stampede**, which takes place the first weekend of July. Started as a contest for local cowboys in the 1920s, the Stampede is now a major professional rodeo.

Details: Williams Lake is located on Highway 97, 203 kilometers (122 miles) north of Cache Creek. Contact the Williams Lake Visitor Infocentre and Chamber of Commerce, 1148 S. Broadway, Williams Lake, 250/392-5025.

NATURE AND ADVENTURE SIGHTS: CHILCOTIN

Chilcotin Lakes
Several long fingers of glacier-fed water lie in the Coast Mountain valleys south of Highway 20. The access roads can be rough, but the lakes—Chilko, Tatlayoko, Taseko, Tatla, and many others—are the

231

ECO-FRIENDLY: CHILCOTIN HOLIDAYS

Kevin Bracewell's grandfather was a packer and guide, and today Bracewell has exclusive guiding rights to a remote area of approximately 5,000 square kilometers (2,000 square miles). Bracewell's territory encompasses the region west of Lillooet and includes Gold Bridge, Spruce Lake, and Big Creek Provincial Park. With partner Sylvia Waterer, Bracewell's Chilcotin Holidays is both a guest ranch and horse-packing outfitter, offering high guide-to-guest ratios (two to seven) and giving visitors an opportunity to experience a way of life that hasn't changed much for over a hundred years.

Bracewell operates his ranch and horse trips with minimal impact and wildlife management in mind, but he also believes that tourism and forestry can coexist. The ranch's woodlot—a source of fuel and building materials—is actively logged, using both selective and mechanized logging techniques. Student guides are given extensive training in forest ecology and forestry practices, using the woodlot as an open-air classroom. The ranch also offers education programs in the woodlot area, emphasizing integrated forestry and wildlife management.

focal points for fishing, paddling, pack trips, and ski touring. These clear, cold waters are the birthplace of millions of Fraser River salmon. To the west, the Homathko River drains southwest from Tatlayoko Lake to the head of Bute Inlet. This region is scattered with cabins, lodges, and guest ranches, many of which are best accessed by small plane or a very tough car.

At the southern edge of the Chilcotin Lakes district is **Ts'yl-os Provincial Park** (pronounced SY-loss), a roadless wilderness of incredibly clear lakes, fast rivers, leaping fish, and snow-capped granite mountains. The 233,000-hectare (576,000-acre) park, encompassing an area once threatened by logging, was established in 1994 when environmental and Native groups succeeded in their fight to preserve and protect the Nemaiah Valley. Many guides and outfitters offer pack and fishing trips in the park (see "Guides and Outfitters").

Details: From Williams Lake, follow Highway 20 west for 221 kilometers (132.5 miles) to Tatla Lake, then turn south toward Tatlayko. Turn east at the community hall, drive 25 kilometers (15 miles), then turn south just before the Chilko River. The road leads to Chilko Lake and Ts'yl-os Provincial Park. For more information contact BC Parks, 281 First Ave. N., Williams Lake, 250/398-4414. For detailed maps, contact BC Ministry of Forests, Williams Lake (see Appendix B). Floatplanes can be chartered in Nimpo Lake, 76 kilometers (45.5 miles) west of Tatla Lake on Highway 20.

Farwell Canyon

The Chilcotin River has carved a graceful slice through a layer-cake of clay, sandstone, and limestone. The frothy blue water and the cottonwood trees on the riverbank contrast with the dun and gold hues of the rock. Hoodoos, sand dunes, and aboriginal rock art are all part of these "badlands," where visitors can enjoy everything from picnicking to hiking to white-water rafting. En route to the canyon you'll pass through **Sheep Range Provincial Park**, a land of rabbit brush and cactus established to protect habitat for a herd of bighorn sheep.

Details: From Williams Lake, follow Highway 20 west for 44.5 kilometers (27 miles). A left turn (south) onto a gravel road leads to the park and canyon.

Gold Bridge/Big Creek Provincial Park

Gold Bridge, in the mountains west of Lillooet, is the point of access for hiking trails in the southern Chilcotin Mountains and, to the north, Big Creek Provincial Park. A 1990 government report called this portion of the Chilcotins "the single most outstanding area of wilderness not presently protected in the southern interior of BC." The government did finally bestow protection upon the northern section of the range in 1994 with the creation of Big Creek Provincial Park, but even today the southern valleys (just north of Gold Bridge) remain unprotected. The area harbors spectacular turquoise lakes, multicolored rock formations, and an array of wildlife, including

BRITISH COLUMBIA

AUTHOR'S TOP PICKS: LONG-DISTANCE HIKES

- **Cape Scott Trail**—*To the north tip of Vancouver Island in Cape Scott Provincial Park.*
- **East Beach Trail**—*Up to a week of walking on the beach in Naikoon Provincial Park.*
- **Juan de Fuca Marine Trail**—*A coastal hike just one hour from Victoria.*
- **Nuxalk-Carrier Grease Trail (Alexander Mackenzie Trail)**—*This 420-kilometer (262-mile) trail approximates the route taken by Alexander Mackenzie on his overland trip to the Pacific in 1793.*
- **West Coast Trail**—*A five-to-seven-day trek along the west coast of Vancouver Island between Port Renfrew and Bamfield.*

---

bears, wolves, California bighorn sheep, and deer. It's also the home of Spruce Lake, one of the world's best trout-fishing lakes.

Details: Gold Bridge is located 100 kilometers (60 miles) west of Lillooet via Bridge River Road. For maps of Chilcotin hiking trails, contact Lillooet Forest District, Bag Service 700, Lillooet, BC V0K 1V0, 250/256-7531 (ask for the Spruce Lake recreation map).

Tweedsmuir Provincial Park and Recreation Area
British Columbia's largest provincial park, located in the Coast Mountains, contains 994,250 hectares (2.45 million acres) of the most amazing, challenging, and soul-soothing mountain country in Canada. The park, with its enormous ice fields, sheer cliffs and canyons, waterfalls, and dense forests, is stunning, especially when seen from the air. If you're planning to hike or paddle in the park without a guide, you'll

have to bring all you own gear and be self-sufficient. Other than 35 drive-in campsites, there are no facilities. A rough access road near the park's headquarters leads to the upper reaches of the Atnarko River Valley and **Hunlen Falls**. The falls' single drop of 260 meters (748 feet) is incredible.

Deep within the park is the remarkable **Rainbow Range**, a string of ancient volcanic peaks streaked with shades of red, ochre, yellow, and purple. The range is visible from Highway 20 approximately 30 kilometers (18 miles) west of Anahim Lake (just as the highway rises into the Coast Mountains, look north). Although it's extremely rugged and remote, the range is accessible via guided horseback trips or by hiking a 20-kilometer (12-mile) trail. The hiking path also offers views of 4,016-meter (13,253-foot) **Mount Waddington**, the highest mountain situated entirely within BC.

Details: Tweedsmuir Provincial Park is located 352 kilometers (211 miles) west of Williams Lake on Highway 20. Park headquarters is located 28 kilometers (17 miles) from the east entrance, and the Rainbow Range trailhead is six kilometers (three and one-half miles) from the east entrance. To reach Hunlen Falls, take the road south from the Young Creek picnic site for 29 kilometers (17.5 miles). For more information contact BC Parks, 281 First Ave. N., Williams Lake, 250/398-4414

NATURE AND ADVENTURE SIGHTS: DISCOVERY COAST

Bella Coola

This tiny community of less than one thousand people is at the head of a long, thin ocean inlet called North Bentinck Arm. The Nuxalk people lived here for thousands of years before Captain George Vancouver, and then Alexander Mackenzie, arrived in 1793. A Hudson's Bay trading post was built here in 1869, and Norwegians settled in the fertile, isolated valley in the 1890s. Until the completion of the Freedom Road (Highway 20) in 1953, the only link Bella Coola had with the outside world was by sea.

Bella Coola is the gateway to an astonishing coastal wilderness. Humpback whales, dolphins and porpoises, bald eagles and acrobatic ravens, salmon and halibut all thrive here. Adventurers flock here for

C. L. Wong

Chilcotin River, Farwell Canyon

the sportfishing, sea kayaking, diving, and boating, and for the slight chance that they might spot a Kermode bear. Outfitters operate trips to Ocean Falls, the Nuxalk community of Bella Bella, the **Fjordland** and **Hakai Provincial Recreation Areas**, and Princess Royal Island. Hakai is the province's largest marine park (although as a "recreation area," some development is allowed), and is well known among adventurous kayakers for its lagoons, reversing tidal rapids, and labyrinthine channels. Fjordland is a magical, peaceful land of beaches, inlets, seals, bald eagles, and glacier-fed streams plunging directly into the ocean.

Details: Bella Coola is located at the west end of Highway 20, 456 kilometers (274 miles) west of Williams Lake. Contact the Bella Coola Visitor Infocentre, Box 670, Bella Coola, BC V0T 1C0, 250/982-0008 (June through September). For information on the Hakai and Fjordland Provincial Recreation Areas, contact the Infocentre in the village of Klemtu on Swindle Island, 250/839-2346.

GUIDES AND OUTFITTERS

Many guest ranches and outfitters offer multi-day backcountry tours on horseback. BC Tourism produces a detailed brochure/catalog with listings and descriptions of numerous guest ranches throughout BC. To obtain a copy, call 800/663-5885. In the descriptions below, rates for accommodations are provided. Some ranches offer day rates for trail rides but most are designed as accommodations/activity packages.

One of the Cariboo's best ranches is **Moondance Guest Ranch**, Box 160, Clinton, BC V0K 1K0, 250/459-7775. The small operation features horseback-riding clinics, lessons for all skill levels, and daylong trail rides. Rates range from $100 to $150 per person. **Big Bar Guest Ranch,** Box 27, Clinton, BC V0K 1K0, 250/459-2333, is located 48 kilometers (29 miles) from Highway 97 in the heart of Cariboo ranching country. A year-round destination, Big Bar specializes in trail rides and rafting on the Fraser in summer, and cross-country skiing, sleigh rides, and ice skating in winter. Rates range from $64 to $112 per person and include meals. The area's oldest guest ranch is **Circle H Mountain Lodge,** Box 7, Clinton, BC V0K 1K0, 604/850-1873. Located in a gorgeous setting, the lodge includes a swimming pool and offers guided horseback rides on its spacious property. Rates are $125 per person, including meals. For total pampering try **Echo Valley Ranch Resort,** Box 16, Jesmond, BC V0K 1K0, 800/253-8831 or 250/459-2386. This adult-oriented establishment features the smooth-riding Tennessee walking horse. Guests can stay in lodge rooms or in cabins. Rates range from $250 to $300 per person, including meals. The **Flying U Ranch,** Box 69, 70 Mile House, BC V0K 2K0, 250/456-7717, is a working cattle ranch dating from 1849. Guests can saddle up and ride the range on their own (maps are provided). The ranch even has its own BC Rail stop.

There's no better way to paddle the Bowron Lakes than with a guide. **Pathways Canada Tours,** 151, 10090-152 St., Suite 116, Surrey, 800/924-2944 or 604/534-5051 www.direct.ca/pathways/index.htm, is based in the Vancouver area but offers weeklong all-inclusive canoe trips on the lakes. The company reserves campsites along the route and caters to all ages and levels of experience.

To hike an interesting portion of the Nuxalk-Carrier Grease Trail (Alexander Mackenzie Heritage Trail), contact **Sea to Sky Adventures,** 106, 11816-88 Ave., Delta, 800/990-8735 or 604/594-7701, www.travel.bc.ca/s/seatosky/. The hike, a strenuous seven-day trip requiring stamina and a decent level of fitness, traverses the Rainbow Range in Tweedsmuir Park. For horseback access to the Rainbow Range and other Tweedsmuir destinations, contact **David Dorsey, Jr. Guide and Outfitter,** Box 3066, Anahim Lake, BC V0L 1C0, 250/742-3539. The Dorsey family has had exclusive guiding rights to the area for three generations. For guided horseback or hiking trips in the pristine Chilcotin area, get in touch with **Chilcotin Holidays,** Gun Creek Rd., Gold Bridge, 250/238-2274, www.chilcotin holidays.com. The company holds the only guiding license in this area and offers pack trips and guest-ranch stays, including winter trips.

An amazing no-holds-barred trip offered by **Canadian River Expeditions**, Box 1023, Whistler, BC V0N 1B0, 800/898-7238 or 2604/938-6651, includes a cruise via sailboat up the coast to Bute Inlet; a floatplane ride to Chilko Lake; a white-water rafting expedition down the Chilko, Chilcotin, and Fraser Rivers to Lillooet; and a train ride back to Vancouver.

For access to Hakai and Fjordland Provincial Recreation Areas, contact **Bella Coola Outfitting Co.**, Box 336, Bella Coola, BC V0T 1C0, 250/982-2933, for sightseeing and fishing; or **Sea Fun Charters**, Box 103, Hagensborg, 800/977-3255, for fishing, diving, or sightseeing on the MV *Sossity*.

CAMPING

In the starkly beautiful dry belt ranch country west of Clinton, camp at **Big Bar Lake** where the ghosts of Natives and cowboys are said to roam. Drive eight kilometers (five miles) north of Clinton on Highway 97, then turn west onto a gravel road for 34 kilometers (20.5 miles). There are 33 sites in two separate campgrounds, with 15 sites on the lakeshore. Facilities are basic. The area is thick with wildlife, and the lake is great for swimming, paddling, and fishing. **Big Bar Guest Ranch**, Box 27, Jesmond, Clinton, BC V0K 1K0, 250/459-2333, also offers a few campsites. Amenities include flush toilets and hot showers. Activities include boating and fishing, horseback riding, and cycling. Fees are $22 per vehicle (two people).

Camping near Barkerville is available in Barkerville Provincial Park (800/689-9025), where there are 170 sites in three campgrounds. Of these, two (Lowhee and Government Hill) offer functional sites with few if any trees. The third, **Forest Rose**, has more trees, plus showers and flush toilets. In Bowron Lakes Provincial Park (800/689-9025) there are more than 100 wilderness campsites along the canoe route and 25 vehicle sites at **Bowron Lake**. Facilities are minimal but you can reserve a spot. **Becker's Lodge**, Box 129, Wells, BC V0K 2R0, 250/992-8864, is a full-service lodge and campground at Bowron Lake. It includes a restaurant, cooking shelter, showers, private beach, and canoe rentals, and they'll even outfit you for a spin around the Bowron Lakes canoe route. Fees start at $15 per vehicle, including hookups.

At Williams Lake, the **Wildwood Campsite**, RR 4, Site 6, Box 50, Williams Lake, BC V2G 4M8, 250/989-4711, has 35 serviced sites, a sani-station, flush toilets, hot showers, laundry facilities, a store, and a freezer for your fish. Fees range from $12 to $15.

Ts'yl-os Provincial Park has two campgrounds with a total of 24 sites. Activities include fishing and hiking. The campgrounds are open from May to October; fees (six dollars per night) are charged from May to September. At Nimpo Lake on Highway 20, there are several private campgrounds including **Nimpo Lake Resort**, 250/742-3239, and **Pine Point Resort**, 250/742-3300. Both these small campgrounds offer hot showers, flush toilets, and fishing gear. In **Tweedsmuir Provincial Park** there are two provincial campgrounds with a total of 42 sites. Facilities include pit toilets, firewood, and sani-stations.

In the Bella Coola area, the **Gnome's Home Campground**, Box 730, Bella Coola, BC V0T 1C0, 250/982-2504, has 40 sites and is open from May through October. Amenities include hot showers, fire pits, and laundry facilities. It's close to all the restaurants and shopping in Hagensborg. Rates are $12 per night plus $1 each for water, sewer, and electricity. The **Bailey Bridge Campsite**, Box 552, Hagensborg, BC V0T 1H0, 250/982-2342, is located on the banks of the Bella Coola River just south of Highway 20. Facilities are minimal (though there are hot showers) but the setting is gorgeous. Rates start at $14 per vehicle.

LODGING

In Gold Bridge, in the Coast Mountains west of Lillooet, is **Tyax Mountain Lake Resort**, Tyaughton Lake Rd., Gold Bridge, 250/238-2221. The large log structure (said to be the biggest in the Pacific Northwest) is a base for ski touring, helicopter skiing, hiking, fishing, and horse trips. The lodge boasts an enormous fireplace, an outdoor hot tub, and a bar and restaurant. There are also several chalets available.

Hills Health and Guest Ranch, 108 Mile Ranch, Comp 26, 100 Mile House, 250/791-5225, e-mail thehills@netshop.net, is a unique wilderness spa in the heart of prime cross-country-ski territory. The ranch's summer activities include hiking, trail rides, swimming (pool or lake), and fishing. The resort's spa features various body and facial treatments, aerobics, and nutritious cuisine. Nightly rates range from $79 to $139 per person.

For luxury accommodations and access to Ts'yl-os Provincial Park, try **Ts'yl-os Lodge**, Box 2560, Williams Lake, BC V2G 4P2, 800/4-TSY-LOS, a true wilderness establishment at the north end of Chilko Lake. The lodge offers overnight fishing and horseback trips to the park, and has a private airstrip so you can just buzz in from Vancouver for the weekend. Daily rates are offered, but the weekly, all-inclusive deals are much more worthwhile: $1,050 to $1,950 includes all meals and equipment. Open May through October.

Tweedsmuir Lodge, RR 1, Bella Coola, BC V0T 1C0, 250/982-2402, has been run by the Corbould family for more than 50 years. They provide guided hikes to Hunlen Falls and portions of the Nuxalk-Carrier Grease Trail, but their real focus is fishing. The lodge and cabins are located at Stuie, a tiny settlement within the park. Rates are $125 per person per night, including meals. Open April through October.

Bella Coola may be a small community, but it has many places to stay. Among them is the **Edlyn Herb Farm Bed & Breakfast**, P.O. Box 282, Hagensborg, BC V0T 1H0, 250/982-2712. Just 10 minutes east of town, the old farmhouse includes three guest rooms and serves up fresh eggs, fruit, and herbs for breakfast. Rates start at $55 per night for a single-bed room and $65 per night for a double. It's for adults only, and no smoking is allowed.

FOOD

For really good home-cooked meals you'll have to be a guest at a ranch or lodge. If you're just passing through, and you want to avoid chains and fast-food restaurants, you've got a challenge. In Lillooet, check out **Elaine's Coffee Garden**, 824 Main St., 250/256-4633, for soups, sandwiches, ice cream, and tasty desserts; a meal for two is about $20. Across the street at 719 Main Street is the **Lillooet Bakery**, 250/256-4889. It serves breakfast, baked items, and terrific coffee.

In Williams Lake, a great place for dessert and coffee is **Rockwells Cappuccino** (Second Avenue South, opposite the Hodgson

Place mall). For lunch or dinner, try **Chef's Corner** (across Second Avenue, 250/398-5622). Their shrimp-smothered crepes and made-to-order omelets are scrumptious. Lunches cost about $10; dinners run around $20.

In Barkerville, stop in at **Wake Up Jake's**, 250/994-3259, for authentic 1870s gold-panners' fare. Caribou stew, fabulous pies and baked goods, and terrific breakfasts are all standard at this inexpensive, fun, and funky establishment. Unfortunately, it's only open May through October.

In Hagensborg, the **Bentinck Arms Pub** in the Bay Motor Hotel (Highway 20, just east of Bella Coola, 250/982-2212) has a pleasant patio and coffee shop, beer, and pub grub.

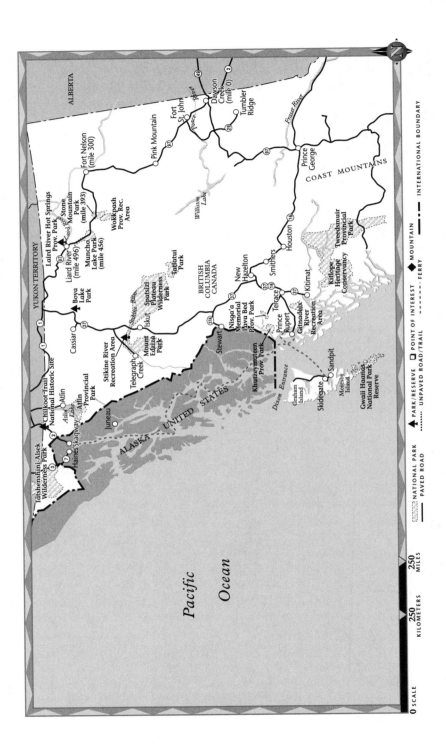

CHAPTER 11

Northern
British Columbia

From the traffic, brewpubs, and university life of Prince George to the absolute isolation and overwhelming majesty of the Tatshenshini-Alsek to the sacred mystery of Haida Gwaii, the North is as complex and diverse as any region in British Columbia. The whole northern half of the province is often dismissed as too difficult to get to, a region of long, dreary drives on rough roads through endless sub-boreal forest. It's true that the North takes some effort and travel here can be expensive and time-consuming, but the reward for your struggle—untainted wilderness teeming with wildlife—is definitely worth any hardship.

Several wilderness parks and recreation areas are located in the northwestern portion of the province, including Khutzeymateen, Spatsizi Plateau, Tatlatui, Mount Edziza, Tatshenshini-Alsek, and others. Note that there is no road access to these parks; you are obliged to get to them by boat, plane, horseback, canoe, or on foot. If you decide to explore the region on your own, you must be wilderness-wise and self-reliant. If you yearn for pristine, remote places but don't have the wilderness skills or the equipment, don't discount the North; there are many guides, outfitters, and wilderness resorts just waiting to introduce you to the magic and wonder of their world.

LAY OF THE LAND

The 200 islands known collectively as Haida Gwaii (Queen Charlotte Islands) stand up to 130 kilometers (78 miles) off the mainland coast across wild Hecate Strait. Like Vancouver Island to the south, Haida Gwaii's western shores are battered by the full force of Pacific storms, while the east side is relatively sheltered. Graham Island, to the north, is the largest island in the archipelago, followed by Moresby Island, to the south.

The remote and misty north coast of the mainland is cut by inlets and spattered with jigsaw-puzzle islands. Just north of the port city of Prince Rupert, the Alaska Panhandle occupies the coast and Canadian soil is entirely inland. Many northern rivers, including the Tatshenshini, Alsek, and Stikine, rise in Canada and flow through Alaska to reach the sea.

The Coast Mountains become increasingly tall toward the north, in the very farthest northwest corner of the province, Fairweather Mountain of the St. Elias Range is the highest point in British Columbia at 4,663 meters (15,388 feet); half the mountain is in BC half is in Alaska. Immense ice fields and glaciers cloak the Coast Mountains; the near-roadless wilderness of the far north is almost unimaginably remote.

East of the Coast Mountains the Stikine Plateau separates the high coastal ranges from the Cassiar Mountains that lie in the interior. The plateau is covered by sub-boreal forest and many lakes such as Burns, Stuart, and Babine. To the east, the Rocky Mountains' northern end is near Muncho Lake. The northeast corner of British Columbia lies east of the Rockies and is unlike any other area of the province. This relatively flat territory is an extension of the Great Plains and is reminiscent of Saskatchewan or the Dakotas.

The Rockies form a drainage divide, sending water flowing east for Hudson's Bay or west for the Pacific. North of the Rockies, the Peace and Liard Rivers also run eastward. You'll encounter the Fraser River once again, as it flows west from its Rocky Mountain birthplace to Giscome Portage just north of Prince George, where the river abruptly turns south. In the far northwest, the Coast Mountains' glaciers spawn several huge rivers: Skeena, Nass, and Stikine. The Tatshenshini and Alsek both rise in the Yukon and flow through the farthest corner of BC, where they join; the Alsek continues on through Alaska to the ocean. The Teslin River rises in the mountains and flows north to the Yukon and, eventually, the Arctic Ocean.

The region's climate is as varied as the landscape, with one common thread: cold. Even on the coast, the summers are short, the winters long and harsh. Although snow is rare at Prince Rupert, in winter the highway leading east to Terrace is among the most dangerous and frequently closed in the province. The farther north you go, the shorter the summers—a fact that makes the Peace Country climate all the more amazing. Lying in a rain shadow, and at a lesser elevation than the mountains to the west, this is BC's major grain-producing region.

HISTORY AND CULTURE

The coastal Native cultures of Haida and Tsimshian were perhaps the most powerful of all the Pacific Northwest aboriginal nations. The Haida were fierce warriors and renowned seafarers who hunted whales from cedar-log canoes. They occupied Haida Gwaii and the southern portion of Prince of Wales Island (Alaska), and have lived here for perhaps 10,000 years. Archaeologists speculate that Haida Gwaii did not experience glaciation, so human society may have established and flourished here longer than anywhere else in BC. Haida Gwaii is so isolated that even the Haida language has no known linguistic relatives. Across Hecate Strait, from Portland Inlet and the mouth of the Nass River to as far south as the territories of the Nuxalk at Bella Bella, the mainland coast was home to Tsimshian. The Tsimshian were concentrated mainly along the Skeena River.

Inland territories were shared by several nations, including the Haisla to the south, the Gitxsan along the Skeena River, and the Nisga'a on the Nass River. Tahltan and Iskut lived in the mountains north of the Nisga'a; a myriad of peoples, including the Tlingit, Tagish, and others, shared the very far north and northwest. Wet'suwet'en and Dakelh homelands lay in the interior forests. In the northeast lived prairie and northern plains peoples: Sekani, Dene, Salteaux, and Cree.

All these peoples experienced European contact in the 1800s. The Haida were contacted by Russian, American, and European traders and experienced three smallpox epidemics between 1790 and 1860, reducing the population from an estimated 7,000 to less than 600. Much of the complex Haida culture was lost, but it was revived again in bits and pieces beginning in the 1950s. The Tsimshian allowed the Hudson's Bay Company to build a trading post in their territory in 1834. Although their population was hit hard by smallpox, the Tsimshian culture survives today largely because of their strong oral tradition of storytelling and family histories.

The Nisga'a territories were so remote that white contact was sparse and sporadic. The tribe experienced a devastating natural disaster—a volcanic eruption and huge lava flow in approximately 1750 that wiped out several villages and may have killed up to 2,000 people. The Gitxsan were buffered by isolation until 1866 when a telegraph line was built through their territory, to be followed later by a railway constructed along the Skeena to the port of Prince Rupert. In the northeast, the Sekani, Salteaux, and Cree are the only First Nations in BC to be governed by a government treaty. Native leaders signed Treaty No. 8 between 1899 and 1914.

Peace River valley

Canneries and whaling stations accounted for much of the coast's early settlement, with logging and prospecting drawing newcomers inland from the sea along the great rivers. Gold fever did not touch this area of the province, except for the very far northwest, when the Chilkoot Trail became a river of humans climbing from Skagway over the mountains to the Klondike. Gold seekers were also drawn to Atlin in 1898, spawning a short-lived population boom in the area. But gold wasn't the only thing people came to find. Other minerals, notably copper, have been mined here. The northeast plains country is the only area of BC where petroleum has been discovered and exploited. The Peace River country is also an agricultural area—the most northerly grain-growing region in the world.

The massive Bennett and Peace Canyon dams located northeast of Prince George were completed in 1968 and 1976 respectively to provide electrical power to BC. Williston Lake, the reservoir created by the Bennett dam, is the world's ninth-largest hydroelectric reservoir. The lake flooded villages, burial grounds, and sacred sites of the Keh Dene people.

FLORA AND FAUNA

There is speculation in the scientific community that Haida Gwaii remained ice-free during the Ice Age, thereby providing a refuge for plants, animals, and humans. Today several plant and animal species are unique to Haida Gwaii. These islands are also renowned for birding and are home to more than 240 resident and migrant species such as peregrine falcons, bald eagles, and tufted puffins.

The coastal forests, especially the Khutzeymateen area north of Prince Rupert, are home to grizzly bears. Kermode or "spirit" bears, white-haired versions of the black bear, are concentrated in an area north of Terrace. Rare glacier bears—black bears with a bluish hue to their fur—live in the Tatshenshini-Alsek area in the province's northwest corner.

In the interior, black and grizzly bears, wolves, moose, and caribou roam the forests. An area of incredible wildlife abundance lies in the northern Rockies in the Muskwa-Kechika region, an area known as the Serengeti of North America. It's home to large herds of elk and

BRITISH COLUMBIA

caribou; concentrations of deer, moose, and sheep; predators such as wolves, bears, and coyotes; and a multitude of smaller mammals.

Mosquitoes and black flies are common throughout BC in the summer, but they are tremendously plentiful in the North. They come in hordes—clouds. They will drive you bananas. A goodly supply of bug dope is essential for outdoor enjoyment in the North. If you're allergic to insect repellants, seriously consider bringing a bug shirt (a shirt with attached hood made from mosquito netting) or a hat with attached netting.

VISITOR INFORMATION

One thing about the North—you'll be doing a lot of driving. Many roads are remote and rough, and it's a long way between towns, so if you're planning to travel here make sure you have a sturdy vehicle and that you know how to change a tire. In-car survival gear doesn't hurt either. Always carry emergency food, blankets, and flares. Another caution: Be alert for wildlife on the road, especially on the Alaska Highway. Hitting a sheep, caribou, elk, or moose can be deadly—for both you and the creature. If you spot wildlife, pull well off the road to take photos. Never approach wild animals.

The city of Prince George lies smack in the center of the province. It's a transportation hub with road, rail, and air links between south and north, east and west. Major roads form a rough triangle through northern BC. The Yellowhead Highway (Highway 16) traverses the entire region from Jasper, Alberta, in the Rocky Mountains on the east side to the port of Prince Rupert on the west coast. Beware of wildlife—especially moose—on the road.

The Stewart-Cassiar Highway (Highway 37) connects with Highway 16 at Terrace and leads through very remote territory in the northwest. It provides access to Mount Edziza and Spatsizi Plateau Provincial Parks and connects with the Alaska Highway at Watson Lake, just north of the BC/Yukon border. Approximately 600 kilometers (360 miles) of the Stewart-Cassiar Highway are paved, but the road remains rough in places. Portions of the highway double as air strips. The first such area is 47 kilometers (28 miles) north of Cranberry Junction; the second is 27 kilometers (16 miles) north of the first (southernmost) Bell-Irving River bridge. Aircraft *always* have the right of way. Pull over and let them land or take off.

Mile 0 of the Alaska Highway (Highway 97) is in Dawson Creek in northeastern BC. It snakes north then west through a remarkable area renowned for its high density of wildlife. The highway passes through Fort St. John and Fort Nelson (both in BC), Watson Lake, and Yukon and then continues west to Johnson's Crossing and Whitehorse and onward to Alaska. The Hart Highway (also numbered as Highway 97) connects Prince George (on Highway 16) with Dawson Creek and the Alaska Highway.

The Alaska Highway

The very northwest corner of the province is accessible only from the Yukon or from Alaska. Highway 3 from Haines, Alaska, travels through BC along the eastern boundary of the Tatshenshini-Alsek Provincial Wilderness Park, then crosses into the Yukon to connect with the Alaska Highway. Highway 2 leads from Skagway, Alaska, over White Pass in the Coast Mountains, then continues on through BC and into the Yukon. The town of Atlin and Atlin Provincial Park in northern BC are only accessible from the Alaska Highway via a gravel road that leads south from the Yukon and into BC.

Prince Rupert is the northernmost terminal for BC Ferries' service. Ferries connect Prince Rupert with Skidegate on Graham Island, Haida Gwaii, where Highway 16 continues along the island's east side. Regular ferry service also connects Prince Rupert with Port Hardy at the north end of Vancouver Island. This 14-hour trip wanders through waters sheltered from the Pacific by offshore islands and passes fishing camps, Native villages, waterfalls, and pristine forest along the way. (See Chapter 3 for details on Port Hardy.)

BC Rail connects Vancouver with Prince George, and VIA Rail

THE PRICE OF PROGRESS

In the 1950s a copper, lead, and zinc mine on the Tulsequah River south of Atlin operated for a mere six years but left a legacy of acid mine drainage—sulfuric acid that's generated when rocks bearing sulfides are exposed to air, rain, and runoff. For 40 years this toxic cocktail has drained into the river, a spawning ground for salmon.

In the old days, ore was sent out by barge for processing. Now, Redfern Resources of Vancouver has purchased the property and wants to re-open the mine. This time, though, they want to build a 160-kilometer (100-mile) access road from Atlin to the mine. The proposed road would open up one of the last remaining wilderness areas in BC and literally pave the way for logging and more mining.

As in other regions of BC, there are numerous points of view on the proposed development and the debate is polarized and acrimonious. Pro-development factions point to the possibility for jobs and economic security for local residents. Environmentalists say the project received only the briefest of reviews by the provincial and federal governments and many questions remain unanswered. Local Tlingit First Nations say the road will destroy an ancient migration route used by their people, and that the development jeopardizes their land-claims negotiations. The battle is international, with Alaskan officials concerned about potential damage to salmon habitat. And Redfern Resources says it has prepared a thorough investigation of impacts on wildlife, fish, hydrology, water quality, and other parameters, and that the proposal should be approved without further delay.

The proposal has deeply divided Atlin residents, pitting neighbor against neighbor, splitting families, and throwing into question the values of wilderness, tourism, and aboriginal traditions.

operates regular passenger rail service along the Skeena line between Prince Rupert on the coast, Prince George, Jasper, Edmonton, and points east including Toronto and Montréal. The White Pass and Yukon Route is a scenic, historic excursion train that once operated between Skagway, Alaska, and Whitehorse, Yukon, passing through northwestern BC en route. The railway company recently decided to operate only between Skagway and White Pass (the Canada/U.S. border) with no onward connection to Whitehorse.

Major airports served by regional airlines are located in Dawson Creek, Fort St. John, Prince George, Terrace, Smithers, Prince Rupert, and Sandspit on Moresby Island, Haida Gwaii. Many northern communities have smaller airports and airstrips served by small airlines and charter aircraft.

For detailed information about northern BC, contact Northern BC Tourism, Unit 11, 3167 Tatlow Rd., P.O. Box 1030, Smithers, BC V0J 2N0, 250/847-5227, fax 250/847-4321, www.travel.bc.ca/region/north. Information is also available from the Peace/Alaska Highway Tourist Association, Box 6850-HB, 9908-106 Ave., Fort St. John, BC V1J 6M7, 250/787-3407.

NATURE AND ADVENTURE SIGHTS: MAINLAND

Atlin

Small houses, big dogs, and a surprising mix of residents make this town of 500 worth the trip. The area's natural beauty and independent lifestyle have attracted artists and craftspeople to Atlin. Established during the Klondike gold rush of the 1890s, Atlin retains that frontier, end-of-the-road feeling—literally. The town is at the end of a 96-kilometer (57.5-mile) gravel road; the other end of the road connects with the Alaska Highway in the Yukon. Come here just to hang out, walk around, and visit the studios of the local artists.

The town is situated on the shore of Atlin Lake, BC's largest natural lake at 140 kilometers long (84 miles); **Atlin Provincial Park** lies at the south end of the lake. There is no road access to the park but you can get there by boat or plane. Covering more than 270,000 hectares (667,000 acres), the park encompasses Coast Mountain wilderness. A

K.D.Wong/Blackbird Design

Atlin

third of the park is under glaciers and snowfields. Popular activities in the park include hiking, camping, fishing, climbing, and photography. For a stunning view book a charter flight to see the Llewellyn Glacier.

Details: From the Stewart-Cassiar Highway near Watson Lake, Yukon, travel west on the Alaska Highway for approximately 375 kilometers (225 miles) to Jake's Corner. Turn south toward Atlin, continuing for 96 kilometers (57.5 miles). For information, contact the Atlin Visitor's Association, Box 365, Atlin, BC V0W 1A0, 250/651-7522 (summer) or 250/651-7470.

Chilkoot Trail National Historic Site

The last great gold rush in North America was the mad dash to the goldfields of Alaska and an area of the Yukon known as the Klondike in the 1890s. There were overland routes, but quicker by far—though no less arduous—was the route from Skagway/Dyea, Alaska, over Chilkoot Pass in the Coast Mountains and down to the banks of Bennett Lake, headwaters of the Yukon River. Gold seekers were required to enter Canada with one ton of supplies, enough to last for a year. Incredibly, thousands of men and women made the backbreaking trip.

Today hikers can make the scenic trek from Alaska to Canada via the Chilkoot Trail. The trail is managed jointly by Parks Canada and the U.S. National Parks Service. You must be in good physical condition and experienced at wilderness survival and backpacking. The weather is extreme and can change rapidly—preparation, including adequate foul-weather clothing, is essential. It's a spectacular but grueling 53-kilometer (33-mile) hike that climbs from sea level to 939 meters (3,246 feet) and takes four or five days to complete. The trail ends on the shores of Bennett Lake, British Columbia, from which a boat ferries hikers to Carcross, Yukon. From there hikers can catch a bus back to Skagway or on to Whitehorse. It's also possible to return to Skagway on the White Pass and Yukon Route Railway (see Appendix A for contact information).

Details: *For more information on the Chilkoot Trail, contact Parks Canada, Yukon Historic Sites, 205-300 Main St., Whitehorse, Yukon, 867/667-3910, or Klondike Gold Rush National Historic Park, Box 517, Skagway, AK 99840, 907/983-2921. Trail fee $35 adults (discounts for youth and seniors); permits are available from Parks Canada. Hikers beginning in Skagway must pre-clear Canadian Customs by visiting or phoning the customs office in Whitehorse, 800/665-8100. Those ending their hike in Skagway must report to U.S. Customs upon arrival.*

Hazelton

There are two towns here: New Hazelton, a mostly white settlement on Highway 16; and Hazelton (or Old Hazelton), a mostly aboriginal town just north of the highway. This settlement is the cultural center of the Gitxsan First Nation, a close-knit, 7,000-year-old community that has survived the ravages of European contact and development with its culture largely intact. Today the 'Ksan model village, a collection of cedar longhouses and totem poles gracing the riverbank, allows visitors to witness the Native settlement as it once was. There is a theater, museum, and gift shop, but the best way to experience 'Ksan is via a guided tour of the cedar houses. Each house's interior is furnished with artifacts depicting a different aspect of ancient Gitxsan life. The tour includes recordings of family songs and stories normally guarded in great secrecy. On Friday evenings in July and August 'Ksan dancers, dressed in ceremonial clothing and masks, perform dances and tell stories.

Highway 62 leads on past Hazelton to the lovely **Kispiox** valley nestled along the fledgling Skeena River. In the village of Kispiox are 15 standing totem poles. More totem poles are in the village of Gitsegukla on Highway 16, 26 kilometers (15.5 miles) west of New Hazelton.

Details: *New Hazelton is located 67 kilometers (40 miles) west of Smithers on Highway 16. Take Highway 62 north from New Hazelton to Hazelton and 'Ksan (the road crosses the Bulkley River on a spectacular one-lane bridge over* *a deep gorge). 'Ksan model village open May–Oct daily 9–6, weekdays 9–5 the rest of the year. Admission is free, guided tours $7. For information call 250/842-5723.*

Kechika-Muskwa

"The Serengeti of North America" is a vast region of northeastern BC protected by provincial parks, ecological reserves, and special management areas. Ostensibly, mining and logging are not allowed in special management areas; time will tell whether the Muskwa-Kechika region remains as unspoiled as it is at present.

The protected region covers 4.4 million hectares (10.9 million acres) in a rough crescent west of Fort Nelson and north from Fort St. John to the Yukon border. Protection of the entire Muskwa-Kechika was the result of years of negotiation among many interest groups in the region; protected status was announced by the provincial government in October 1997. The majority of the Muskwa-Kechika is utter wilderness—a maze of peaks, lakes, game trails, and glaciers. Access to the backcountry is best accomplished in the company of a guide. In the words of BC Parks, "We don't have the staff, resources, or facilities to keep an eye on everyone who goes into the backcountry here." In other words, if you intend to hike, canoe, or otherwise venture off the road, you must be totally self-sufficient. Brochures and information on the area are available from the Peace/Alaska Highway Tourist Association.

Besides the Rocky Mountain scenery, the best thing about the Muskwa-Kechika region is the abundance of wildlife. The region is home to an estimated 4,000 caribou, 2,000 moose, 15,000 elk, 7,000 stone sheep, and 3,500 grizzly and black bears. You'd have to keep your eyes closed to avoid seeing wild creatures in the Muskwa.

Within the region are several adjoining provincial parks and recreation areas, all accessible from the Alaska Highway. **Stone Mountain Provincial Park** is the most southerly of these. The dramatic scenery of this park includes alpine tundra and broad glacial valleys. Summit Lake, which is within the park, is the starting point for some terrific, if primitive, wilderness hiking. There are no facilities or maintained trails. **Wokkpash Recreation Area** lies southwest of Stone Mountain.

The northern end of the Rocky Mountains is marked by **Muncho Lake**, a drop of liquid jade with a backdrop of dramatic peaks. Unlike glacial lakes, which derive their color from tiny rock fragments suspended in the water, Muncho Lake's green hue comes from copper dioxide.

Liard River Hot Springs Provincial Park is an astonishing place, well worth the long journey. Two steaming-hot mineral pools create their own microclimate and local ecology and provide habitat for plants normally found much farther south, including the insect-eating sundew. The pools can get as hot as 49 degrees Celsius (120 degrees Fahrenheit).

Stone Mountain Provincial Park

Alpha Pool has huts for changing; Beta Pool is smaller and can be reached by a short hike. The setting is especially magical in winter, when icicles and frost cling to the vegetation.

Details: Fort Nelson is located at Mile 300 of the Alaska Highway, 460 kilometers beyond Dawson Creek. Contact the Visitor Infocentre at Bag Service 399, Fort Nelson, BC V0C 1R0, 250/774-6400 or 250/774-2541 (off-season).

Stone Mountain Provincial Park straddles the Alaska Highway, 112 kilometers (67 miles) beyond Fort Nelson. Wokkpash Provincial Recreation Area adjoins Stone Mountain to the southwest (no road access or facilities). Muncho Lake is off the Alaska Highway at Mile 427, approximately 670 kilometers from Fort Nelson. Laird River Hot Springs is at Mile 497 of the highway, 790 kilometers north of Fort Nelson. For information on all Muskwa-Kechika parks and recreation areas call 250/787-3407.

Nisga'a Memorial Lava Bed Provincial Park

In 1998 the Nisga'a (NISH-ga) First Nation completed negotiations with the federal and provincial governments to establish a Native homeland and self-governing region in traditional Nisga'a lands on the Nass River north of Terrace. This provincial park was created to commemorate a volcanic explosion and lava flow that occurred in about 1750. According to Nisga'a legend, the molten lava, forest fires, and loss of perhaps 2,000 lives was nature's way of getting even for the acts of young boys who were tormenting salmon in the Nass River. Today 39 square kilometers (15 square miles) of the valley floor is blanketed by a thick layer of gray-black lava that is only just beginning to break down and support new life. Trees, grasses, ferns, mosses, and lichens are gradually reclaiming the bleak, hard surface. This is a fascinating, sacred place. The village of Gitwinksihlkw (Canyon City), formerly accessible only by a swinging pedestrian bridge suspended high over the Nass River, is now linked via a new vehicle bridge adorned with four excellent totem poles.

Details: Take the Nisga'a Highway north 64 kilometers (38.5 miles) from Terrace (this is a rough road, not suitable for RVs or trailers). For more information contact BC Parks, 250/847-7320, or the Nisga'a Tribal Council, 250/633-2601.

Prince Rupert

The end of the road! Highway 16 terminates here in this "City of Rainbows," a good euphemism for "it rains a lot here." Prince Rupert is Canada's rainiest city, but don't let that stop you. The **Museum of Northern BC,** 100 First Ave. E., 250/624-3207, is excellent, providing insight on the culture and life of the Tsimshian First Nation. Rupert is the best access point for **Khutzeymateen Provincial Park**, a remote coastal wilderness park that is Canada's only grizzly bear sanctuary. Accessible only by air or boat, the park lies 45 kilometers (27 miles) north of Prince Rupert in the northern reaches of what's become known as the Great Bear Rain Forest. Only guided tours have access to the park; see "Guides and Outfitters."

Nearby Port Edward grew up around the **North Pacific Cannery**, BC's oldest surviving cannery (from 1899) and now a museum. Salmon canneries once dotted the coast from Vancouver to Alaska, but with declining salmon stocks and the advent of much larger fishing vessels the need for hundreds of small canneries disappeared. Today the North Pacific Cannery is a national historic site.

AUTHOR'S TOP PICKS: HOT SPRINGS

- **Ainsworth**—*This place is fully developed with pools, a cave (an abandoned mine shaft), and a hotel. It has the highest level of mineral saturation among BC's hot pools, without the sulfur smell.*

- **Harrison**—*A resort town complete with lake, big hotels, sandy beach, and very hot water.*

- **Hot Springs Cove**—*Accessible by boat, kayak, or floatplane from Tofino, this is Vancouver Island's only known hot spring. Bathing suits are optional.*

- **Liard**—*The two hot pools here create an astonishingly tropical microclimate. Summertime interpretive programs accompany soakings. In winter the entire area becomes a wonderland of steam and frost.*

- **Radium**—*Facilities here include a bathing pool, changing room, gift shop, and café. Accommodations and services are available in the adjacent town of Radium.*

Details: Prince Rupert is located on Highway 16, 140 kilometers (84 miles) west of Terrace and 725 kilometers (435 miles) from Prince George. For information contact Box 669, Prince Rupert, BC V8J 3S1, 250/624-5637.

For the North Pacific Cannery Village Museum, take the road from Highway 16 to Port Edward, a distance of 10.5 kilometers (6 miles). Admission is $5. For information call 250/628-3538.

Air or boat charters for Khutzeymateen Provincial Park can be obtained in Prince Rupert. For information call 250/847-7320.

Smithers

If you drive west from Prince George through the seemingly endless expanse of rolling country clothed in forests of spruce and pine, you'll

K. D. Wong/Blackbird Design

Twin Falls at Smithers

be heartened when you see the land begin to rise. As if by magic, you'll suddenly find yourself in the mountains again with the sporty town of Smithers just down the road. Smithers, set at the foot of 2,621-meter (8,649-foot) Hudson Bay Mountain, is a town full of healthy-looking people who love to ski, hike, fish, cycle, and climb. The town is home to numerous outdoor-supply shops where you can rent a bike, stock up on camping gear, or buy a fishing license. A popular local hike is to **Twin Falls**, an easy half-kilometer walk from the parking lot at the end of the Kathlyn Lake road just west of town.

Details: Smithers is on the Yellowhead Highway (Highway 16), 371 kilometers (222.5 miles) west of Prince George. For information contact the Smithers and District Chamber of Commerce, Box 2379, Smithers, BC V0J 2N0, 250/847-9854.

Spatsizi Plateau Wilderness Provincial Park
This park is among the largest protected areas anywhere in Canada. Covering more than 650,000 hectares (1.6 million acres), the park

has no facilities and no road access and is not a place for the inexperienced. For competent campers and backpackers, though, it's a veritable paradise on Earth with the glaciated peaks of the Skeena Mountains, the rolling, forested expanse of the Spatsizi Plateau, and great herds of caribou and elk. The park's remoteness deters all but the most dedicated wilderness seekers; fewer than 1,000 people visit Spatsizi each year. The name *spatsizi* means "red goat" in the Dene language; the area's mountain goats, normally snow-white, pick up a reddish color from rolling in the red soils of the plateau (the soils are colored from iron oxides). The adjoining **Tatlatui Provincial Park** protects an additional 106,000 hectares (261,000 acres) and includes the headwaters of the Finlay River, which eventually flows into Williston Lake (the huge reservoir formed by the Bennett dam). Access is by floatplane.

The Stikine River flows westward along the northern boundary of Spatsizi Park, crossing Highway 37 north of Iskut and continuing through the settlement of Telegraph Creek and Mount Edziza Provincial Park (see below). The **Stikine River Provincial Recreation Area** is a narrow corridor on both sides of the river, a band of relatively protected land connecting Spatsizi and Mount Edziza Parks. The recreation area includes the **Grand Canyon of the Stikine**, a narrow gorge 80 kilometers (48 miles) long where the great river surges between 300-meter (990-foot) rock walls. The canyon's east end marks the pullout point for raft and canoe trips coming down the Stikine from Spatsizi Park.

Details: Spatsizi Plateau Wilderness Provincial Park is located 300 air kilometers (180 miles) north of Smithers. For information contact BC Parks Skeena District Office, Bag 5000, 3790 Alfred Ave., Smithers, BC V0J 2N0, 250/847-7320. Outfitters and tour guides can be hired in Smithers, Terrace, and several places along Highway 37.

Tatshenshini-Alsek Wilderness Provincial Park

The remote northwest corner of BC was declared a provincial wilderness park in 1995. In so doing, the BC government used this crucial piece of land to complete an enormous protected area encompassed by Canada's Kluane National Park and Alaska's Wrangell/St. Elias and Glacier Bay National Parks. Together, these four parks form the largest international protected area in the world; BC's portion alone covers 958,000 hectares (2.3 million acres). The parks, a UNESCO world heritage site, contain the earth's largest nonpolar ice fields.

The Tatshenshini River, once threatened by a proposed copper-mine development, is now protected from its headwaters in the Yukon to its confluence with the Alsek River just before the Alsek crosses into Alaska and flows west to the Pacific. This is one of Canada's last wild rivers: no bridge crossings, no roads, no facilities or development, no mines, no logging. Just bears, salmon, wind, glaciers, North America's tallest mountains, and endless forest. The surrounding wilderness is at once humbling and affirming.

This is no place for amateurs. Rather, it's wild, dangerous, and a long way from help. To journey here on your own, you must be experienced, self-reliant, and well supplied. Rafting the entire 260-kilometer (156-mile) river system from Dalton Post in the Yukon to Dry Bay, Alaska, takes about 6 days, though a 10-day trip gives lots of time to explore and enjoy the many wonders of this awesome land.

Details: The only direct access to Tatshenshini-Alsek Provincial Park is by rafting down the Tatshenshini River. For information contact BC Parks, 800 Johnson St., Victoria, 250/387-5002, or a travel outfitter (see "Guides and Outfitters").

Telegraph Creek

Similar to Atlin in the far northwest, Telegraph Creek is difficult to get to and therefore attracts a certain type of independent character. The lower town, its false-front buildings facing the Stikine River, has a frontier feel to it. Europeans settled here in 1861 with the discovery of gold in the river gravel. Steamships on the Stikine could travel no farther upriver, and the town grew as a supply point. Later, ambitious plans to build a telegraph line over land between Paris and New York included a station in Telegraph Creek (hence the town's name), but the grand project died when a telegraph cable was successfully laid across the Atlantic in 1866. The town continued to supply gold seekers headed for points even farther north, especially to the Klondike in 1898.

The access road for Telegraph Creek passes along the northern boundary of **Mount Edziza Provincial Park**, on the opposite side of the Stikine River from the road and the town. The park encompasses the cone of an extinct volcano, Mount Edziza, created by successive eruptions perhaps 4 million years ago. Eruptions continued up to about 1,500 years ago; much of the landscape is still devoid of vegetation. The aptly named Spectrum Range is a series of multihued volcanic peaks. Guided hiking or horse packing trips are available in Telegraph Creek, Dease Lake, or Iskut. There is no road access or facilities, just wilderness and lots of it.

Details: Turn onto Telegraph Creek Road from Highway 37 at Dease Lake, 492 kilometers (295 miles) north of Highway 16. Then drive west for 113 kilometers (68 miles). Accommodations in Telegraph Creek are limited; phone ahead for reservations (see "Lodging").

Mount Edziza Provincial Park park is accessible from Kinaskan Lake Provincial Park on Highway 37. You can boat across the lake to the head of the Mowdade Trail, which leads 24 kilometers (14 miles) north into Mount Edziza. For more information contact BC Parks, Skeena District Office, Bag 5000, 3790 Alfred Ave., Smithers, BC V0J 2N0, 250/847-7320.

Terrace

Located on Highway 16 about halfway between New Hazelton and Prince Rupert, Terrace makes a good base of operations for anyone venturing south to Kitlope Provincial Park or north to Nisga'a Memorial Lava Bed Provincial Park. The region's other claim to fame is the Canadian record for a one-day snowfall: 118 centimeters (46.5 inches) fell in a single 24-hour period in 1974 at Lakesle Lake just south of Terrace. In February 1999, Terrace received 110 centimeters (43.3 inches) in 24 hours.

Kitlope Provincial Park, a wilderness area that embraces grand Coast Mountain scenery and adjoins the northern section of Tweedsmuir Provincial Park, preserves a huge chunk of coastal rain forest. The park is operated jointly by BC Parks and the Haisla First Nation, who were instrumental in saving the region from logging in 1994.

Continuing along Highway 16 west of Terrace, the road clings to the north bank of the wide Skeena River. About midway between Terrace and Prince Rupert is Exchamsiks Provincial Park, with campsites and a boat launch. This is the starting point for exploration of **Gitnadoix River Recreation Area**, which covers 58,000 hectares (143,500 acres) of lakes, rivers, and marshes on the Skeena's opposite shore. Access to the Gitnadoix is by boat only. For experienced canoeists, this is a fabulous place to paddle and explore. You'll have harbor seals for company—they swim more than 100 kilometers (60 miles) up the Skeena looking for salmon.

Details: Terrace is located on Highway 16, 210 kilometers (126 miles) west of Smithers. For information contact 4511 Keith Ave., Terrace, 250/635-2063.

For access to Kitlope Provincial Park, take Highway 37 south from Terrace 54 kilometers (32 miles) to the village of Kitamaat. For information call 250/847-7320 or contact the Haisla Tribal Council, Box 1101, Kitamaat Village, BC V0T 2B0, 250/639-9382.

For Gitnadoix Provincial Recreation Area, launch from Exchamsiks River Provincial Park on Highway 16, 55 kilometers (33 miles) west of Terrace. Currents in the Skeena are very strong, and the crossing to Gitnadoix is for experienced boaters only. For information contact BC Parks, Skeena District Office, Bag 5000, 3790 Alfred Ave., Smithers, BC V0J 2N0, 250/847-7320.

NATURE AND ADVENTURE SIGHTS: HAIDA GWAII

Gwaii Haanas National Park Reserve

In the 1980s, the southern portion of Moresby Island was being logged when the Haida First Nation and environmental activists from around the world fought to save the massive trees and culture of the Haida homeland. The ancient village of Sgan Gwaii (also called Ninstints) had already been declared a UNESCO World Heritage Site for the presence of standing totem poles. In 1985 the BC and Canadian governments established protection for the southern end of Moresby Island and several adjacent islands by making them a national park reserve. Today the area is managed jointly by Parks Canada and the Haida.

Among the main attractions of Gwaii Haanas are the stunning forests (Windy Bay on Lyell Island has some very large trees); the huge populations of sea birds, bald eagles, and killer whales; the array of marine life in the shallow coves; and the Haida villages. Among the village sites are Skedans (also called K'una or Koona), Cumshewa, Tanuu, and, the most famous of all, Sgan Gwaii (Ninstints). **Sgan Gwaii** is an eerie, mystical, humbling place—a ghost town like no other. Located on a tiny island off the southwest tip of Moresby Island,

Holly Quan

Mists at Haida Gwaii

the village faces a quiet lagoon. The remains of totem poles leaning at crazy angles are spread along the crescent beach. The village was abandoned after the smallpox epidemic of the 1860s; the lush rain forest has been reclaiming it ever since.

Other park highlights include **Hot Springs Island** (located just south of Lyell Island on the east side of the park, its healing hot waters are a welcome relief for paddlers) and **Burnaby Narrows**, a neck of water between Burnaby and Moresby Islands. The cold, nutrient-rich waters of Hecate Strait flush back and forth through this channel and create a living carpet of sea life—sea stars, snails, anemones, clams, and more.

To really see the best of Gwaii Haanas, consider visiting with a guided sailing or kayaking tour (see "Guides and Outfitters"). If you're determined to visit on your own, you must be experienced. The area is subject to rapid weather changes, high winds, large tidal variations, difficult currents, and frequent ocean swells. Excellent paddling, navigation, and rescue skills are required.

Details: If you intend to travel into the park on your own, you must register with park wardens. Entry fees are $10 per day for day trips, $10 per night for stays of one to five nights, $60 flat fee for stays of 6 to 14 nights, and $80 flat fee for stays of 15 nights or longer. At present there are no designated campsites. Beach camping is permitted except in special areas such as Sgan Gwaii. Contact Gwaii Haanas National Park Reserve, P.O. Box 37f, Queen Charlotte, BC V0T 1S0, 250/599-8818, e-mail gwaiicom@qcislands.net.

Naikoon Provincial Park

Covering a large part of Graham Island's northeast corner, Naikoon is a great place to observe sea life and hike along remote, pristine beaches. A path along **East Beach** traverses the park from the settlement of Tlell in the south to Tow Hill at the northeastern tip of the island. The beach is 94 kilometers (56.5 miles) long and requires between four and six days to hike (remember to pack fresh water). Rose Spit, an ecological reserve at the northeast tip of the island, is 17 kilometers (10 miles) past Tow Hill.

Details: From Skidegate, take Highway 16 north for 36 kilometers (21.5 miles) to Tlell and park headquarters. For the north entrance, continue past Tlell on Highway 16 for 61 kilometers (36.5 miles) to Massett. For more information contact BC Parks, Skeena District Office, Bag 5000, 3790 Alfred Ave., Smithers, BC V0J 2N0, 250/847-7320, or call the local park office in Tlell, 250/557-4390.

GUIDES AND OUTFITTERS

For guides and outfitters in the Muskwa-Kechika region, contact **Northern BC Guides Association**, Box 6370, Fort St. John, BC V1J 4K6; or **Canadian Alpine Expeditions**, Box 150, Moberly Lake, BC V0C 1X0, 250/788-9330. **Duke's Air Service**, 250/776-7500, provides charter flights to various points within the Muskwa-Kechika region.

Many outfitters offer rafting trips on the Tatshenshini. **Canadian River Expeditions**, P.O. Box 1023, Whistler, BC V0N 1B0, 800/898-7238, www.whistler.net/canriver, also offers trips on the Skeena, Chilko, Chilcotin, and Fraser Rivers, plus hiking and rafting trips in the northern Rockies. Their emphasis is on interpretation, shore walks, natural history, and low-impact camping. Most trips have only moderate rapids—these are nature-study adventures, not white-water-thrills trips. Similar trips are offered by **Arctic Edge Expeditions**, Box 4850, Whitehorse, Yukon Y1A 4N6, 867/633-5470; and **Tatshenshini Expediting**, 1602 Alder St., Whitehorse, 867/633-2742.

The River League, Suite 201, 1112 Broughton St., Vancouver, 800/440-1322 or 604/687-3417, www.riverleague.ca, offers an entirely different kind of wilderness rafting trip. They lead expeditions on threatened rivers such as the Taku, Whiting, and Turnagain in northwestern BC. The company maintains a solid conservation ethic while showing people endangered wildernesses they hope will someday earn protection.

For remote access to northwestern wilderness parks contact **Harbour Air Seaplanes**, 4760 Inglis Dr., Richmond, or call them in Iskut, 250/234-3526, to arrange charter flights into Spatsizi Plateau and Mount Edziza Provincial Parks. **Iskut River and Trail Adventures**, Iskut, BC V0J 1K0, 250/234-3331; and **Stikine Canyon Trail Rides**, General Delivery, Dease Lake, BC V0J 1LO, 250/771-4301, offer access to Spatsizi Plateau and Tatlatui Provincial Parks.

K. D. Wong/Blackbird Design

Tatshenshini River

ECO-FRIENDLY:
BLUEWATER ADVENTURES

In 1974, Dan Culver started operating white-water rafting trips, one of the first such operations in British Columbia. Culver next branched into sailing expeditions in the Vancouver area, then discovered whale-watching in the Inside Passage and pioneered sailing trips to northern Vancouver Island. When he sold the rafting side of his business to focus on sailing, Culver adopted the name Bluewater Adventures to draw attention to the oceangoing nature of his expeditions.

In 1983, Culver bought the Island Roamer, *a 63-foot ketch that allowed for trips to remote destinations, notably Haida Gwaii. Culver sold the whole business to his captain and chief guide, Randy Burke, in 1988; Burke continues to head the company and has purchased a second vessel, the 65-foot* Snow Goose, *a power vessel that was built as a research ship.*

In-depth knowledge of marine environments is Bluewater's claim to ecotourism fame. Even a visit to the company's Web site provides a treasury of information on wildlife, marine ecosystems, Native culture, and interactions between them. Sailing trips to Haida Gwaii include an onboard naturalist or Native culture expert. Respect and appreciation in a casual, fun atmosphere are hallmarks of a Bluewater Adventure tour.

The company practices what it preaches. Bluewater Adventures has developed a code of ethics for operating in wilderness settings, aimed at minimal-impact use of the marine and terrestrial environments that the tours encounter.

Maple Leaf Adventures, 19-2625 Muir Rd., Courtenay, 250/240-2420, is based on Vancouver Island but offers sailing trips to the Kitlope coastal area south of Terrace. Operators offering guided tours to the grizzly bear sanctuary in Khutzeymateen Provincial Park include **Adventure Canada**, #101, 2025 W. Broadway, Vancouver, 800/387-1483.

Several operators offer guided hikes of the Chilkoot Trail. Contact **Sea to Sky Trails**, 105C, 11831-80th Ave., Delta, 800/990-8735 or 604/594-7701. If you're hiking the trail on your own, you can arrange for a water taxi across Lake Bennett at trail's end by contacting **Chilkoot Boat Tours**, RR 1, Site 20, Comp 34, Whitehorse, Yukon Y1A 4Z6, 867/668-7766.

Houseboating is popular on Atlin Lake. To rent a fully equipped houseboat, complete with kitchen, laundry, toilets, and showers, call **Norseman Adventures**, Box 184, Atlin, BC V0W 1A0, 250/651-7535. A five-day rental costs between $995 and $1,495, depending on how many people are onboard.

In the Smithers area, take single- or multi-day guided hikes with instruction on animal tracking and observation with **Take-a-Hike Tours**, Box 372, Telkwa, BC V0J 2X0, 250/846-5551. They emphasize small groups and low-impact camping; winter ski touring on groomed trails is also available. Accommodations are available in rustic log cabins (no running water).

Without a doubt, the best way to see Gwaii Haanas National Park Reserve is with a guided tour, since historic Haida villages are often off-limits to individual travelers. For an exceptional sailing adventure aboard the vessel *Island Roamer*, contact **Bluewater Adventures**, #3-252 E. First St., North Vancouver, 888/877-1770 or 604/980-3800, www.bluewateradventures.bc.ca. Several outfitters operate guided kayaking trips in the park as well—try **Ecosummer Expeditions** and **Ecomarine Ocean Kayak Centre**. For contact information on both of these Vancouver-based outfitters see Chapter 6, "Guides and Outfitters."

CAMPING

There are many provincial and Forest Service campgrounds throughout the northern part of BC. There are also lots of privately owned campgrounds, most of which have more amenities and services than

AUTHOR'S TOP PICKS: CANOEING

- **Arrow Lakes**—*Sheltered lake paddling in the Kootenays on two long and narrow reservoirs.*

- **Bowron Lakes**—*One of North America's best canoe routes follows six major lakes and a number of short stretches of river connected by short portages.*

- **Gitnadoix River Recreation Area**—*This large protected area just east of Prince Rupert is accessible only by paddling across the Skeena River.*

- **Powell Forest Canoe Route**—*A terrific family trip using 10 lakes, this route can be paddled all at once or in sections, depending on how much time you have and how experienced you are.*

the provincial campgrounds. Wilderness camping is allowed in Gwaii Haanas National Park Reserve. Contact the warden's office to purchase a backcountry camping permit.

For those traveling the Alaska Highway, a good overnight stop is the 33-site campground at **Buckinghorse River**, located at Mile 173 (200 kilometers/120 miles northwest of Fort St. John). **Stone Mountain Campground**, with 28 sites and only basic facilities, is another good place to rest. It's at Mile 373 (130 kilometers/78 miles beyond Fort Nelson). **Liard River Hotsprings Provincial Park** (for reservations call 800/689-9025) offers 53 lovely sites and easy access to the hot mineral pools. It's wheelchair accessible and amenities include pit toilets, picnic tables, fire pits, wood, and water. For information on all of the above campgrounds, contact BC Parks, #250, 10003-110 Ave., Fort St. John, 250/787-3407.

Between Prince George and Smithers are numerous opportunities for camping, boating, and fishing. A fine choice for camping is **Babine Lake Resort**, Box 528, Burns Lake, BC V0J 1E0, 250/964-4692. The resort sells fishing licenses and offers a smokehouse for preserving your catch. It's open May through October and charges $15 to $17 per vehicle (water and electric hookup are extra). If you want to stay in Smithers, try the **Riverside Recreation Centre**, Box 4314, Smithers, BC V0J 2N0, 250/847-3229. Set on a golf course, this RV park is especially handy if you brought your clubs. It's open April through October and charges $15 to $18 per site.

Seeley Lake Campground, on Highway 16 just west of New Hazelton, is a wooded and very private provincial campground. Its 20 sites are suitable for RVs, tents, or trailers. Amenities are basic, but the perks—excellent boating and fishing on Seeley Lake—make it worth a stop.

Lakesle Lake Provincial Park Campground, 800/689-9025, on Highway 37 just south of Terrace, may be the world's biggest suburban backyard. You'll find kids on skateboards, bikes, and in-line skates, lots of lawn chairs and loud music, and a lake full of boats. But you'll also find that it's very clean, forested, and well operated—the noise stops after dark and the resident campground managers patrol the 156 sites for trouble. It's actually a very pleasant place to stay—a good stopover between Hazelton and Prince Rupert.

Naikoon Provincial Park on Graham Island, Haida Gwaii, has two campgrounds. Agate Beach's 21 sites are close to the water and somewhat exposed; the 30 sites at Misty Mountain are treed and more private. Pit toilets are the only facilities at either campground. For those hiking the East Beach Trail, wilderness camping is permitted and there are shelters at Cape Ball River, Oeanda River, and Fife Point.

LODGING

The **Cow Bay B&B**, 20 Cow Bay Rd., Prince Rupert, 250/627-1804, in Prince Rupert is a wonderfully cozy place. It has three beautiful guest rooms, one of which comes with its own bathroom. Fresh flowers, lively art, homemade breads, and a large fireplace make this place feel like home. Prices start at $80 per room.

All accommodations in Haida Gwaii are on Graham Island. **Dorothy and Mike's Guest House**, 3125 Second Ave., Queen Charlotte City, 250/559-8439, includes gardens and ocean views and is a great home base for exploring the island. You'll have a full kitchen for making your own meals, and the choice of either a private or shared bath. Rates range from $35 to $60 per night. Also in Queen Charlotte City is **Grace's Place**, 3113 Third Ave., Queen Charlotte City, 250/559-4262. A self-described "nutty landlady," Grace has outfitted her place with antiques and down quilts. Some units have kitchen facilities; all have private bathrooms. Rates range from $50 to $70 per night.

For accommodations in the remote northwest, and access by horseback or plane to Spatsizi Plateau or Mount Edziza Provincial Parks, contact **Red Goat Lodge**, Box 101, Iskut, BC V0J 1K0, 888/733-4628 or 250/234-3261. This modern facility in the wilderness is operated as a B&B with breakfast and an evening treat included in the price. There are also hostel units (dormitory-style accommodations and shared bathrooms) and a campground with laundry facilities and hot showers. Rates for the B&B start at $85 per night; campsites are just $9.35 per night.

The local hangout in Telegraph Creek is **RiverSong Café, Lodge, General Store and Outfitters**, 250/235-3196. It offers rooms, meals, river rafting on the Stikine, and all the information you need to enjoy the region's wilderness parks. The building was originally erected by the Hudson's Bay Company as a trading post. Rates start at $50.

If you plan to make the trip all the way out to Atlin, stay "downtown" at **Norland House B&B**, Box 135, Atlin, BC V0B 1A0, 250/651-7585, a restored historic cabin. Hosts Bob and Lynn Coutts serve complementary wine and treats in the afternoon. Breakfast costs extra. A slightly less expensive but still comfy B&B is the **Fireweed Inn**, Box 316, Atlin, BC V0B 1A0, 250/651-7729. Breakfast is included. For a unique do-it-yourself romantic stay, choose Sidka Tours' **Glacier View Cabins**, Box 368, Atlin, BC V0B 1A0. The cabins, a short drive outside of town, offer amazing views of Llewellyn Glacier. Bring your own breakfast supplies. Sidka Tours will also show you around town on a motorbike or canoe.

The best place to stay in Dawson Creek may be the **Trail Inn**, 1748 Alaska Ave., Dawson Creek, 800/663-2749 or 250/782-8595. It's a typical motel but is clean and well run, offers complimentary continental breakfast and coffee, and is a bargain at around $65 per night. Way up at Liard, check out **Trapper Ray's Liard Hotsprings Lodge**, Mile 497, Alaska Hwy., 250/776-7349, a friendly European-style lodge; the associated campground has pull-through sites, a sani-station, and sells gas, propane, and diesel. Rates start at $60 for the lodge rooms and range from $8 to $10 per night for camping.

FOOD

Fine dining is a rare experience in the North, but there are small cafés and family-owned restaurants that are worth seeking out. Hours can be erratic, especially in isolated areas, and many establishments are open only seasonally. As with accommodations, larger towns and cities offer more choices.

Alaska Café & Pub, at Alaska Highway Mile 0 in Dawson Creek, 250/782-7040, has Victorian-style decor. Burgers and beer rule for lunch, but the dinner menu is more varied, with steak, schnitzel, and delicious European desserts. The main attraction is the pub's keyboard player, who is blind and knows every song in the book. The restaurant's owners are refurbishing the Dew Drop Inn next door.

Buffalo Brewing Company is a brewpub and restaurant at 611 Brunswick St., Prince George, 250/564-7100. The menu features salmon as the star attraction, and the beer list is quite large. If you eat in the pub (as opposed to the more formal restaurant side) you can crack peanuts and toss the shells onto the floor.

In the trendy Cow Bay area in Prince Rupert, check out **Chatham Sound Seafood**, 7 Cow Bay Rd., 250/627-4000, for fabulous fresh or smoked cod, halibut, salmon, and shellfish. Should you actually catch a fish of your own, Chatham Sound will fillet, smoke, or can your catch and ship it home for you.

APPENDIX A
TRAVEL BASICS

WHAT TO BRING

British Columbia, especially in the metro areas, is a modern shopper's paradise—if you forget your toothbrush or decide you need a new pair of skis, you won't have any trouble finding what you need. The farther you roam from the Vancouver, Victoria, and Nanaimo population centers, however, the harder it gets to find the right equipment for specialized outdoor activities. If you're traveling on your own, bring what you think you'll need with you. If you're traveling with an outfitter, make sure you know what they provide and what they require you to bring.

You should carry some basic gear on every outing, no matter how short or close to home it is. Essentials to ensure your safety and comfort when traveling in the backcountry include extra clothing, food and water, a first-aid kit, waterproof matches, flashlight (with extra batteries), and a map and compass.

Be sure you have adequate health insurance before you leave home. If you take prescription medication and may require a refill while in BC, bring a copy of your prescription with you. Large urban centers (and many smaller cities and towns) have walk-in clinics for minor medical problems. In an emergency, go to the nearest hospital.

ENTRY AND EXIT REQUIREMENTS

When entering Canada, citizens of the United States should carry identification such as a birth certificate or passport (a driver's license is not sufficient). Citizens from all other nations must carry passports, and some must also have visas. For information on entering Canada, contact Canada Customs, General Inquiries, First Floor, 333 Dunsmuir St., Vancouver, BC V6B 5R3, 604/666-0545 or 604/666-0272.

All firearms must be declared upon entry to Canada; carrying unregistered firearms is a criminal offense. Restricted firearms (those that cannot legally be brought into Canada) include pistols, revolvers, and all fully automatic weapons. Rifles and shotguns used for hunting can be brought into the country only if you intend to hunt. If you are turned back at the border for carrying restricted firearms, you can usually store your guns at firearms dealers in U.S. border towns.

U.S. citizens may bring 1.1 liters (1 quart) of hard liquor or wine or up to 8.1 liters (a case) of beer into Canada for personal use. Canada Customs has a zero-tolerance policy regarding narcotics, including marijuana. Items being brought into Canada for personal use, such as sports gear, electronics, cameras, and musical instruments should be declared at the border to avoid possible duty charges or seizure when leaving the country.

Pets older than three months can accompany you into Canada, but you must have a certificate of rabies vaccination. Horses are subject to veterinary checks at border crossings; because vets are not normally stationed at the border, phone ahead to make an appointment at the crossing you will be using and ask that a vet be present to check out your horse.

The laws governing what items can be taken home from Canada vary depending upon your country of origin—you should know the import and duty-free laws of your own country before leaving home. American citizens who stay in Canada for 48 hours or longer may take up to $400 worth of goods back to the United States duty free. For those who have been in Canada less than 48 hours, the limit is $200.

HEALTH AND SAFETY

Generally speaking, British Columbia is a safe place to travel. Exceptions include Vancouver's rough east end along East Hastings and in parts of Chinatown. Theft and vandalism of vehicles bearing out-of-province license plates is an increasing problem throughout Vancouver; if you're staying at a Vancouver hotel take everything out of your car. Campgrounds can be notorious for theft from tents and vehicles. Always lock your car and carry valuables (wallet, credit cards, passport) with you at all times. Leave your jewelry at home.

The Royal Canadian Mounted Police (RCMP) provide policing services throughout BC, supplemented by municipal police in Vancouver, Victoria, and several other large urban centers. Within the national parks, park wardens also have certain police powers, especially regarding traffic violations and poaching. In the event of an emergency, dial 911 for fire, ambulance, and police. Some areas of the province do not yet have 911 service; if you don't get an answer by dialing 911, immediately dial 0 for the operator. Local emergency phone numbers are listed on the inside front covers of phone books.

Bears

When traveling in BC's backcountry, beware of bears. Bears are territorial and may defend themselves against perceived competitors, including humans. They will also defend a carcass. Female grizzlies are vigorous protectors of their young. Among the most dangerous situations a hiker can encounter is to unknowingly come between a sow and her cubs.

Don't let the presence of bears deter you from venturing into BC's magnificent wilderness—just follow some commonsense rules. The best defense against a bear attack is to be aware of your surroundings and make lots of noise—shout, whistle, sing, whatever—especially when hiking through heavy brush or along watercourses. A surprised bear is a dangerous bear!

If you see a bear at a distance, stop, look around you (for cubs, nearby trees, obstacles, and escape routes), and retreat slowly and quietly. Take a very wide detour around the area (at least one kilometer). If you must pass by the bear, first make loud noises to warn the bear of your presence. The bear will likely depart the area. If the bear does not retreat, leave the area quickly and find an alternative route.

Carrying pepper-spray bear repellent is a controversial measure that tends to instill a false sense of security. Pepper spray will not prevent an attack and can only be used effectively at very close range, when you have an equally good chance of getting a dose yourself. On the other hand, a bear with a face full of pepper spray virtually always abandons the attack. If you decide to buy pepper spray, make sure the container has enough capacity for several blasts, and that the concentration of capsicum is at least 10 percent.

Attaching bear bells or other noise-making devices to your boots, pack, or clothing has a similarly sedating effect—on you. If you count on the bells too much you may neglect to be watchful in potentially dangerous situations. Beside, the tinkling sound of bear bells is simply not loud enough to warn a bear of your approach.

Water Safety

There are two high and two low tides within each 25-hour period (approximately). The lowest tides occur between June and September. Tide tables and charts are available from all major marine suppliers along the coast and from Canadian Hydrographic Service, Box 6000, W. Saanich Rd., Sidney, BC V8L 4B2, 250/363-6390. Remember when you use these tables to add one hour to the published times to account for daylight saving time (April through October).

The shattered nature of the BC coastline makes for numerous underwater hazards; a marine chart is a must for paddling or sailing in coastal waters. There are 10 lighthouses along the west coast, plus numerous buoys and fog signals. They are described in a Coast Guard booklet entitled *Lights, Buoys, and Fog Signals* (Canadian Coast Guard Service, 10060 Pacific Centre, 700 W. Georgia St., Vancouver, BC V7Y 1E1).

Currents on the west coast of Vancouver Island are not as extreme as those in the Inside Passage and Gulf Islands. Some areas are renowned for fast tidal currents. Check locally for hazardous currents before going swimming, paddling, or diving.

The Canadian Armed Forces are responsible for search and rescue in coastal waters. The Canadian Coast Guard also patrols coastal waters and operates a number of special search-and-rescue vessels. VHF Channel 16 (156.8 MHz) is monitored 24 hours a day by the Coast Guard and can be used for distress calls. In an emergency call collect: 250/388-1543 (Victoria) or 604/732-4141 (Vancouver). The emergency number for the Rescue Coordination Centre is 800/567-5111.

In 1999 the Canadian Coast Guard released a new edition of their *Safe Boating Guide,* which outlines safety rules that came into effect in the summer of 1999. Obtain a copy by calling the Coast Guard at 800/267-6687, or visit their Web site at www.ccg-gcc.gc.ca.

TRANSPORTATION—TO BRITISH COLUMBIA

There are 22 points of entry for vehicles entering BC from the United States. There are also several points of road access from Alberta, the Canadian province that lies to the east of BC, and from the Yukon, to the north.

By Bus
Major coach lines serve British Columbia from the United States and from other Canadian provinces. Among these are:
- **Borderline Stage**: 509/684-3950
- **Brewster Transportation and Tours**: 800/661-1152 or 403/762-6700
- **Gray Line of Seattle**: 206/626-6090
- **Greyhound**: 800/661-1202 (in BC), 800/661-8747 (rest of Canada), or 604/662-3222
- **Quick Shuttle**: 800/556-7122 or 604/244-3744
- **Spokane-Trail Vanlines**: 250/368-8400

By Rail
AMTRAK service is available between Seattle and Vancouver. For rates and schedules, call 800/USA-RAIL or 604/585-4848. For information about VIA Rail Canada, BC Rail, and the Rocky Mountaineer, see page 280.

By Air
Many international airlines provide service to the Vancouver International Airport and the Victoria Airport. Among them are: Air Canada, WestJet (service in western Canada only), Canadian Airlines, United Airlines, American Airlines, Horizon Air, Northwest Airlines, Quantas, Air New Zealand, Japan Air Lines, Cathay Pacific, KLM, Lufthansa, and many others.
- **Air Canada**: 800/663-3721 or 604/688-5515
- **Canadian Airlines International**: 800/665-1177 or 604/279-6611
- **Horizon Air**: 800/547-9308
- **WestJet**: 403/250-5839

- **United Airlines**: 800/241-6522
- **American Airlines**: 800/433-7300
- **Northwest Airlines**: 800/441-1818
- **Quantas**: 800/227-4500
- **Air New Zealand**: 800/663-5494
- **Cathay Pacific**: 800/268-6868
- **KLM**: 800/441-1818
- **Lufthansa**: 800/563-5954
- **British Airways**: 800/247-9297
- **Delta Air Lines**: 800/241-4141

By Boat

If you are arriving in Canada via private or charter boat, you must clear Canadian Customs. Ports of entry are located at Victoria, Vancouver, Nanaimo, Courtenay/Comox, Campbell River, Sidney, Port Alberni, Powell River, Kitimat, Ucluelet, White Rock, Prince Rupert, Bedwell Harbour, and Stewart. In addition, for those paddling up the Columbia River from Washington State, there are Canada Customs offices in Trail, BC.

Ferry travel along the west coast is a very popular way to access BC. Regularly scheduled ferry services operate between Alaska and BC coastal destinations, and between Washington State and BC coastal destinations. Note that some of these services take passengers only or operate in the summer months only. BC Ferries does not operate internationally.

International ferry services include:
- **Alaska Marine Highway (Alaska State Ferries)**: 800/642-0066 (U.S.) or 907/465-3941 (Canada)
- **Black Ball Transport, Inc.**: 250/386-2202 (Victoria) or 360/457-4491 (Port Angeles, WA)
- **Clipper Navigation, Ltd.**: 800/888-2535 or 250/382-8100 (Victoria) or 206/448-5000 (Seattle)
- **Victoria Line**: 800/668-1167 (Canada) or 800/683-7977 (U.S.)
- **Victoria Rapid Transit, Inc.**: 250/361-9144 (BC), 360/452-8088 (Port Angeles), or 800/633-1589 (Washington)
- **Victoria/San Juan Cruises**: 800/443-4552

- **Washington State Ferries**: 800/84-FERRY (Washington), 250/381-1551 or 250/656-1531

TRANSPORTATION—WITHIN BRITISH COLUMBIA

Driving

Seatbelts must be worn by all adults traveling in a motor vehicle; child restraints/car seats are required for children weighing less than 9 kilograms (20 pounds). Cyclists and motorcyclists must wear helmets. Radar detectors are permitted in BC. The minimum legal driving age is 16 and the minimum legal drinking age is 19. The maximum blood-alcohol level is 0.08 percent. BC police forces practice the Stop Check program—random checks for impaired drivers. If you are stopped you may be asked to take a Breathalyzer test. Impaired driving (i.e. driving when you have a blood-alcohol content of 0.08 percent or greater) is a criminal offense.

Speed limits in BC are posted in kilometers per hour and are strictly enforced. Photo-radar systems are used in BC to monitor vehicle speeds. Common speed limits are:
- Highway: 90 km/h unless otherwise posted; high-speed highways in the Vancouver area may be up to 100 km/h
- Urban areas: 50 km/h unless otherwise posted
- School zones/playground zones: 30 km/h

Paved and unpaved roadways run throughout the province. If you're driving your own vehicle, be sure it's in good repair, especially if you're traveling to remote destinations. You can rent cars, vans, and RVs from numerous rental agencies throughout BC. If you are traveling in the summer, or if you require a specialized vehicle such as a multi-passenger van or four-wheel drive, you should reserve your vehicle ahead of time. Major rental agencies that operate in BC include Avis, Budget, Hertz, and National/Tilden.

Logging Roads

You can obtain information about logging roads from BC Forest Service, Range, Recreations and Forest Practices Branch, 1450 Government St., First Floor, Victoria, BC V8W 3E7, 250/387-1946. For regional Forest Service offices, see Appendix B.

When using a logging road, you must be aware that the roads exist for the purpose of transporting trees from logging areas to sawmills. This is accomplished by logging trucks, which are long, wide vehicles that always have the right-of-way on logging roads and often travel in the middle of the road at high speed. (Logging trucks are in radio contact with one another, to avoid collisions. Consequently, traveling behind a logging truck, while unpleasant, is relatively safe—the driver is likely to relay your position to other drivers.) Logging roads are rough, narrow, winding, and often either muddy or dusty. Some rules to live by:

• Drive with your headlights on at all times! (Make sure to turn your headlights off when you leave your vehicle—don't come back to a dead battery and a long walk out after your backcountry jaunt.)
• Wear your seatbelt.
• Be watchful for logging trucks both behind you and in front of you, and always yield to oncoming or overtaking trucks by moving over to the right-hand side of the road or pulling off.
• Do not overtake or pass a logging truck unless it is parked or stopped.
• Consider avoiding logging-truck traffic altogether by planning your trip for a weekend, holiday, or after working hours (8 to 5 Monday through Saturday).
• Most logging roads are passable for two-wheel-drive passenger cars but some require four-wheel-drive vehicles. Logging roads are generally not suitable for motorbikes, mountain bikes, RVs, campers, or trailers.
• When venturing onto a logging road, make sure your gas tank is full and you have a spare tire. A full container of windshield-washing fluid doesn't hurt either.
• Watch for road damage such as potholes, slides, and washouts.
• Park well off the road and always lock your vehicle.

Buses

Numerous bus lines operate between destinations in BC. In cases where the route includes a ferry crossing the bus fare usually includes the ferry fare. Bus lines operating within BC include:

- **Azure Transport, Ltd.**: 250/537-4737
- **Canim Lake Stage Lines**: 250/397-2562
- **City Link Bus Lines**: 604/878-1290 or 604/793-1290
- **Dewdney Trail Stages**: 800/332-0282 or 250/426-4662
- **Farwest Bus Lines**: 250/624-6400
- **Greyhound Lines of Canada**: 800/661-1202, 800/661-8747, or 604/662-3222
- **Island Coach Lines**: 250/385-4411
- **Knight Limousine Service**: 250/475-2010
- **Maverick Coachlines**: 250/662-8051 or 604/255-8051
- **Northland Buslines**: 250/996-8421
- **Perimeter Transportation**: 800/663-4265, 604/273-9023, or 604/261-2299
- **Pacific Coach Lines**: 800/661-1725
- **Peace Coaches, Inc.**: 250/785-5945
- **Seaport Limousine**: 250/636-2622
- **West Coast Trail Express**: 250/477-8700

Trains

There are several excursion trains meant for scenic enjoyment, tourists, and train buffs. They usually offer only round-trip fares with no stops. Others are regular passenger services and are more suitable for travelers wishing access to destinations in the interior. Rail lines operating scheduled services within BC include:

- **BC Rail**: 800/339-8752, 800/663-8238, or 604/631-3500
- **Esquimalt and Nanaimo Railway**: 800/561-8630 or 250/383-4324
- **Rocky Mountaineer Railtours**: 800/665-7245
- **VIA Rail**: 800/561-8630

Planes

Often the most efficient way to get around British Columbia, especially in the northern part of the province or along the coast, is by air. Flying by plane or helicopter is sometimes the only way to get into remote wilderness areas. You can charter an aircraft from virtually any place in BC by simply going to the local airport or airstrip. Further information on charter air access is given in association with specific remote areas listed in this book. Airlines operating scheduled services within BC are:

- **Air BC**: 800/663-3721 or 604/688-5515
- **Air Nootka**: 250/283-2255
- **Airspeed Aviation**: 604/852-9245
- **Awood Air, Ltd.**: 604/273-3521
- **Baxter Aviation**: 800/661-5599
- **Canadian Regional**: 800/665-1177 or 604/279-6611
- **Central Mountain Air**: 800/663-3905
- **Coval Air**: 604/681-0311
- **Cypress Airlines**: 604/276-9500
- **Harbour Air**: 800/663-4267
- **Helijet Airways**: 604/273-1414
- **Island Hopper**: 250/753-2020
- **Kenmore Air**: 800/543-9595
- **North Vancouver Air**: 800/228-6608 or 604/278-1608
- **Pacific Coastal Airlines**: 800/663-2872 or 604/273-8666
- **Shuswap Air**: 800/663-4074
- **Vancouver Island Air**: 250/287-2433 or 250/949-6800
- **Wells Gray Air Service, Ltd.**: 250/674-3115
- **West Coast Air**: 800/347-2222
- **Wilderness Airline, Ltd.**: 800/665-9453 or 604/276-2635

Boats

British Columbia is served by an extensive network of marine and interior-waters ferries. BC Ferries operates 24 year-round routes. Reservations are taken for Vancouver/Gulf Islands, Inside Passage (Vancouver or Port Hardy/Prince Rupert), Discovery Coast (Bella Coola/Port Hardy), and Queen Charlotte Islands (Prince Rupert/Skidegate). For schedules and fares and to make reservations, call 250/386-3431 (Victoria), 888/223-3779 (anywhere in BC), or 604/444-2890; or check out the BC Ferries Web site at www.bcferries.bc.ca. To make a reservation for the Vancouver/Nanaimo ferry, call 888/724-5223 from anywhere in British Columbia.

Summer lineups for some routes can be very long. To avoid waiting, travel early in the day. More detailed information about ferry ports and crossings is given in each destination chapter.

Marine transport is also available via working freighters, some of which accept passengers. Among these are:

- **Alberni Marine Transport Company**: 250/723-8313. (Alberni Inlet to Barkley Sound)
- **Juan de Fuca Express Water Taxi**: 888/755-6578 or 250/755-6578 (Port Renfrew/Bamfield)
- **Nootka Sound Service, Ltd.**: 250/283-2325 or 250/283-2515

If you are sailing your own boat or have rented a bare boat (no skipper or crew, just the boat) you must be familiar with reading marine charts and tide tables. These, plus two invaluable publications (*British Columbia Small Craft Guide*, volumes 1 and 2, and *Sailing Directions—British Columbia Coast*, volumes 1 and 2) are available from marine supply shops and Canadian Hydrographic Service, Box 6000, West Saanich Rd., Sidney, BC V8L 4B2, 250/363-6390.

COMMUNICATIONS

Language
English is spoken throughout BC. In theory, Canada is officially bilingual (French being the second language), but French is not widely spoken in BC. In the Lower Mainland (including Victoria and Nanaimo) the high population of Asian peoples means that Japanese and several Chinese dialects are spoken. German is becoming more widespread, even in remote interior and northern areas.

Telephone Service and Internet Access
There are two area codes in BC. Area code 604 encompasses Vancouver and the Lower Mainland, plus the Sunshine Coast and Whistler. Elsewhere in BC, including Victoria, the area code is 250. Cellular phone service is excellent in Vancouver, Victoria, and the surrounding urban areas. In the rest of the province, cell coverage is sporadic. Internet access is available in most large urban centers.

Mail Service
Canada Post operates the mail system and there are major postal outlets in all cities and towns. Secondary postal outlets (such as Mail

Boxes Etc.) can also be found in major urban centers; these privately operated businesses offer most postal and business services. Major couriers in Canada include UPS, Federal Express, and many others.

MONEY MATTERS

Currency

The basic unit of currency in Canada is the Canadian dollar. Common denominations of folding money are $5, $10, $20, and $50. Common coins are one-dollar (known as the "loonie," this is a gold-colored coin picturing a loon on the "tails" side), two-dollar (a silver coin with a gold-colored center, often called the "toonie"), the penny (1¢), nickel (5¢), dime (10¢), and quarter (25¢). (All prices in this books are given in Canadian dollars.)

U.S. currency is widely accepted throughout Canada at stores, restaurants, gas stations, and hotels. You will get a more favorable exchange rate at a bank or currency-exchange outlet than from a merchant or restaurant. All other foreign currencies must be exchanged for Canadian currency. This can be done at any bank, or at currency exchanges in large cities and airports. Travelers' checks in Canadian or U.S. dollars are also widely accepted but you must have sufficient identification, such as a credit card or driver's license, to cash them. Personal checks are accepted only with two forms of identification, one of which must be a picture ID such as a driver's license or passport.

Banks

There are five major banks in Canada. Hours vary but you can generally depend on finding an open bank between 10 and 4 Monday through Friday. Some banks in urban areas have Saturday hours. Credit unions and trust companies keep longer hours but offer fewer services; in the case of credit unions, service may be restricted to members only. All financial institutions are closed on statutory holidays. Automated teller machines (ATMs) are now widespread throughout BC.

Credit Cards

Major credit cards accepted in BC include VISA, MasterCard, and American Express. Some establishments also accept Diners' Club and Discover cards. Some restaurants, even in the large cities, do not take credit cards; nor do some remote lodges or most campgrounds. All BC government liquor stores are operated on a cash-only basis.

Taxes and Tipping

Canadians are burdened with high taxes, including the widely cursed federal Goods and Services Tax (GST). This inescapable 7 percent surcharge is applied at the time of purchase to nearly everything, even services such as haircuts, shoe repair, vehicle repair, accommodations . . . the list goes on. Groceries are generally exempt. It is possible for foreigners to get a GST rebate on some items. You can claim an on-the-spot rebate of up to $500 at any duty-free shop. For claims of more than $500, you have to file some bothersome paperwork, but if you've spent enough money it's probably worth your time. Obtain a rebate form from any duty-free shop or from a Canada Customs office when you enter the country. Most BC infocentres also have the rebate forms. For information on GST rebates, call 800/66-VISIT from within Canada or 613/991-3346 from outside Canada.

British Columbia levies a provincial sales tax of 7 percent on most items except food, books, and children's clothing. The provincial sales tax does not apply to services.

Tipping for services is generally practiced, especially in restaurants, hotels, and for cab rides. It's also customary to tip your tour guide or travel outfitter. The accepted rate is 15 percent.

Business Hours

Business hours vary widely throughout BC. Government and other offices are usually open by nine and close by five Monday through Friday. Government offices are generally closed on weekends and holidays. Businesses may choose to remain open on statutory holidays, although almost every business shuts down on Christmas Day, New Year's Day, and Easter Sunday.

Stores are usually open from 9 to 5 Monday through Thursday; some are open later on Friday. Most stores operate on Saturdays but may close early. In urban areas there is a trend toward Sunday shopping, usually with shorter hours (10 to 4) Restaurants may close for one day per week and between meals. Pubs are usually open from 11 or noon until closing time—last call is usually at one in the morning.

Generally speaking, the more remote the location, the shorter or stranger an establishment's business hours are likely to be. In addition, many hotels, restaurants, services, and outfitters in remote locations operate on a seasonal basis. Only a few outfitters operate winter-only services.

CUISINE

When it comes to food, anything goes in BC. The general rule is the farther you are from Vancouver the more limited your food choices will be. If you're a strict vegetarian headed for the far north you might consider packing a private stash of tofu.

In the urban areas of Vancouver, Victoria, and Nanaimo the variety and quality of ethnic foods available is amazing. There is a large Asian population in the lower mainland, reflected by the many Asian restaurants. Vegetarian restaurants are also much in evidence in many localities.

BC's farms and orchards produce everything from wheat (the Peace River area in northeastern BC is the northernmost wheat-growing region in the world) to apricots (the south end of the Okanagan Valley is the only place in Canada where apricots can survive). The vineyards of the Okanagan and the lower mainland yield grapes for an ever-expanding, ever-improving winemaking industry. Increasingly, food producers are turning to organic and sustainable agriculture. Locally grown organic produce, eggs, dairy products, poultry, and meats are available in most towns and urban areas. Most towns even have a cappuccino bar or two. Microbreweries are everywhere.

Politically correct or not, the fish of choice in BC is salmon. Due to decreasing wild salmon stocks you may find yourself eating farm-raised (aquaculture) salmon in restaurants. You can buy fresh fish and seafood directly from the people who caught them (go to the docks in Steveston, New Westminster, Prince Rupert, or any number of fishing villages on the coast); however, it's illegal to buy fish from Native fishermen out of season. When in doubt, get thee to a grocery store.

TIME ZONES

There are two time zones in BC. The Pacific time zone covers most of the province from the coast eastward. A small portion of southeastern BC lies in the Mountain time zone.

During the summer months, both Pacific and Mountain time switch to daylight saving time. From early April until late October all clocks in the province are set ahead one hour from standard time. However, a small area of the Kootenay region, including the city of Creston, refuses to participate in daylight saving time and remains on Pacific standard time all year long.

CLIMATE

Terrestrial weather systems in BC are controlled by several factors: season, latitude, altitude, and geography. Storm patterns and prevailing winds usually move from west to east, less often from north to south.

Coastal weather tends to be wet, with high rainfall and frequent fog. Winter temperatures tend to be moderate—freezing and snowfall are rare—but summers tend to be warm rather than hot. Throughout the interior, even in the north, summers are short and warm to hot, with cool nights. Weather in the mountains can be highly variable; sunny mornings don't guarantee sunny afternoons. Remember also that it can snow at any time of year, especially at higher elevations.

Dressing for the weather can be tricky. Depending on the season, and where you are traveling in the province, you may find yourself needing a lot of different clothes, or a very versatile wardrobe. It's a good idea to have a windproof jacket or vest. And don't lose track of your rain gear—you'll need it eventually. Especially in the backcountry or in alpine environments, the key to comfort, if not survival, is staying dry. Another caution: protect yourself from the intense alpine sun. Use a hat and good sunscreen, with a protection factor of at least

15. Alpine nights are cool. Fleece clothing is a good idea for staying comfortable at high elevations.

The rain-shadow effect is prevalent throughout BC. Rain shadows occur when Pacific storm systems are forced to pass over mountain ranges. As the moisture-laden Pacific air mass rises, the air temperature cools; the moisture condenses and falls as rain or snow on the windward side of the mountains. The air mass passes over on its eastward journey, warming up again as it descends the lee side of the mountains, resulting in climate conditions that are generally, sometimes markedly, warmer and drier than on the opposite side of the mountain range. This effect is seen especially on Vancouver Island, where the west coast is subject to heavy precipitation while the east coast is dry.

For 24-hour weather information call 604/664-9010 (for information on Vancouver and region), 604/664-9032 (for areas outside Vancouver and the Lower Mainland), 250/656-3978 or 250/656-2714 (Victoria), or 250/245-8877 (Nanaimo). When traveling in BC you can also contact the weather information service at the local airport. Look in the blue pages (government listings) of the local phone book under Environment Canada or Weather Information.

Marine weather forecasts can be obtained from:
- **Weatheradio Canada** (broadcasts from various locations at various frequencies; call the Coastal Weather Office for a list)
- **Coastal Weather Office**: 250/356-6629 (Victoria), 250/94-6559 (Port Hardy), or 604/666-7502 (Vancouver)
- **Canadian Coast Guard**: 250/656-7515 or 656-2714 (Victoria) or 604/270-7411 (Vancouver)
- **Continuous marine broadcast**: Canadian Coast Guard VHF frequencies WX1: 162.55; WX2: 162.40; WX3: 163.475; 21B: 161.65. Also AM channel 1260 (Long Beach, Pacific Rim National Park Reserve) and Marine VHF channel 22.

HOLIDAYS

Ten statutory holidays are recognized in BC:
- New Year's Day—January 1
- Good Friday—Friday before Easter

- Easter Sunday
- Victoria Day—a Monday in May, on or about May 24
- Canada Day—July 1
- BC Day—first Monday in August
- Labor Day—first Monday in September
- Thanksgiving Day—first Monday in October
- Remembrance Day—November 11
- Christmas Day—December 25

Boxing Day (December 26) and Easter Monday (the Monday immediately after Easter) are recognized by most government offices, businesses, and banks. Shops and restaurants are usually open on these days.

EVENTS AND FESTIVALS

British Columbia is literally swarming with special events and festivals, especially in the summer. Virtually every community celebrates its heritage, harvest, or some other significant event. Large centers have numerous celebrations, many of them ethnic in origin. Among the most popular festivities are:

- **Abbotsford International Air Show** (mid-August), 604/852-8511—The show, held at the Abbotsford airport, includes flying demonstrations and displays of vintage and modern aircraft.
- **Canadian International Dragon Boat Festival** (June), 604/683-2000—Some 2,000 paddlers and 100,000 spectators enjoy the spectacle on the waters of False Creek in Vancouver.
- **Cloverdale Rodeo** (July), 604/576-9461—This is one of hundreds of small-town rodeos that take place throughout BC from April through October. The Cloverdale attracts professional competitors from Canada, the United States, and Australia.
- **First Peoples Festival** (August), 250/387-3701 or 800/661-5411—This Native arts and cultural celebration is held at the Royal BC Museum in Victoria.
- **Ironman Canada Triathlon** (August), 250/490-2464—Competitors swim, cycle, and run their way to glory in Penticton.
- **Kamloops Powwow** (mid-August), 250/828-9801—Many aboriginal celebrations and festivals occur throughout the year in all parts of

BC. This event is a large one, attracting dancers, competitors, and spectators from Canada and the United States.

- **Nanaimo Marine Festival** (late July), 250/756-0106—OK, here's a good one: A bunch of lunatics in homemade vessels resembling bathtubs race from Nanaimo on Vancouver Island across the Strait of Georgia to Vancouver.
- **Pacific National Exhibition** (mid-August to Labor Day), 604/254-1631—The original country fair gone big-time, PNE includes midway rides and games, agricultural shows, crafts displays, and concerts in Vancouver.
- **Swiftsure Sailing Race** (late May), 250/953-2033—Competitors race in and around Victoria's Inner Harbor.
- **Vancouver Folk Music Festival** (mid-July), 604/683-2000—A weekend of top-name entertainers, speakers, a children's stage, food, and crafts at Jericho Beach Park.
- **Victoria Folkfest** (late June or early July), 250/953-2033—Not to be outdone, Victoria also holds an annual celebration of folk and ethnic music.
- **Williams Lake Stampede** (July 1 weekend), 250/392-7404—An authentic rodeo if ever there was one.

METRIC SYSTEM

Canada uses the metric system to measure such things as distance, speed, temperature, volume, height, weight, and area. The best way to keep your head clear is by not converting—just go with the flow and live in metric while you're in Canada.

Metric equivalents are as follows:
2.5 centimeters (cm) = 1 inch
1 meter (m) = 3.3 feet
1 kilometer (km) = 0.62 mile
1 square kilometer (square km) = 0.39 square mile
1 kilogram (kg) = 2.2 pounds
1 liter (l) = 0.88 Imperial quarts or 0.946 U.S. quarts (when buying gasoline, figure about four liters to a U.S. gallon, then remember that Canadian dollars are cheap and you're actually getting a bargain)

To convert Celsius to Fahrenheit, multiply the Celsius temperature by 1.8 and add 32.

PARK AND CAMPGROUND USER FEES

National parks fees vary depending upon the park, the season, your age, how many people are in your group, and what services you're purchasing. Fees for each national park are outlined in this book in the "Details" section that follows each park's listing. Common to all of the national parks in BC (except Pacific Rim and Gwaii Haanas) is an entry fee, usually four or five dollars per adult per visit.

If you intend to visit and use a number of national parks you should consider purchasing a Western Canada Parks Pass. The pass is accepted at all national parks in BC, Alberta, Saskatchewan, and Manitoba, and is good for a year. Passes cost $35 per adult, or $70 for a group of two to seven people. Once purchased, your pass must be prominently displayed in your vehicle whenever you're in a national park. Vehicles without either a Western Canada Pass or a day pass will be ticketed and fined. To obtain a park pass, call 800/748-7275 or buy one upon entering any of the national parks. For additional information check out the Parks Canada Web site at www.parkscanada.pch.gc.ca.

All national parks levy camping fees. "Front country" campground (roadside) fees vary depending on location and services offered. Fees range from $12 to $21, plus $3.50 for wood. Camping in the backcountry (remote walk-in sites, backcountry huts, or shelters) requires the purchase of a backcountry permit, usually $6 per person per night to a maximum of $30. Annual backcountry camping passes are available for $42 per adult. Note that having a backcountry pass does not entitle you to a remote camping spot—many popular backcountry destinations also require reservations. See the "Details" section of each national park listing for more information on camping.

At present there are no entry fees for provincial parks in BC, but most do charge for camping. Campground fees vary depending upon the park's popularity and the services available. The most heavily used campgrounds and the ones that have amenities such as playgrounds, hot showers, RV hookups, and sani-stations (sewage disposal) cost up to $15 per site per night. Often there are limits to how long you can occupy a site (usually seven nights in a row). The simpler camp-grounds—those with only water and firewood—are usually free, but in some places there is a charge, usually $8 per site per night. BC Parks does not charge for campsite reservations.

Early in 1999 the BC Forest Service announced that it would begin charging a fee for camping in Forest Service sites, regardless of location or services (most Forest Service campgrounds have minimal services, usually just potable water and pit toilets, sometimes fire-wood). Forest Service campground permits now cost $8 per site per night, or you can buy an annual pass for $27 (a bargain, considering the nightly fee). Passes are sold wherever hunting or fishing licenses are available. There is no charge for day use of campgrounds and recreation sites.

APPENDIX B
ADDITIONAL RESOURCES

TOURIST INFORMATION

Tourism British Columbia/Super, Natural British Columbia
Parliament Buildings, Victoria, BC V8V1X4
800/663-6000 or 250/663-6000, www.travel.bc.ca

Cariboo-Chilcotin Tourist Association
Box 4900, Williams Lake, BC V2G 2V8
800/663-5885 or 250/392-2226, cariboo@netshop.net

High Country Tourist Association
#2, 1490 Pearson Place, Kamloops, BC V1S 1J9
800/567-2275 or 250/372-2770, hcta@tourvan01.tbc.gov.bc.ca

Kootenay Country Tourist Association
610 Railway St., Nelson, BC V1L 1H4
800/661-6603 or 250/352-6033, kcta@netidea.com

North by Northwest Tourism Association
Box 1030 #11, 3167 Tarlow Rd., Smithers, BC V0J 2N0
250/847-5227, nxnw@mail.netshop.net

Okanagan/Similkameen Tourist Association
1332 Water St., Kelowna BC V1Y9P4
250/860-5999, osta@avinc.com

Peace River/Alaska Highway Tourism Association
Box 6850, #10631-100 St., Fort St. John, BC V1J 4J3
250/785-2544

Rocky Mountain Visitors Association
Box 10, 1905 Water Ave., Kimberley, BC V1A 2Y5
250/427-4838, bcrockies@cyberlink.bc.ca

Tourism Vancouver Island
#302-45 Bastion Square, Victoria, BC V8W 1J1
250/382-3551, tavi@island.bc.ca

Vancouver, Coast and Mountains Tourism Association
#204, 1755 W. Broadway, Vancouver, BC V6J 4S5
604/739-10153, VCM_tourism@mindlink.bc.ca

NATIONAL PARKS

Parks Canada Information Service
Western Regional Office, Room 522, 220-Fourth Ave. S.E., Box 2989
Station M, Calgary, AB T2P 3H8
403/292-4401, www.parkscanada.pch.gc.ca

Glacier National Park
Box 350, Revelstoke, BC V0E 2S0
250/837-7500

Gwaii Haanas/South Moresby National Park Reserve
Box 37, Queen Charlotte City, BC V0T 1S0
250/559-8818

Kootenay National Park
Box 220, Radium, BC V0A 1M0
250/347-9615

Mount Revelstoke National Park
Box 350, Revelstoke, BC V0E 2S0
250/837-7500

Pacific Rim National Park Reserve
Box 280, Ucluelet, BC V0R 3A0
250/726-4212

Yoho National Park
Box 99, Field, BC V0A 1G0
250/343-6324

PROVINCIAL PARKS

BC Provincial Park
Second Floor, 800 Johnson St., Victoria, BC V8V1X4
250/387-5002, www.env.gov.bc.ca/bcparks

Cariboo District
#281 First Ave. N., Williams Lake, BC V2G 1Y7
250/398-4414

Garibaldi/Sunshine District
Box 220, Brackendale, BC V0N 1H0
604/898-3678

Kootenay District
Box 118, Wasa, BC V0B 2K0
250/422-4200

Lower Mainland District
1610 Mount Seymour Rd., North Vancouver, BC V7G 1L3
604/929-1291

Okanagan District
Box 399, Summerland, V0H 1Z0
250/494-6500

Peace-Liard District
#250, 10003-110 Ave., Fort St. John, BC V1J 6M7
250/787-3407

Prince George District
Box 2045, 4051 18th Ave., Prince George, BC V2N 2J6
250/565-6340

Skeena District
Bag 5000, 3790 Alfred Ave., Smithers, BC V0J 2N0
250/847-7320

South Vancouver Island District
RR 6, 2930 Trans-Canada Highway, Victoria, BC V9B 5T9
250/391-2300

Strathcona District
Box 1479, Parksville, BC V9P 2H4
250/954-4600

Thompson River District
1210 McGill Rd., Kamloops, BC V2C 6N6
250/851-3000

BC FOREST SERVICE

The BC Forest Service can provide maps and information about logging roads, back roads, Forest Service campgrounds, and fire bans. For specific information, contact the appropriate office in the region where you intend to travel.

Cariboo Forest Region
200, 640 Borland St., Williams Lake, BC V2G 4T1
250/398-4345

Kamloops Forest Region
515 Columbia St., Kamloops, BC V2C 2T7
250/828-4131

Nelson Forest Region
518 Lake St., Nelson, BC V1L 4C6
250/354-6200

Prince George Forest Region
1011 Fourth Ave., Prince George, BC V2L 3H9
250/565-6100

Prince Rupert Forest Region
3726 Alfred Ave., Bag 5000, Smithers, BC V0J 2N0
250/847-7500

Vancouver Forest Region
4995 Canada Way, Burnaby, BC V5G 4L9
604/660-7500

🌲 BRITISH COLUMBIA

MAPS

Recreation maps are available from the British Columbia Ministry of Forests and from BC Provincial Parks. These very detailed maps show locations of logging roads and Forest Service campgrounds and list handy reference phone numbers. Excellent 1:50,000-scale National Topographic Survey (NTS) maps are published by the federal department of Energy, Mines, and Resources. NTS maps are available from numerous sport shops, bookstores, and other sources or from:

Geological Survey of Canada
100 W. Pender, Vancouver, BC V0B 1R8

Dominion Map, Ltd.
541 Howe, Vancouver, BC V6C 2C2

Outdoor Recreation Council of BC
Suite 334, 1367 W. Broadway, Vancouver, BC V6H 1A9
604/737-3058

Environmental and Conservation Groups/BC Environment
780 Blanshard St., Victoria, BC V8V 1X5
250/387-9767

Carmanah Forestry Society
1431 Richardson St., Victoria, BC V8S 1R1
250/381-1141

Greenpeace
1726 Commercial Dr., Vancouver, BC V5N 3A4
604/253-7701, www.greenpeace.org

Sierra Club of Western Canada
1525 Amelia St., Victoria, BC V8W 2K1
250/386-5255

Western Canada Wilderness Committee (WCWC)
20 Water St., Vancouver, BC V6B 1A4
604/683-8220
Suite 301, 19 Bastion Square, Victoria, BC V8W 1J1
250/388-9292
info@wildernesscommittee.org, www.wildernesscommittee.org

RECOMMENDED READING

Travel and Adventure Guides

Baldwin, John. *Exploring the Coast Mountains on Skis.* West Vancouver: Gordon Soules Book Publishers, Ltd., 1994.

Fairley, Bruce. *A Guide to Climbing and Hiking in Southwestern British Columbia.* West Vancouver: Gordon Soules Book Publishers, Ltd., 1986

Langford, Dan, and Sandra Langford. *Cycling the Kettle Valley Railway.* Calgary, Rocky Mountain Books, 1997.

Lebrecht, Sue, and Susan Noppe. *Adventuring around Vancouver Island.* Vancouver: Greystone Books, Douglas & McIntyre, 1997.

MacFarlane, Quan, Uyeda, and Wong. *The Official Guide to Pacific Rim National Park Reserve.* Calgary: Blackbird Naturguides, 1997.

McGee, Peter, ed. *Kayak Routes of the Pacific Northwest Coast.* Vancouver: Greystone Books, Douglas & McIntyre, 1998.

Obee, Bruce. *The Pacific Rim Explorer.* Vancouver: Whitecap Books, 1986.

Payne, Matthew, and Adam Vasilevich. *Juan De Fuca Marine Trail.* Vancouver: Unnum Press, 1997.

Polischuk, Darrin. *Mountain Biking British Columbia.* West Vancouver: Okanagan Mountain Biking and Gordon Soules Book Publishers, Ltd. 1996.

Schmidt, Jeremy. *Adventuring in the Rockies.* Toronto: A Sierra Club Travel Adventure Guide, Key Porter Books, 1997.

Seagrave, Jayne. *Provincial and National Park Campgrounds in British Columbia.* Surrey, BC: the Heritage House Publishing Company, Ltd., 1997.

Sierra Club of Western Canada, Tim Leadem, ed. *The West Coast Trail and Nitinat Lakes.* Vancouver: Douglas & McIntyre, 1992.

Smith, Stuart. *Canadian Rockies Whitewater.* Jasper, Alb.: Headwaters Press, 1995.

Snowden, Mary Ann. *Island Paddling.* Victoria: Orca Book Publishers, 1990.

Stoltmann, Randy. *Hiking Guide to the Big Trees of Southwestern British Columbia.* Vancouver: Western Canada Wilderness Committee.

Trepanier, Carl. *The Vancouver Area Diving Guide.* West Vancouver: Gordon Soules Book Publishers, Ltd., 1994.

Voss, Jennifer. *Stikine River: A Guide to Paddling the Great River.* Calgary: Rocky Mountain Books, 1998.

Wainwright, Jack. *Canoe Trips British Columbia.* Delta, BC: Summit Productions, 1994.

White, Gordon R. *Stein Valley Wilderness Guidebook.* Vancouver: Stein Valley Wilderness Alliance, 1991.

Woodsworth, Glenn. *Hot Springs of Western Canada.* West Vancouver: Gordon Soules Book Publishers, Ltd., 1997.

Wriget, Richard T. *Bowron Lake Provincial Park, the All-Season Guide.* Surrey, BC: Heritage House Publishing Company, Ltd., 1994.

Natural History

Cannings, Richard, and Sydney Cannings. *British Columbia: A Natural History.* Vancouver: Greystone Books, Douglas & McIntyre, 1996.

Hoyt, Erich. *Orca the Whale Called Killer.* Camden East, Ontario: Camden House, 1984.

Kavanagh, James. *Nature BC: An Illustrated Guide to Common Plants and Animals.* Vancouver: Lone Pine Publishing, 1993.

Lyons, C. P., and Bill Merilees. *Trees, Shrubs, and Flowers to Know in British Columbia and Washington.* Vancouver: Lone Pine Publishing, 1995.

MacKinnon, Andy, Jim Pojar, and Ray Coupé, eds. *Plants of Northern British Columbia.* Victoria: BC Ministry of Forests and Lone Pine Publishing, 1992.

McConnaughey, Bayard H., and Evelyn McConnaughey. *Pacific Coast.* New York: National Audubon Society Nature Guides, Alfred A. Knopf, 1985.

Parish, Roberta, Ray Coupé, and Dennis Lloyd, eds. *Plants of the*

Southern Interior British Columbia. Victoria: BC Ministry of Forests and Lone Pine Publishing, 1996.

Pojar, Jim, and Andy MacKinnon. *Plants of Coastal British Columbia.* Victoria: BC Ministry of Forests and Lone Pine Publishing, 1994.

Porsild, A. E. *Rocky Mountain Wild Flowers.* Ottawa, Ontario: National Museum of Natural Sciences, Parks Canada, 1986.

Short, Steve, and Bernie Palmer. *Best of BC.* Vancouver: Whitecap Books, 1992.

Turner, Nancy J. *Food Plants of British Columbia Indians Coastal Peoples.* Victoria: Royal British Columbia Museum, 1975.

Turner, Nancy J. *Plants in British Columbia Indian Technology.* Victoria: Royal British Columbia Museum, 1979.

Underhill, J. E. *Guide to Western Mushrooms.* Surrey, BC: Hancock House.

Van Tighem, Kevin. *Bears.* Canmore, Alb.: Altitude Publishing Canada, Ltd., 1997.

History and Travel Essay

Careless, Ric. *To Save the Wild Earth.* Vancouver: Raincoast Books, 1997.

Czajkowski, Chris. *Diary of a Wilderness Dweller.* Vancouver: Orca Book Publishers, 1996.

Danford, Barrie. *McCullough's Wonder: The Story of the Kettle Valley Railway.* Vancouver: Whitecap Books, 1978.

Gayton, Don. *Landscapes of the Interior.* Gabriola Island, BC: New Society Publishers, 1996.

Hoagland, Edward. *Notes from the Century Before.* Vancouver: Douglas & McIntyre, 1969.

McAllister, Ian, Karen McAllister, and Cameron Young. *The Great Bear Rainforest.* Madeira Park, BC: Harbour Publishing, 1997.

Moore, Patrick. *Pacific Spirit: The Forest Reborn.* West Vancouver: Terra Bella Publishers Canada, Inc., 1995.

Poole, Michael. *Ragged Islands: Paddling the Inside Passage.* Vancouver: Douglas & McIntyre, 1991.

Wood, Daniel, and Beverley Sinclair. *Western Journeys.* Vancouver: Raincoast Books, 1997.

Aboriginal Culture

Coull, Cheryl. *A Traveller's Guide to Aboriginal B.C.* Vancouver: Whitecap Books and *Beautiful British Columbia Magazine*, 1996.

Kirk, Ruth. *Wisdom of the Elders.* Vancouver: Douglas & McIntyre and the Royal British Columbia Museum, 1986.

Kremer, Pat. *Native Sites in Western Canada.* Canmore, Alb.: Altitude Publishing Canada, Ltd., 1994.

Kremer, Pat. *Totem Poles.* Canmore, Alb.: Altitude Publishing Canada, Ltd., 1995.

Magazines, Newspapers, and Newsletters

BC Outdoors, 780 Beatty St., Suite 300, Vancouver, BC V6B 2M1

Beautiful British Columbia, 929 Ellery St., Victoria, BC V9A 7B4

Beautiful British Columbia Traveller, 929 Ellery St., Victoria, BC V9A 7B4

Canadian Geographic, 39 McArthur Ave., Vanier, Ontario K1L 8L7

Explore: Canada's Outdoor Adventure Magazine, #420, 301-14th St. N.W., Calgary, Alberta T2N 2A1

The Georgia Straight, 1770 Burrard St., Second Floor, Vancouver, BC V6J 3G7, 604/730-7000

Outdoor Canada: The Total Outdoor Experience, 35 Riviera Dr., Unit 17, Markham, Ontario L3R 8N4

The Outdoor Report, 334, 1367 W. Broadway, Vancouver, BC V6H 4A9

INDEX

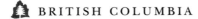

Guidebooks that really guide

City•Smart™ Guidebooks

Pick one for your favorite city: *Albuquerque, Anchorage, Austin, Calgary, Charlotte, Chicago, Cincinnati, Cleveland, Denver, Indianapolis, Kansas City, Memphis, Milwaukee, Minneapolis/St. Paul, Nashville, Pittsburgh, Portland, Richmond, Salt Lake City, San Antonio, San Francisco, St. Louis, Tampa/St. Petersburg, Tucson.*
US $12.95 to 15.95

Retirement & Relocation Guidebooks

The World's Top Retirement Havens, Live Well in Honduras, Live Well in Ireland, Live Well in Mexico.
US $15.95 to $16.95

Travel•Smart® Guidebooks

Trip planners with select recommendations to *Alaska, American Southwest, Arizona, Carolinas, Colorado, Deep South, Eastern Canada, Florida, Florida Gulf Coast, Hawaii, Illinois/Indiana, Kentucky/Tennessee, Maryland/Delaware, Michigan, Minnesota/Wisconsin, Montana/Wyoming/Idaho, New England, New Mexico, New York State, Northern California, Ohio, Pacific Northwest, Pennsylvania/New Jersey, South Florida and the Keys, Southern California, Texas, Utah, Virginias, Western Canada.* US $14.95 to $17.95

Rick Steves' Guides

See *Europe Through the Back Door* and take along guides to *France, Belgium & the Netherlands; Germany, Austria & Switzerland; Great Britain & Ireland; Italy; Scandinavia; Spain & Portugal; London; Paris;* or *Best of Europe.* US $12.95 to $21.95

Adventures in Nature

Plan your next adventure in *Alaska, Belize, Caribbean, Costa Rica, Guatemala, Hawaii, Honduras, Mexico.*
US $17.95 to $18.95

Into the Heart of Jerusalem

A traveler's guide to visits, celebrations, and sojourns.
US $17.95

The People's Guide to Mexico

This is so much more than a guidebook—it's a trip to Mexico in and of itself, complete with the flavor of the country and its sights, sounds, and people. US $22.95

JOHN MUIR PUBLICATIONS
A DIVISION OF AVALON TRAVEL PUBLISHING
5855 Beaudry Street, Emeryville, CA 94608

Please check our web site at www.travelmatters.com for current prices and editions, or see your local bookseller.

ABOUT THE AUTHOR

Holly Quan was born in Edmonton, Alberta, and grew up in Calgary. A freelance writer since 1988, she writes about travel, food, and environmental issues for local, national, and international publications. She is an avid hiker, skier, and horseback rider, and she lives in Calgary.